卐

SIEG HEIL!
SIEG HEIL!
SIEG HEIL!
SIEG HEIL!
SIEG HEIL!
SIEG HEIL!
SIEG HEIL!
SIEG HEIL!
SIEG HEIL!
SIEG HEIL!

Books by STEFAN LORANT

Wir von Film   (*Berlin, 1928*)

So sehen wir aus   (edited) (*Berlin, 1930*)

I Was Hitler's Prisoner   (*London, 1934*)

Chamberlain and the Beautiful Llama   (*London, 1940*)

Lincoln, His Life in Photographs   (*New York, 1941*)

The New World   (*New York, 1946*) (*Revised Edition, 1965*)

FDR, A Pictorial Biography   (*New York, 1950*)

The Presidency   (*New York, 1951*)

Lincoln, A Picture Story of His Life   (*New York, 1952*) (*Revised Editions, 1957, 1969*)

The Life of Abraham Lincoln   (*New York, 1954*)

The Life and Times of Theodore Roosevelt   (*New York, 1959*)

Pittsburgh, The Story of an American City   (*New York, 1964*)

The Glorious Burden—The American Presidency   (*New York, 1968*)

Sieg Heil!—An Illustrated History of Germany from Bismarck to Hitler   (*New York, 1974*)

SIEG HEIL!

(HAIL TO VICTORY)

An Illustrated History of Germany

from Bismarck to Hitler

BY STEFAN LORANT

How does tyranny arise? That it comes out of democracy is fairly clear. Does the change take place in the same sort of way as the change from oligarchy to democracy? Oligarchy was established by men with a certain aim in life: the good they sought was wealth, and it was the insatiable appetite for money-making to the neglect of everything else that proved its undoing. Is democracy likewise ruined by greed for what it conceives to be the supreme good?
—*Plato, The Republic VIII 562*

BONANZA BOOKS, NEW YORK

First Edition—January, 1974
Second Printing—March, 1974
Bonanza Edition—1979—15,000 copies

This edition is published by Bonanza Books, a division of Crown Publishers, Inc., by arrangement with Stefan Lorant.
a b c d e f g h
BONANZA 1979 PRINTING
Manufactured in the United States of America

Layout and typography by Stefan Lorant

Library of Congress Cataloging in Publication Data

Lorant, Stefan, 1901-
 Sieg Heil! = Hail to victory.

 Bibliography: p.
 Includes index.
 1. Germany—History—1871-1918—Pictorial works.
2. Germany—History—20th century—Pictorial works.
I. Title.   II. Title: Hail to victory.
DD232.L67 1979   943.08′022′2   78-31662
ISBN 0-517-27787-5

A Note of Thanks

FOR ALMOST FIFTY YEARS I have edited magazines and published books in which the main emphasis was on pictures.

During these five decades I acquired many friends. The works of many of the world's great photographers were first published in my magazines. I printed the early photographs of Dr. Erich Salomon, of Robert Capa, of Brassai, of André Kertész, of Hanns Hubmann, Kurt Hutton, Helmuth Kurth, Felix Man. Those of them who were still alive graciously allowed me the use of their pictures in this volume. Dr. Salomon's son Peter sent me prints from his late father's original negatives; Cornell Capa let me have some of his brother's classic photographs, and Gunther Sander furnished me with portraits taken by his father.

The bulk of the seven hundred and more illustrations came from five principal sources: from my own picture collection, which I began in the middle of the nineteen-twenties; from the picture archive of the Süddeutsche Verlag in Munich, which has grown from its modest beginning under my initial direction in 1929 of a few hundred prints to the largest photographic archive in the world with eight million photographs; from the magnificent historical collection of the Landesbildstelle in Berlin; from the files of United Press International in New York; and from captured German materials deposited in the Library of Congress and the National Archives in Washington.

At the Süddeutsche Verlag my old friend Hans Schuhmann and his charming assistant Mrs. Lydia Bohne responded to my many requests with courtesy and patience; they guided me in locating pictures which otherwise I would not have been able to discover.

At the Landesbildstelle Dr. Frederich Terveen gave much of his time to help with my research. He is a photographic editor of superb competence. His arrangement of the voluminous historical material on the German past is ingenious and practical; photographs of every description can be easily found at his institution. The quality of the prints — done by Werner Heymsodt — is excellent. The help given by the able picture librarians, particularly Mrs. Constance Strech, made the search easy.

At United Press International my good friend Jack Fletcher, the chief of the photographic collection, and his knowledgeable lieutenants, Arthur Lee and Joseph Luppino, and also archivist William Stribling were digging out rare material for me.

At the Library of Congress my old friends Milton Kaplan and Virginia Daiker — whom I have frequently consulted during the past quarter century — gave me their advice, pointing my search in the right direction.

At the National Archives Dr. Robert Wolf shared with me his profound knowledge of the period; James W. Moore cooperated in securing photographic prints.

In all the countries in which I did my pictorial research I encountered courtesies and received friendly cooperation. But I would like to say a special "thank you" to Dr. Walter Wieser and the staff of the Österreichische National Bibliothek in Vienna; to the staff of the Bibliothèque Nationale in Paris; to the Institut für Zeitgeschichte in Munich and its director, Dr. Anton Hoch; to Dr. Wolfgang Mommsen and the staff of the Bundesarchiv in Coblenz, particularly to photolibrarian Herbert Walther; to Dr. Ronald Klemig and the staff of the Staatsbibliothek in Berlin; to Mr. E. Hine and the staff of the Imperial War Museum in London; to H. Quaschinsky and the staff of the monumental picture library Zentralbild in East Berlin; to the staff of the Hoover Institution in Stanford, California.

Several photographic agencies in Berlin and Paris supplied me with material. In Berlin I was allowed to go through the files of the Ullstein Picture Library, which is under the able management of Liselotte Bandelow; in Paris my old friend Alex Garai at Keystone came up with photographs from the old files.

Young Heinrich Hoffmann, the son of Heinrich Hoffmann, Hitler's personal photographer, led me through his well-catalogued archive in Munich and let me have many original prints and enlargements from his father's negatives.

For snapshots of writers taken in the period, I am grateful to Mrs. Thomas Mann, to Mrs. Helene Weigel-Brecht, to Mrs. Liesl Frank-Lustig, to Mrs. Kurt Tucholsky, who sent me unposed pictures of their late husbands.

John Heartfield, the German artist, after escaping from the clutches of the Nazis, showed up at my London office in 1939, bringing with him his photomontages. I published a selection of them in *Lilliput,* and on the cover of *Picture Post* I printed the montage which served as a model for Idabelle Kleinhans' painting for the jacket of this book.

Much nonsense has been concocted by psychiatrists and psychoanalysts on Hitler's character. Most of them based their analyses on imaginary "facts and events." Talks with my friend Dr. Margaret Brenman-Gibson straightened me out on some of her colleagues' fallacies.

Marlene Dietrich and her husband Rudolph Sieber — friends for five decades — allowed me to use Marlene's early pictures. We fondly remember the times when I — as a youngster — made the first screen test of Marlene in Berlin. (How I wish I had that film!) And thanks to Josephine Baker, the toast of Berlin in tho twentios, for her telling photograph on the Berlin stage with curtain decoration by Benno von Arendt, the man who later became the race-hating artistic coordinator for the Nazis.

My friend Eli Wallach, captain in the U. S. Army in the Second World War, allowed me to see his "liberated" photographs from Germany. I wish I had space to use them all. And thanks to Anne Jackson, who put her charmed amulet around my neck and let me wear it when luck was needed.

During the four years I was working on the book, I was given steady encouragement by my friend Dr. Paul Dudley White, who was keenly interested in the progress of the work, prodding me on when my own morale flagged. Even during his last fatal illness he sent me notes from his hospital bed, inquiring about the work. I feel grieved that I cannot show him the results.

At W. W. Norton and Company I received many courtesies. Evan W. Thomas, my editor, guided me with pertinent criticism and suggestions; through all vicissitudes we kept our friendship. The common sense and sweet disposition of Rose Franco were always a balm. The eagle eyes of Kendra K. Ho, the copy editor of the manuscript, discovered typographical errors both in English and German. If any of them have remained, the blame is mine. Ben Gamit, Jr., did the mechanicals with patience and good humor. But my deepest gratitude goes to James L. Mairs, production director and senior editor of the company, who with energy, patience, and imagination handled all the complexities of "putting the book to bed." A brilliant craftsman, a perceptive and knowledgeable editor, he understood the technical problems and offered solutions to them. He was a rock of strength; his good taste and judgment infallible. It was my good fortune to have his assistance during the strenuous weeks of going to press and to profit by his enthusiasm and good will.

Photographic works and reproductions were done by my good friends in Pittsfield, Great Barrington, and Lenox: Joel Librizzi, Richard C. Gilson, and Lucien Aigner. Their ready cooperation, together with their skill and artistry, overcame many technical difficulties.

My friend Kenneth Adams at Murray Printing Company supervised and helped with the production process. During the past two decades we have worked on three of my books; I always listen to his advice and to his suggestions; they always make sense. Many thanks, Ken.

Lynne Foy, an outstanding artist and a lovely member of the Murray staff, has drawn the charts and was a whiz in the completion of the mechanicals.

Fran McNamara and Mike McSweeney at Wrightson Typographers in Boston were immensely helpful with the on-the-spot setting and correcting of the final copy. It was a pleasure working with them; they are true craftsmen who set high standards for themselves and their company.

My deep appreciation to my friends Theodore W. Kheel and Raymond Gregory, who helped to disentangle legal matters, and to clever and wise Michael D. Hess, who lowered the barricades and brought an end to all misunderstandings. I am particularly grateful to Ray for his unfailing good sense and his endless patience and support.

My secretary, Sally Bergmans, not only typed the manuscript, counted the characters in every line of the text, and fitted the captions under every picture, but pointed out my discrepancies and mistakes, offered editorial corrections, and suggested improvements. During the grueling hours of work she kept her cheerfulness, never complaining whether the typing had to be done at night or on Sunday, her job was always magnificent. My deep gratitude to her.

John Furbish kept the picture files in order, prepared a chronology of events, and helped with the research. Carol Edwards did odds and ends cheerfully, ably, and intelligently.

The acknowledgment would not be complete without a mention of my family. They were my true collaborators. Laurie, my wife, read every line of the copy and made valuable critical suggestions. She assisted in the research, typed when the need arose, and sustained me during the four years I spent on the work. And our boys were helpful too. One early morning before dawn Mark, then seven years old, padded into my study and, seeing me in a low mood at my desk, offered: "Don't worry, Daddy, you worked hard and people will like the book." By then Christy, his older brother, appeared in the doorway and nodded soberly, "That's right." Thank you, boys, for your confidence.

"Farview"
Lenox, Massachusetts   STEFAN LORANT

THE KING IS IN TROUBLE

FOR A THOUSAND years Germany was a conglomeration of lands strewn across the map of Europe—a patchwork without organic connections. It consisted of 314 independent states and 1,475 estates and was held together by the absolute rule of the emperor and his troops.

The Roman empire—the National Socialists' "first Reich"—was an elective monarchy, its monarch chosen by seven electors. Friedrich von Hohenzollern became elector in 1415, but it took another three centuries before the Hohenzollerns made their mark on German history. By then they already possessed the duchy of Prussia, granted to them by the Polish crown.

The first outstanding Hohenzollern prince was Friedrich Wilhelm, the "great elector" (the ruler of Brandenburg-Prussia from 1640 to 1688). An astute politician and skilled organizer, he militarized Prussia, building a strong army of 30,000 men. His son and successor, Friedrich III (from 1688 to 1713), desired to become a king, and was allowed to crown himself in 1701 as king *in* (but not *of*) Prussia. Proclaiming himself Friedrich I, he imitated the French court, even taking a mistress though he had no use for her.

His incompetent rule was followed by the competent one of his son Friedrich Wilhelm I (1713–1740). Pious and moral, Friedrich Wilhelm I, the soldier king, welded Prussia into a military garrison. He introduced economy and iron discipline and left the legacy of a large, efficient, and well-trained army.

His son Friedrich II ruled for forty-six years (from 1740 to 1786), meting out defeat to the Habsburgs, conquering Silesia, dividing Poland, and vastly extending the borders of his realm. By his death Prussia had become a dominant power in Europe.

Frederick the Great was succeeded by two inept kings: his nephew Friedrich Wilhelm II (1786–1797) and Friedrich Wilhelm III (1797–1840). They squandered away the advantages they inherited from their great predecessor.

It was under Friedrich Wilhelm III that the Prussian army suffered defeat by Napoleon at Jena in 1806; six years later at Leipzig they took their revenge. With Napoleon's demise the "thousand-year-old first Reich" ended. The Deutsche Bund—a confederation of thirty-nine states replaced it.

The two Friedrich Wilhelms were followed by yet another, Friedrich Wilhelm IV (1840–1861), who considered democracy a revolt against God. After a series of strokes he became mentally deranged; his brother Wilhelm acted as regent, becoming king when Friedrich Wilhelm died in 1861.

At his coronation in Königsberg, where the first Prussian king was crowned a hundred and sixty years before, Wilhelm I was already sixty-four years old. He had grown up as a soldier, and his main interest was the military. He believed in the mission of Prussia and the unity of the German lands. He was determined to reform the army and increase the number of recruits. Since the introduction of universal military service in 1815, Prussia's population had risen from 11 to 18 million, yet the number of recruits had remained static.

The new king wanted to retain the three-year service period and also to link the Landwehr—originally formed as a militia against Napoleon—with the standing army. The liberal faction in the diet opposed his proposals, and an impasse developed with neither side willing to compromise.

In the election of 1861 the liberals increased their strength. The new diet refused to pass the army reform bill or to vote for an increase in military appropriations. When the opposition demanded a detailed budget from the government, the diet was dissolved and a new election called for May 6, 1862. Again the electorate strengthened the liberals. Once more the diet refused to vote for increased military expenditures. Once more the majority insisted on only two years' service. Once more they demanded that the king leave the Landwehr untouched. The quarrel developed into a constitutional crisis of great magnitude.

Wilhelm was in a dilemma. What was he to do? To disregard the constitution and rule autocratically, or to abdicate? He had already drafted his abdication when General Roon, his conservative war minister persuaded him to recall Otto von Bismarck, who was representing Prussia in France, and to appoint him minister president. The king was not enthusiastic about the idea, but he consented. Roon sent a message to Bismarck in Paris: "*Periculum in mora. Dépêchez-vous.*" (There is danger in delay. Hurry up.) Bismarck rushed to Berlin. On September 22 and the next day, he conversed with the king and was appointed.

The new minister president held that if the budget could not be agreed upon by the chamber of deputies, the upper house, and the king, the government could still collect taxes and use the money until an agreement was reached. In his first speech as the king's minister, Bismarck told the chamber: "The great questions of our day cannot be solved by speeches and majority votes . . . but by iron and blood."

8

1861, October 18:
THE CORONATION OF WILHELM I
AS PRUSSIAN KING IN KÖNIGSBERG.

THE NEW BROOM

THE NEW MINISTER PRESIDENT was born in 1815—the year of Napoleon's final defeat. He came from a land-owning gentry family. In his youth he was tall and slim; later he became fat because of his love of food and drink. At seventeen he entered Göttingen University, completed his studies in Berlin, and passed his first examination in law. Disliking the idea of becoming a civil servant, he returned to Pomerania, where he successfully managed his family's run-down estate. He joined a religious group and married one of the Pietists, Johanna von Puttkamer, in 1847. That same year he substituted in the Landtag for the ill deputy from his district.

In 1851 he was appointed as Prussian envoy to the Federal Diet. He stayed in Frankfurt for seven years, learning diplomacy and statesmanship. After the death of the king in 1861, the new monarch—in his effort to establish good relations with the liberals in the Diet—removed the conservative Bismarck from Frankfurt and sent him as Prussian ambassador to St. Petersburg. He stayed there for three years; from there he was transferred to Paris.

He was forty-seven when he became minister president. An imposing personality, he spoke many languages, had a ready wit, and the ability to make quick decisions; he had little interest in political ideology. Once he wrote to a friend: "I will be either the greatest scoundrel or the greatest man in Prussia." Though he was a poor public speaker with a high-pitched soft voice his writing was clear and lucid. Only one other political writer of his age matched him—Abraham Lincoln.

Bismarck was highly emotional; a promiscuous lover, a passionate gambler, and a voracious reader, he cried easily, suffered from hysterical outbursts, cholecystitis, jaundice, and convulsions. Golo Mann calls him "a nervous barbarian." He behaved arrogantly, hated unforgivingly; he felt that he lived in a hostile world, surrounded by enemies and conspirators. "If I have an enemy in my power, I must destroy him."

He had a clear political program: to keep Prussia powerful and in the hands of the Junkers. In a brilliant essay on his hero, Henry Kissinger observed: "Within five years of coming to power in 1862, he had solved the problem of German unity along the lines of the memorandum he had written during the previous decade. He first induced Austria to separate herself from the secondary German states and to undertake a joint expedition with Prussia against Denmark over the status of Schleswig-Holstein. With Austria isolated from its traditional supporters, Bismarck brought ever increasing pressure on her until in exasperation she declared war. A rapid Prussian victory led to the expulsion of Austria from Germany. Prussia was now free to organize North Germany on a hegemonic basis."

Gladstone's harsh opinion is the ultimate one of the "Iron Chancellor": "He made Germany great and Germans small."

1863 September:

THE CONGRESS OF THE GERMAN PRINCES IN FRANKFURT wanted to reform their confederation. But as Bismarck dissuaded his king from attending, nothing came of it.

Emperor Franz Josef of Austria (in white tunic) ascended the throne in 1848, ruling until 1916; to his right, the king of Bavaria; to his left, the blind king of Hanover.

THE POWER IN THE LAND:

OTTO VON BISMARCK
was appointed as head of the Prussian cabinet in September 1862.

THE THREE WARS

Two years after Bismarck became Prussian minister president, he induced Austria to join him in a war on Denmark and to take Schleswig-Holstein. In another two years—in 1866 —he forced a war on Austria, defeating her at Sadowa. (Seven decades later Anton Kuh quipped: "Hitler became Austria's revenge on the Germans for her defeat at Sadowa.") And in 1870 Bismarck prepared for war against France.

Bismarck's three wars—in 1864, in 1866, and in 1870–71—led to the foundation of the Second Reich. After the first war, against Denmark, he solidified his position and laid plans to fight his political opposition. The second war, against Austria, enabled him to oust Austria from leadership among the German states and to make Prussia the dominant force in the German confederation. And the third war, against France, paved the way for the unification of Germany.

With Austria's defeat by Prussia, the Habsburg influence over the south German states waned. But the new situation created new difficulties with France. Napoleon III told Lord Clarendon that if the south German states joined the North German Confederation, "our guns will go off by themselves." The French dreaded a united Germany on their northern frontier.

Bismarck was convinced that war with France was inevitable and also that such a war would bring about German unity. When talking to foreigners, he emphasized how he hated war. (Wilhelm II and Hitler followed his example.) But to friends like the

THE ATTACK...

Contemporary drawing for Enselin & Laiblen

THE WAR IN 1870: GERMAN INFANTRY INVADES A FRENCH VILLAGE.

Illustrated London News, September 24, 1870

THE SMALL VILLAGE OF BAZEILLES NEAR SEDAN IS BURNED.

...AND THE RESULT

Contemporary drawing for Harper's Weekly

FOR HUNDREDS OF FRENCH SOLDIERS THERE WAS NO RETREAT.

Illustrated London News, *September 17, 1870*

THE FRENCH RAISE THE WHITE FLAG OF SURRENDER AT SEDAN.

German liberal Carl Schurz, who had left his country after the 1848 revolution and in America became one of the founders of the Republican party, he confided in 1867 that war would come within two years.

Only a spark was needed to ignite the conflict. And the controversy over the succession to the Spanish throne provided this spark. After the military coup and after the deposition of Queen Isabella II, the Spanish monarchists sought a new ruler. Bismarck, who tried to put a Hohenzollern prince on the Spanish throne, promoted the candidacy of Prince Leopold von Hohenzollern-Sigmaringen, a scion of the Catholic southern branch of the Hohenzollerns.

When the French learned that Leopold had accepted the candidacy (with the consent of the Prussian king, the titular head of the Hohenzollern family), their tempers flared. Threatened on their northern border by the menace of Prussia, and now facing a Spain ruled by a German prince on their western border, they feared for their security.

The French government instructed its ambassador in Prussia, Count Benedetti, to seek an interview with the Prussian king, who at that time was taking the cure at Ems. Benedetti conferred with Wilhelm, who, seeing the outcry in France, was ready to settle the dispute in an amicable way. He induced Leopold to withdraw his candidacy. With that the crisis seemed to be solved. If only France and Bismarck had let sleeping dogs lie.

The French government ordered

13

Benedetti to seek a further interview with the Prussian emperor, and when the monarch delayed the meeting, the French ambassador posed himself in the Kurgarten to force an accidental encounter. The trick worked. Wilhelm spotted him and engaged him in conversation. The envoy seized the opportunity to press the emperor for an assurance that Leopold would never again be allowed to be a candidate for the Spanish throne. The king refused to give the promise and told Heinrich von Abeken of the foreign office to inform Bismarck of the incident.

Abeken's telegram from Ems reached Bismarck while he was at dinner with General Moltke, the chief of the general staff, and Roon, the Prussian minister of war. The three men were in a depressed mood; as Leopold had withdrawn his candidacy the day before, their expectations for war had gone up in smoke. But as they studied the message, their spirits revived. Quickly Bismarck set about to edit the telegram, shortening it, changing its emphasis, to the point where he felt it would "have the effect of a red flag on the Gallic bull."

GUNFIRE DEVASTATED THE PARIS SUBURB OF ST. CLOUD.

1870, Winter:
GERMAN WOMEN IN A MANNHEIM

After reading it, Moltke remarked: "In the original it sounded like a *chamade* (a signal for negotiations by the besieged), but now it is like a fanfare, a reply to a challenge." Roon exclaimed happily: "The old God still

CHURCH MAKE MATTRESSES AND ROLL BANDAGES FOR THE SOLDIERS FIGHTING ON THE FRENCH BATTLEFIELD.

lives—it will not let us perish in shame." And Moltke, looking with a joyous countenance toward the ceiling, pounded his chest: "If I can lead our army in such a war—I won't mind if the devil fetches 'my old carcass' afterward." (So Bismarck noted their reactions in his reminiscences.)

The effect of the telegram's publication surpassed Bismarck's expectations. On the next day—July 14, Bastille Day—France mobilized. And five days later—on the nineteenth—she declared war on Prussia.

The news woke the German states from their lethargy. Württemberg, Hesse, and Baden joined Prussia and her northern confederates in the war

THEY LED THE TROOPS: CROWN PRINCE FRIEDRICH WILHELM (WITH BEARD, LEFT CENTER), COMMANDER OF THE

against France; Bavaria—with some hesitation—followed soon thereafter.

The Prussian general staff was prepared; their military machine was well oiled, their plans had been carefully worked out. In less than a fortnight 400,000 German soldiers were in readiness in the battle zone. The French too were prepared and confident in their armed superiority. But they moved slowly and with much confusion. It was not till the first week of August that the two armies encountered each other in a major engagement. On August 4 the Germans scored their first victory at Weissenburg and followed it up at Wörth and Spichern, and a fortnight later at Mars-la-Tour and Gravelotte. The French forces under General Bazaine had to retire behind the defenses of Metz. There they were neutralized, bottled up by the Germans, unable to move.

The French government ordered General MacMahon to relieve Bazaine's army. MacMahon protested, predicting the worst, but he had to obey.

The French army faced the Germans on the last day of August at Sedan. In forty-eight hours the outcome of the war had been decided; the Germans had won it. On September 2 well over 100,000 encircled French troops surrendered. Among the captives was the emperor Napoleon.

The victory at Sedan brought the rule of Napoleon and the Second Empire to an end. Two days later a new French republic was proclaimed in Paris, and a "Government of National Defense" was organized. The new government wanted to pursue the fight against the Germans; though they battled for four more months, they could not convert defeat into a victory.

By the end of January 1871 an armistice was declared; on March 1 the

THE FRENCH CAPITULATE

Painting by Anton von Werner

AFTER THE VICTORY AT SEDAN. On September 2, 1870, the morning after the decisive battle, Bismarck rides to meet Napoleon III to parley with him.

Painting by Wilhelm von Camphausen

THE VICTOR AND THE VANQUISHED. Bismarck discusses the peace with French emperor Napoleon III at the cottage of Madame Fournaise in Donchery.

GERMAN 3RD ARMY, AND HIS STAFF.

preliminaries to the peace treaty were signed and ratified by the newly elected French national assembly.

As in the interim the French government troops were engaged in a fierce fight against the Commune in Paris, the peace treaty was not signed until May 10. A month later Alsace-Lorraine was legally united with the German Reich, an event of far-reaching significance. The loss of that territory rankled in the minds of the French —they swore *revanche*, and they had it four decades later. After the First World War Alsace-Lorraine became French again.

Painting by Anton von Werner

THE GERMAN AND FRENCH NEGOTIATORS. From left to right: Capt. d'Orcey, Gen. Favre, Gen. Castelneau, Gen. von Wimpffen, Gen. von Podbielski, Field Marshal von Moltke, Bismarck, Capt. von Winterfeld, Capt. Count Nostitz, Maj. Krause, Lt. Col. von Schellendorff, Lt. Col. du Vernois, Maj. Blume, Maj. de Claer.

FOUNDATION
OF THE
REICH

1871, January 18:
GERMAN OFFICERS at the proclamation of the Reich. Third from left (in dark uniform) is the young Lieutenant Paul von Beneckendorff und von Hindenburg, who fifty-four years later in 1925 followed Friedrich Ebert as second president of the Weimar Republic.

ON JANUARY 18, 1871, AT TH

IT WAS THE anniversary of the crow
ing of the first Prussian king in 17
Now, 170 years later, another Pru
sian king was to become German ka
ser. Not a civilian was among the m
in uniform, save the painter Ant
von Werner, who sketched the even

PRUSSIAN GUARD
IN VERSAILLES.

THE FRENCH CAPITULATE

Painting by Anton von Werner

AFTER THE VICTORY AT SEDAN. On September 2, 1870, the morning after the decisive battle, Bismarck rides to meet Napoleon III to parley with him.

Painting by Wilhelm von Camphausen

THE VICTOR AND THE VANQUISHED. Bismarck discusses the peace with French emperor Napoleon III at the cottage of Madame Fournaise in Donchery.

Painting by Anton von Werner

THE GERMAN AND FRENCH NEGOTIATORS. From left to right: Capt. d'Orcey, Gen. Favre, Gen. Castelneau, Gen. von Wimpffen, Gen. von Podbielski, Field Marshal von Moltke, Bismarck, Capt. von Winterfeld, Capt. Count Nostitz, Maj. Krause, Lt. Col. von Schellendorff, Lt. Col. du Vernois, Maj. Blume, Maj. de Claer.

GERMAN 3RD ARMY, AND HIS STAFF.

preliminaries to the peace treaty were signed and ratified by the newly elected French national assembly.

As in the interim the French government troops were engaged in a fierce fight against the Commune in Paris, the peace treaty was not signed until May 10. A month later Alsace-Lorraine was legally united with the German Reich, an event of far-reaching significance. The loss of that territory rankled in the minds of the French —they swore *revanche*, and they had it four decades later. After the First World War Alsace-Lorraine became French again.

FOUNDATION
OF THE
REICH

1871, January 18:
GERMAN OFFICERS at the proclamation of the Reich. Third from left (in dark uniform) is the young Lieutenant Paul von Beneckendorff und von Hindenburg, who fifty-four years later in 1925 followed Friedrich Ebert as second president of the Weimar Republic.

ON JANUARY 18, 1871, AT THE

IT WAS THE anniversary of the crowning of the first Prussian king in 1701. Now, 170 years later, another Prussian king was to become German kaiser. Not a civilian was among the men in uniform, save the painter Anton von Werner, who sketched the event.

PRUSSIAN GUARD
IN VERSAILLES.

CHURCH MAKE MATTRESSES AND ROLL BANDAGES FOR THE SOLDIERS FIGHTING ON THE FRENCH BATTLEFIELD.

lives—it will not let us perish in shame." And Moltke, looking with a joyous countenance toward the ceiling, pounded his chest: "If I can lead our army in such a war—I won't mind if the devil fetches 'my old carcass' af-

terward." (So Bismarck noted their reactions in his reminiscences.)

The effect of the telegram's publication surpassed Bismarck's expectations. On the next day—July 14, Bastille Day—France mobilized. And five

days later—on the nineteenth—she declared war on Prussia.

The news woke the German states from their lethargy. Württemberg, Hesse, and Baden joined Prussia and her northern confederates in the war

THEY LED THE TROOPS: CROWN PRINCE FRIEDRICH WILHELM (WITH BEARD, LEFT CENTER), COMMANDER OF THE

against France; Bavaria—with some hesitation—followed soon thereafter.

The Prussian general staff was prepared; their military machine was well oiled, their plans had been carefully worked out. In less than a fortnight 400,000 German soldiers were in readiness in the battle zone. The French too were prepared and confident in their armed superiority. But they moved slowly and with much confusion. It was not till the first week of August that the two armies encountered each other in a major engagement. On August 4 the Germans scored their first victory at Weissenburg and

followed it up at Wörth and Spichern, and a fortnight later at Mars-la-Tour and Gravelotte. The French forces under General Bazaine had to retire behind the defenses of Metz. There they were neutralized, bottled up by the Germans, unable to move.

The French government ordered General MacMahon to relieve Bazaine's army. MacMahon protested, predicting the worst, but he had to obey.

The French army faced the Germans on the last day of August at Sedan. In forty-eight hours the outcome of the war had been decided; the

Germans had won it. On September 2 well over 100,000 encircled French troops surrendered. Among the captives was the emperor Napoleon.

The victory at Sedan brought the rule of Napoleon and the Second Empire to an end. Two days later a new French republic was proclaimed in Paris, and a "Government of National Defense" was organized. The new government wanted to pursue the fight against the Germans; though they battled for four more months, they could not convert defeat into a victory.

By the end of January 1871 an armistice was declared; on March 1 the

THE FRENCH CAPITULATE

Painting by Anton von Werner

AFTER THE VICTORY AT SEDAN. On September 2, 1870, the morning after the decisive battle, Bismarck rides to meet Napoleon III to parley with him.

Painting by Wilhelm von Camphausen

THE VICTOR AND THE VANQUISHED. Bismarck discusses the peace with French emperor Napoleon III at the cottage of Madame Fournaise in Donchery.

GERMAN 3RD ARMY, AND HIS STAFF.

preliminaries to the peace treaty were signed and ratified by the newly elected French national assembly.

As in the interim the French government troops were engaged in a fierce fight against the Commune in Paris, the peace treaty was not signed until May 10. A month later Alsace-Lorraine was legally united with the German Reich, an event of far-reaching significance. The loss of that territory rankled in the minds of the French —they swore *revanche*, and they had it four decades later. After the First World War Alsace-Lorraine became French again.

Painting by Anton von Werner

THE GERMAN AND FRENCH NEGOTIATORS. From left to right: Capt. d'Orcey, Gen. Favre, Gen. Castelneau, Gen. von Wimpffen, Gen. von Podbielski, Field Marshal von Moltke, Bismarck, Capt. von Winterfeld, Capt. Count Nostitz, Maj. Krause, Lt. Col. von Schellendorff, Lt. Col. du Vernois, Maj. Blume, Maj. de Claer.

FOUNDATION OF THE REICH

1871, January 18:

GERMAN OFFICERS at the proclamation of the Reich. Third from left (in dark uniform) is the young Lieutenant Paul von Beneckendorff und von Hindenburg, who fifty-four years later in 1925 followed Friedrich Ebert as second president of the Weimar Republic.

ON JANUARY 18, 1871, AT THE

IT WAS THE anniversary of the crowning of the first Prussian king in 1701. Now, 170 years later, another Prussian king was to become German kaiser. Not a civilian was among the men in uniform, save the painter Anton von Werner, who sketched the event.

PRUSSIAN GUARD
IN VERSAILLES.

Painting by Anton von Werner

PALACE OF VERSAILLES, WILHELM OF PRUSSIA WAS CROWNED KAISER WILHELM I OF THE GERMAN REICH.

To the kaiser's right stood the crown prince; at the foot of the pedestal, Prime Minister Bismarck and General Moltke, the army chief of staff.

The ceremony—in the words of Professor Otto Pflanze—signified "the union of three traditions: Hohenzol-lern authoritarianism, Prussian militarism, and German nationalism."

And when everything was over Bismarck wrote his wife that the "kaiser-birth" had been difficult because "kings, like women in such situations, have peculiar desires before they give the world what they cannot hold back in any case. As *accoucheur* I often had the urge to become a bomb and explode so that the building would go down in ruins. Necessary business doesn't affect me, but unnecessary business makes me bitter."

19

THE COMMUNE
IN PARIS

THE TOPPLED COLUMN—a memorial to Napoleon's military victories—at the Place Vendôme after the bloody fighting on May 16, 1871, viewed by the people.

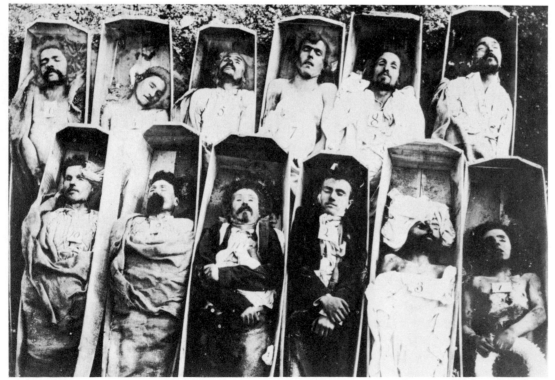

Courtesy of Helmut Gernsheim

THE BODIES OF MURDERED COMMUNARDS who offered resistance in the Père Lachaise Cemetery on May 28, the last day of the fighting, before their burial.

1871, May 26

A PHOTOMONTAGE OF THE COM-

THE WAR WAS LOST, the monarchy toppled. In the elections for a new republican assembly, the country districts sent conservative, monarchist representatives, while the city of Paris voted for deputies with republican principles.

The National Guard in the capital was an army within an army; it had to be dissolved. When the order was ignored, government troops were sent against the recalcitrants. But the guard

Montage by E. Appert, Paris

MUNIST MASSACRE. IN RETALIATION GOVERNMENT TROOPS KILLED THOUSANDS OF COMMUNARDS.

forced them and the government to flee the city. On March 18 Paris was in the hands of the guard's central committee, which proclaimed a commune (as self-governing cities were named in the Middle Ages and in the French Revolution).

Lenin later said: "The Commune developed spontaneously. It was neither consciously nor methodically prepared." It came into being as a response to the sufferings under the siege, the defeat in the war, unemployment, the people's anger at bureaucratic inefficiencies, the reactionary composition of the national assembly. The underlying reason was the deep dissatisfaction in the ranks of the working class, which was ripe for a proletarian revolution.

From Versailles the exiled government—encouraged by Bismarck—sent fresh troops against the National Guard and the Commune.

Victor Hugo wrote: "Paris will die so France can live." But it was not to be. On May 16 government troops entered the city and wiped out all resistance. Frightful atrocities were committed by both sides: government troops shot their prisoners, the guard executed its hostages. On May 28 the rule of the Commune came to an end after seventy-two bloody days. The 20,000 victims who perished were remembered for generations to come.

1871, June 16:

THROUGH BERLIN'S BRANDENBURG GATE the victorious German troops enter the capital. The 65-foot-high neo-Grecian portal replacing the medieval gateway to the city was built between 1788 and 1791 by Karl Gotthart Langhans for the Prussian king, Friedrich Wilhelm II, the obese, woman-chasing nephew of Frederick the Great. For the top of the edifice Johann Gottfried Schadow, the celebrated sculptor of his age, created a statue of the Goddess of Victory's chariot drawn by four horses. Ever since this day in 1871, it has been traditional for German troops to march between the columns of the gate on their return from war.

THE VICTORS RETURN

BERLIN MADE elaborate preparations to celebrate the return of the victors in the war. Bleachers were built for a hundred thousand spectators.

The date was the sixteenth of June. A month earlier—on May 10—Bismarck and French foreign minister Jules Favre had signed the peace treaty in Frankfurt.

Soon after noon the parade began led by the three heroes of the war: War Minister Roon, who was made a count; Chief of Staff Moltke, who became a field marshal; and Bismarck, whom the kaiser had made a prince.

They were followed on horseback by the emperor, the crown prince, and the emperor's twelve-year-old grandson, Prince Wilhelm, riding on a pony. Behind them and the other princes came the infantry—each man decorated with the Iron Cross—the cavalry, and the artillery.

Emanuel Geibel wrote a poem for the occasion; "Und gründ in unsrer Mitte / Wehrhaft und fromm zugleich / In Freiheit, Zucht und Sitte / Dein tausendjährig Reich!" ("And establish in our midst a militant but devout, a free and disciplined thousand-year-old Reich!") Six decades later that last phrase became the Nazis' propaganda slogan.

22

Sieg Heil!
The people of Berlin
hail their victory
in the war.

BISMARCK'S DOMESTIC POLICIES

FOR BISMARCK foreign policy came first; domestic issues afterward. In the Reichstag he could seldom rely on a safe majority, thus he was forced to make concessions, to water down his original proposals.

The three major domestic political issues arising during his chancellorship were the Kulturkampf, social legislation, and the tariff question.

The Kulturkampf ("the campaign for cultural freedom"), as the movement against the Catholics was called, began after the declaration of papal infallibility in questions of faith and morals, and with the pope's *Syllabus of Errors*, which condemned the "errors of liberalism." For the pope the accomplishments of European civilization since the Middle Ages were the work of the devil and should be destroyed.

In the ensuing struggle Bismarck led the attack, allying himself with Germany's "old Catholics," who were against the Vatican's decrees. He in-

troduced measures against church interference with state affairs; declared education and marriage civil matters. For seven years the quarrel went on,

BISMARCK'S POLICIES LAMPOONED:

AT THE WHEEL. The Liberal spoke says: "Don't be too satisfied. As soon as the wind changes I will be on the top of the wheel."

ending only when the tariff issue forced Bismarck to abandon it. As the liberals who supported him were for free trade, Bismarck needed the help of the Catholic party for his tariff legislation. Thus peace between church and state was re-established and Bismarck had the Catholic Center supporting the tariff.

After two attempts were made on the emperor's life in 1878, the chancellor, blaming the Socialists for the outrages, introduced stringent measures against the Social Democrats, whom he wanted to destroy. (His action served as a model for Hitler, who in 1933 used the Reichstag fire as a pretext to destroy the Communists.)

But Bismarck did not bring in only antilabor legislation; he also championed bills—for reasons of his own—to protect and insure the workers against accidents, against sickness, old age, and disability—legislation which other industrial states copied and adopted decades later.

KULTURKAMPF. Many German Catholics refused to recognize the dogma which followed the decrees of the 1870 Vatican Council, declaring the pope's infallibility in matters of faith. Bismarck, using the controversy to political advantage, introduced radical changes in the relations between church and state. He proposed taking birth, death, and marriage registration from the clergy.

HE FOUGHT THE POWER OF THE SOCIAL DEMOCRATS. But he proposed a scheme for workers' sickness, accident, and old age insurance. Following an attempt on the emperor's life in 1878, Bismarck dissolved the Reichstag and in the following election his political antagonists lost heavily. Forced to go underground, the Social Democratic press printed its papers in foreign countries.

24

BISMARCK AND THE CROWN PRINCE
who in 1888 became Kaiser Wilhelm II.

1887, March 22:
THE NINETIETH BIRTHDAY OF KAISER WILHELM I was celebrated with great pomp and ceremony. It seemed as if the whole city of Berlin had come to his palace at Unter den Linden to wish him a happy birthday. In the photograph above, the figures of the aged emperor and his empress, Augusta, are shown at the second floor corner window—painted in by the photographer.

THE OLD KAISER DIES

AT 8:20 the morning of March 9, 1888, a fortnight before his ninety-first birthday, Kaiser Wilhelm I died in Berlin. He had been king of Prussia for twenty-seven years and emperor of a united Germany for seventeen years.

A conservative autocrat, his personal life and outlook were those of a bourgeois rather than a reigning monarch. He watched with eagle eyes over the expenses of his household. Distrusting his servants, he made a pencil mark on the wine bottle to show the level of its contents after each meal. He would not install a bathroom in his palace; when he felt like taking a bath, a tub was brought in from a neighboring hotel. He loved music halls and visited them often. Before he went, he carefully changed his pants; dinner trousers were too good to wear at the theater.

He was first and last a military man. His interests were those of a soldier; his mind centered around his army. He cared little about the people and nothing about their needs. In the 1848 revolution, when he advocated the use of raw force against the revolutionaries, he received the nickname *"Kartätschenprinz"* (Prince of Grapeshot), which he never lived down.

A mediocre personality, Wilhelm I is remembered mainly because his chancellor was Bismarck. The two made a perfect combination: the king,

Photograph by Sophus Williams, Berlin

HIS LAST PHOTOGRAPH. On March 3, 1888, six days before his death, the almost ninety-one-year-old monarch accepts the homage of his people from the window of his palace.

HIS LAST SIGNATURE

In the document the kaiser orders an end to the Reichstag session.

WILHELM I DIED ON MARCH 9, 1888.

an absolute monarch deriving his power from God, a figurehead, and Bismarck, his servant, charting the course of the empire.

They did not always see eye to eye about policies. Occasionally Bismarck had to use all his powers of persuasion to convince the monarch of the rightness of his course. The kaiser was against getting into the war of 1864, which led to the annexation of Schleswig-Holstein; he argued hotly against the war with Austria in 1866, but after the battle of Sadowa he had to be restrained from marching at the head of the victorious army to Vienna and wresting some territory from defeated Austria. Bismarck had difficulty holding him back.

When Wilhelm I died he was succeeded on the throne by his son Friedrich, who was married to the eldest daughter of the English queen Victoria and Prince Albert. A tragic figure, he lived for decades in the shadow of his father, and when his own time came he was already fifty-seven and dying of throat cancer. During the last months of his life, he was unable to speak; too ill to attend his father's funeral, he watched the procession from the palace window. As emperor he took the name Friedrich III, but his very brief reign lasted only ninety-nine days. He died on June 15, 1888, as a last gesture placing his wife's hands into those of Bismarck.

THE NEW KAISER

HE WAS VAIN and shallow; his withered arm made him feel inferior. Though gifted, he never troubled to work hard and until his death remained a dilettante living in a make-believe world. He believed—as did his forebears—that the king's power came directly from heaven; thus his decisions were inspired by God. Bismarck described him: "From Friedrich I he inherited a love of display, vanity, and autocratic nature; from Friedrich Wilhelm I a taste for tall fellows, from Friedrich the Great only the love of interfering in his officials' business, from Friedrich Wilhelm II a mystic turn and a strong sexual impulse, from Friedrich Wilhelm IV the compulsion to talk too much."

He was a consummate actor; his instinct for the theatrical was unerring. He was the product of two cultures, inheriting the characteristics of the Prussian Junker from his father, while his English mother imbued him with respect and love for English liberalism.

Nationalism and militarism—served up with pomp and splendor—were hallmarks of his reign. He did everything on a monumental scale. When his doctor said he had a little cold, he retorted: "No, it is a big cold." His wife bore him six sons and a daughter and was able to satisfy his voracious sexual appetite. His father disliked him; his mother thought him "selfish, domineering, and proud."

FRIEDRICH III (1831–1888), who died after a reign of 99 days.

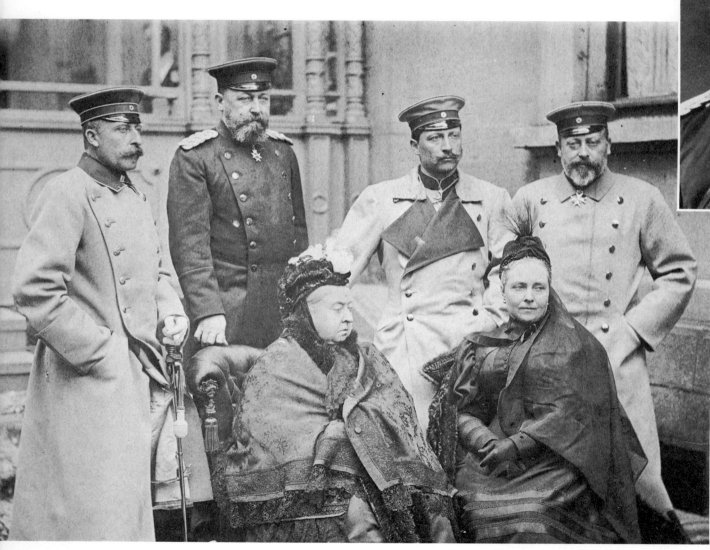

Photograph by J. Russell & Sons, London

GRANDMOTHER: Queen Victoria of England, the grandmother of Kaiser Wilhelm II, is surrounded by her children: Arthur, the Duke of Connaught; Alfred, the Duke of Saxony, Coburg, and Gotha; Edward, the Prince of Wales; and Victoria, the mother of Wilhelm II. He stands behind his grandmother and mother.

THE POWER IN THE LAND:

WILHELM II, who succeeded his father, Friedrich III, in June 1888.

A DEBATE IN THE REICHSTAG ON MAY 18, 1889, about a month after Hitler was born. Bismarck in the chancellor's seat, next to him, State Secretary Boetticher. This superb shot was taken decades before high-speed photographs were commonplace.

BISMARCK'S REICHSTAG

WHILE Bismarck was chancellor, six parties dominated the Reichstag.

On the right were the Conservatives, representing the old feudal ideal of Prussian society, hostile to industrialization and mechanization. They regarded Bismarck as too liberal.

The Free Conservatives (Reichs party), the party of the large landowners outside Prussia, were behind Bismarck. (In 1887 the Conservative and Liberals reached a working alliance—a "cartel"—in support of him.)

The strongest party was the National Liberals, the party of intellectuals, professionals, and the wealthy bourgeoisie. On all major issues they were behind Bismarck.

The Progressive party came into being after Bismarck introduced his tariff and anti-Socialist legislation in 1880. They represented "the alliance of iron, coal, and yarn with grain." Antimilitarist, antiprotectionist, for laissez faire in politics and economics, they steadfastly opposed socialism.

The Center party was the political arm of the Catholic church—at times with the right, at times with the left, and as such opposing Bismarck.

The only party on the left—the Social Democrats—grew from 2 deputies in 1871 to 35 in 1890. They consistently were against the chancellor, holding on to their platform of universal suffrage, proportional representation, a graduated income tax, the eight-hour day.

The minorities were represented by a number of small parties representing Alsace-Lorraine, Posen, Silesia; there were also delegates of the Danes, of the Guelphs of Hanover (who fought their state's incorporation into Prussia), and of anti-Semites.

30

BISMARCK
WITH MEMBERS
OF THE BUNDESRAT.

Das heiligste Recht einer Nation ist das
als solche zu bestehen und anerkannt zu werden.

Photographs by J. F. Klinger, Braunau am Inn

THE MOTHER OF HITLER—Klara Pölzl—Alois Hitler's third wife, bore her husband six children, of whom only Adolf, the fourth, and Paula, the youngest, survived. She was born on August 12, 1860, was married on January 7, 1885, and she died when forty-seven years old on December 21, 1907, not long after an operation for cancer of the breast. She was buried in Linz.

THE FATHER OF HITLER was the illegitimate son of the peasant girl Maria Anna Schicklgruber. He married three times, first a woman fourteen years older, then a girl twenty-four years younger, and finally his last wife, twenty-three years younger. He had his name changed to Hitler in 1876. He was born on June 7, 1837, and died of a stroke at sixty-five on January 3, 1903.

A BOY BORN TO THE HITLERS

WHEN ADOLF HITLER was born on April 20, 1889, in the Austrian city of Braunau am Inn, his thrice-married father was fifty-two years old.

The elder Hitler was a customs officer, a loyal servant of the emperor, whom, like all Austrians, he emulated in appearance and manner. Gruff and pedantic, he ruled his home just as the emperor ruled his palace—with an iron hand. And just as Franz Josef did not know how to be an understanding father to his son Rudolf, so Alois Hitler did not comprehend how to guide his son Adolf. "I honored my father," recalled the son, "but I loved my mother."

He did well in elementary school; but when he entered the Realschule he failed the first grade and had to repeat it. The father confronted his son. In *Mein Kampf* Hitler tried to present the scene as a clash of personalities. He claimed that his father tried to make him a civil servant, while he wanted to become an artist. But more likely the elder Hitler was angered at his son's failure in school.

ADOLF HITLER'S FIRST PICTURE, TAKEN IN BRAUNAU ON MARCH 9, 1890.

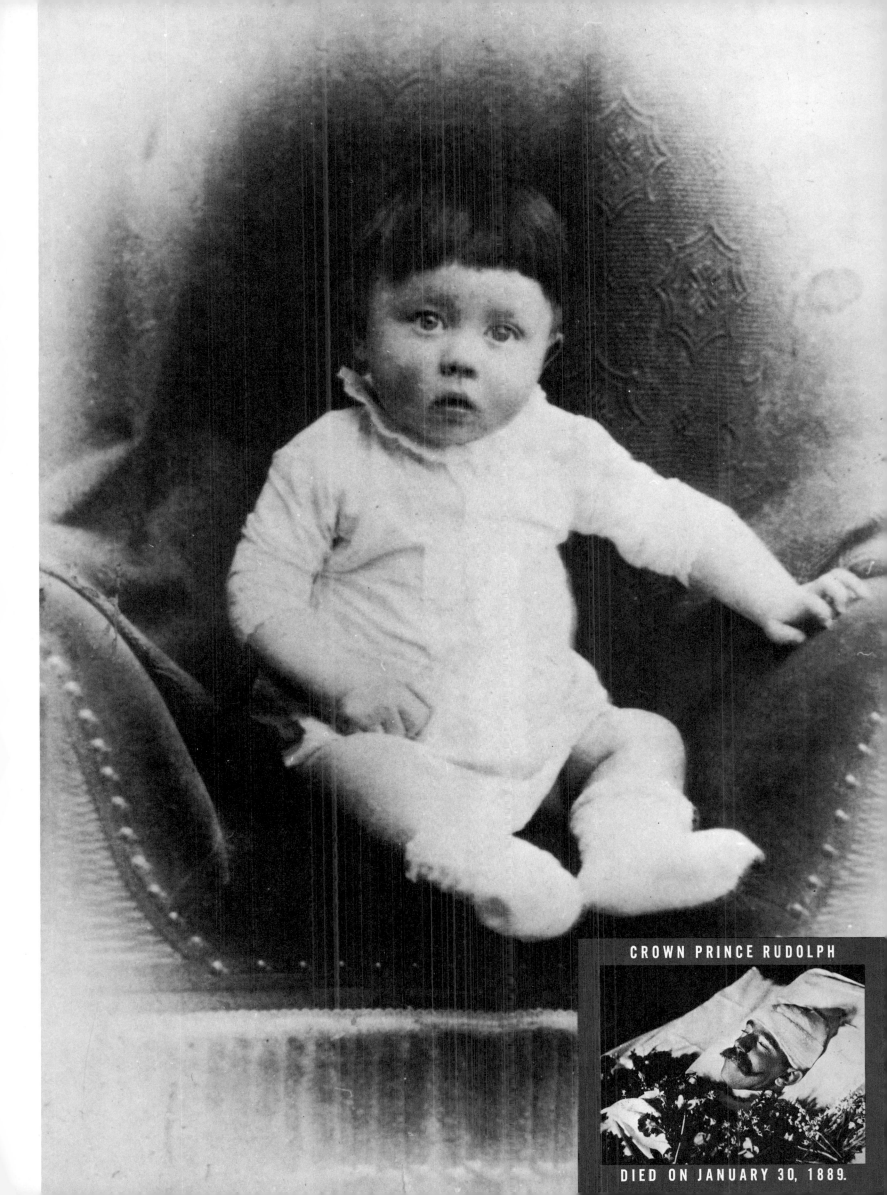

CROWN PRINCE RUDOLPH

DIED ON JANUARY 30, 1889.

BISMARCK RESIGNS

"THE KAISER," said Bismarck in 1888, "is like a balloon. If you don't hold fast to the string, you never know where he'll be off to."

Yet Bismarck would not stay in Berlin to hold on to the string—most of the time he spent at Friedrichsruh, his country estate.

The new emperor, eager to assert himself, was frustrated. His courtiers filled his ears with gossip, putting Bismarck in a bad light. "If Frederick the Great had had a chancellor like Bismarck," they told the emperor, "he would not have been called great."

That Wilhelm would sooner or later clash with his chancellor was inevitable. He wanted to be his own master and to forge ahead, while Bismarck struggled to preserve what he had already achieved. By 1890 Bismarck had served as chancellor for nineteen years; the time was ripe for a change.

On January 24—the birthday of Frederick the Great—Wilhelm called a privy council meeting in which he demanded immediate social legislation: Sunday rest for workers and re-duced working time for women and children. Bismarck opposed it and the two clashed head on.

The kaiser was adamant not to let Bismarck renew his anti-Socialist legislation. "I will crush anyone who opposes me in this undertaking."

The final break came over an old decree issued in 1852 which proclaimed that ministers must consult with the head of the cabinet before communicating with the emperor. Wilhelm wanted its revocation. When Bismarck refused, he had to resign.

1890, March 29:
"THE OLD PILOT LEAVES SHIP." The cartoon by John Tenniel in the English *Punch*, on Bismarck's resignation.

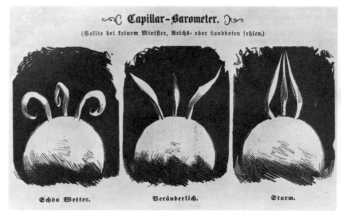

1881, March 13:
"THE BAROMETER which should be on the desk of every minister," reads the caption to this drawing in *Kladderadatsch*, the German political-satirical weekly. Cartoonists made fun of the old chancellor's almost total baldness.

1890, March 27:
FAREWELL! In this cartoon which appeared in *Kladderadatsch* after his resignation, Bismarck hands the cartoonist the insignia of his office—the three hairs on his bald pate.

BISMARCK LEAVES THE CAPITAL. A distinguished group of ambassadors and a host of his political associates came to the Lehrter Station on March 19, 1890, to bid farewell to the chancellor, who described his departure as "a first-class funeral."

Bismarck was succeeded in office by General Count Leo von Caprivi, who served until 1894, at which time the seventy-five-year-old Count Hohenlohe took the reins, holding the post until 1900, when he was replaced by Count Bernhard von Bülow.

RECONCILIATION AND DEATH

AFTER HIS RESIGNATION, Bismarck—full of fighting spirit—stayed at his estate in Friedrichsruh, where he received friends and deputations and wrote articles against the kaiser's policies for the *Hamburger Nachrichten*. His supporters, the National Liberals, secured him a seat in the Reichstag, but he never attended the sessions.

The first years of his retirement were filled with work on his memoirs. Aided by Lothar Bucher, he completed the task in the short space of two years. But publication had to wait until after his death. The first two volumes—put into their final version by Horst Kohl—appeared in 1898; the third volume, containing details of the chancellor's quarrel with the kaiser, was issued in 1919, a year after Wilhelm II's abdication.

For a while after their rift both the kaiser and Bismarck let their anger burn fiercely. When the old man went to Vienna in July 1892 for his son Herbert's wedding, Wilhelm wrote to the Austrian emperor (with whom Bismarck was to have an audience), asking him "as a true friend not to make my situation more difficult by receiv-

1894, January 26:
BISMARCK IN BERLIN. Returning to the capital for the first time since his resignation, the old chancellor, leaning on the arm

ing the rebellious servant before he has approached me and said his peccavi." But a year later, when Bismarck became gravely ill, the courtiers around the kaiser pressed for a reconciliation.

So Bismarck was asked to Berlin to take part in the kaiser's thirty-fifth birthday celebration on January 27, 1894.

On the day of the meeting the kaiser was as nervous as a bridegroom. He was up early, inspected the room

1895, April 1:
THE KAISER
AT BISMARCK'S
80TH BIRTHDAY.

of Prince Heinrich, the kaiser's brother, takes the salute of the honor guard. Behind them walks his doctor, Ernst Schweninger.

Bismarck had not seen the kaiser in four years and could not refuse the invitation to Wilhelm's 35th birthday. The kaiser desired to show the country that the two were not enemies. As the prince made his entrance, Wilhelm kissed him on both cheeks.

where he was to receive his old foe; he rearranged the vases, darted outside to inspect the honor guard, then was back again, fidgeting, pacing the floor. Watching the old chancellor's arrival from the window, he posed himself in the center of the room, waiting for the doors to be flung open. And when Bismarck entered, he held out both hands and kissed the old man on both cheeks.

No sooner was the meeting concluded than the kaiser—never at a loss to make political capital of sentimental occasions—left the palace and took a ride in his coach, showing himself to the people of Berlin, who cheered their great-souled emperor.

During the following years Wilhelm visited Bismarck on several occasions at his home, but every time the discussion veered toward political matters, he turned the conversation to lighter subjects.

On July 30, 1898, Bismarck died, eighty-three years old. Resentful to-ward his master's grandson to the end, he willed that his tomb was to bear the inscription: "A true German servant of the emperor Wilhelm I."

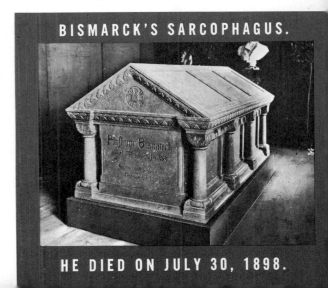

BISMARCK'S SARCOPHAGUS.

HE DIED ON JULY 30, 1898.

HOW THEY LIVED

WORKING MEN SPENT MANY EVENINGS EXERCISING IN THEIR CLUBS.

A COBBLER SHOP AT HOME KEPT THE MEN BUSY AND CHILDREN AMUSED.

THE SIXTY-EIGHT MILLION GERMANS were in four social and economic classes. On the top, having an income the equivalent of $2500 a year and more—an enormous sum for that time —were the aristocracy, the wealthy landowners and industrialists, also doctors, lawyers, professors and prominent artists. Then came the upper middle class—some three million families with incomes between $650 and $2500—landowners with medium-sized holdings, owners of commercial enterprises, higher officials, members of the liberal professions. The third stratum was the lower middle class— farmers, artisans, small tradespeople, minor officials and skilled workers, with incomes ranging between $450 to $650. And at the bottom of the pyramid were the workers, wage earners and peasants earning less than $250 yearly, some six million families.

Class distinctions were sharply drawn. A worker did not tip his hat to his social equal, but bowed deeply down to the ground when a *Regierungsrat* passed by. The image of the kaiser was predominant. Wilhelm II was imitated in appearance and manner. His *"Es ist erreicht"* mustache (it is achieved) was affected by millions of his subjects. The people felt deference to the royal family, enjoyed being governed with ostentatious pomp, and were content with a paternalistic monarchy. "For every pfennig that the German pays in taxes, he exploits and receives a pfennig's worth of government," observed the American Ray Stannard Baker in 1901.

It took half of the Germans to control the other half. Records of every person were meticulously kept, with full details about his occupation, wealth, and social standing. Every change in the citizen's status was dutifully noted by the mushrooming bureaucracy. If someone moved to a new residence, the police had to be notified and a card filed; if someone

IT WAS A MAN'S WORLD. THEY PREFERRED EACH OTHER'S COMPANY TO THAT OF WOMEN—EVEN ON SUNDAYS.

hired a servant girl, she had to be registered on a yellow form.

There were hundreds of petty regulations which proscribed what was forbidden. It was *verboten* to walk on the grass, *verboten* to enter a place reserved for children, *verboten* to bicycle on a path, and so on and on. If one violated the regulation one had to pay a fine (some as low as 2 cents).

The making of a German citizen was the making of a German soldier, and indeed, the making of the German nation. Every male had to serve in the army. The life of a young German was divided into four military terms: the actual service period, the reserve period, the Landwehr period, and the

IN THE GARDEN OF MUNICH'S HOFBRÄUHAUS SHORTLY BEFORE THE WAR.

39

MOVIE HOUSE IN BERLIN'S FRANKFURTER ALLEE IN THE EARLY 1900s.　MOTHER GOES SHOPPING ACROSS THE

Landsturm period. The formative years of a young man were his years in the service. There he was taught obedience and orderliness; he became used to hard work, plain living, and frugality. On the other hand in those years his individuality was weakened, his initiative deadened, and he acquired a lifelong habit of dependence upon authority.

The coming of the industrial age transformed the nation of peasants into a nation of industrial and white-

collar workers. The increase of the population—which prior to the nineteenth century was stagnant—saw a sudden threefold increase within a few decades. People left the land and moved into the cities.

Industrial production surged forward. By the end of the 1871 war German production outdistanced that of France. By the beginning of the new century it surpassed that of Great Britain. And when World War I broke out, Germany was the second largest

1913:
BERLIN. Friedrichstrasse is decorated for the celebration of the kaiser's 25th Jubilee.

SANDWICHMAN ADVERTISES SOUPS FOR 15 AND MEAT DISH FOR 30 PFENNIG.　THE　EMPRESS　GOES　SHOPPING—

Photograph by Heinrich Zille
OLD KNOBELSDORFF BRIDGE IN BERLIN.   ONE OF THE EARLY TWENTY-MINUTE MOVIES STARRING HENNY PORTEN.

industrial nation in the world, close behind the United States.

Workers toiled 11, 12, 13 hours a day, often on Sundays as well.

For the lower classes Sundays made the other six days of the week bearable. They were spent at an inn over pale beer and wurst, while a small string band played favorite tunes.

The pay for a first-rate master carpenter was equivalent to a dollar a day; an unskilled worker made half of that. Workers lived in crowded quarters, with seldom more than two rooms for a family of four. Rent in tenements came to $2.50 a month. The total food for a family of four came to about 35 cents a day.

The lower classes did not take part in the government. They had no influence in making the laws. The Socialists, whose number grew before the war, were severely constrained.

Yet on the whole, the people were content. There was peace, they had their work and their steady incomes.

1916:
MUNICH. Many persons taking part in the Schützenfest stream through the Karlstor.

ND HER DEVOTED SUBJECTS GIVE A CHEER.   THE WOMEN ENJOY THEMSELVES ON SUNDAYS AT THEIR ARCHERY CLUB.

THE TWELVE-YEAR-OLD ADOLF HITLER, photographed in June 1901 with the first class of the Linzer Realschule. He had flunked his class the year previously and now he was repeating it.

The bearded principal is Dr. Oscar Langer. It was usual that students with lower grades were placed at the back in the class picture; Adolf happens to be in the top row—the last boy on the right.

TWO BOYS GROW UP

AFTER FIVE YEARS in elementary schools and four in the Realschule, Hitler was through with his education.

Not long before his fourteenth birthday, his father died. For a while he struggled on in school, then went to Vienna to become a painter. But when he failed his entrance examination at the Academy of Art, the idea of becoming an artist evaporated. His mother died when he was eighteen—and from then on he was alone.

The other boy's life was far easier —as heir to the throne, he had few worries. On his tenth birthday, he was made a lieutenant in his father's regiment. He grew up in the palace, acquired a fondness for cars, horses, and women. Had he not been born a Hohenzollern, the world would never have heard of him.

43

THE TEN-YEAR-OLD SON OF THE KAISER— the crown prince—is invested as a lieutenant in the First Guard Regiment in the traditional ceremony at Potsdam.

KAISER MANEUVERS

1906: WITH YOUNG WINSTON CHURCHILL.

1910: WITH EX-PRESIDENT T. ROOSEVELT.

THE KAISER loved military maneuvers; they were the great events in his life. To show off his military prowess he invited friends from home and abroad to watch them. At one of the maneuvers young Winston Churchill was his guest, at another ex-President Theodore Roosevelt, whom he presented with a set of photographs, scribbling on them facetious captions about peace and pacifists.

After Bismarck's resignation Wilhelm II set out on a "new course." It was *Weltpolitik.*

Bismarck was content to keep Germany's power base in Europe. He did not look for political pastures in other parts of the world. He wanted peace and security at home. To achieve this he built up a system of alliances — the Triple Alliance with Austria and Italy, and the Reinsurance Treaty with Russia. With England he was on friendly footing; he had no desire to enlarge the German fleet or to acquire colonies — two later moves which so upset the British.

The weakness of this system was that the alliances depended upon his personal diplomatic skill. Once he was shorn of his power the political house of cards collapsed — and his successors did not have the ability to rebuild it.

The kaiser was a romanticist; he was determined to move Germany from a continental to a world power. Dominated by dreams of world supremacy, he encouraged the movements for colonies and he fiercely advocated a naval expansion.

Germany needed new sources of raw material, new markets for products and new areas for investment. And the kaiser went after these goals with great energy.

Proponents of the country's new role in world affairs — like court chaplain Stöcker or Major General Bernhardi — eloquently supported such policies. In his National Socialist catechism Stöcker posed the question: "What is nationalism?" and he answered: "The efforts of the German people to spread their influence over the globe." Bernhardi argued in his book *Germany and the Next War* for the elimination of France, the foundation of a Central European Federation under Germany, and the acquisition of colonies as the way to world power.

The trouble with all this was that the character of the kaiser was ill-suited for the implementation of these policies. He had, as von Holstein once remarked, "dramatic rather than political instincts" and no patience to think earnestly and consistently about the problems. His tutor Hinzpeter said of him that he had "never learnt the first study of a ruler, hard work." A weak and vacillating man, he made decisions emotionally, not rationally.

With him at the helm of the state the foreign policy of Germany sailed a zigzag course — at one time steering toward friendship with England, another time with Russia, always moored to the Austrian alliance. That such aims were incompatible with each other and incongruous did not seem to bother him.

Wilhelm, the grandson of the English queen, had a love-hate relationship with England. He regarded his uncle Edward, who followed his grandmama Queen Victoria on the throne, as "Satan," the "intriguer and mischief-maker in Europe." He courted his cousin Nicholas, the czar of Russia, attempting to lure "dear Nicky" into a treaty. He was after Victor Emmanuel, the king of Italy, to keep his partnership in the Triple Alliance.

Forever on the move — he was called the Reise-Kaiser (the traveling kaiser) — his mind changed with the wind. He could never hold his tongue, he blurted out impolitic remarks, and

KAISER WILHELM II JOKES WITH PRINCE MAX EGON ZU FÜRSTENBERG AND THE AUSTRIAN MILITARY ATTACHÉ.

his "oratorical derailments" were a steady embarrassment to his government. After the English raided Transvaal late in 1895 and were routed by the Boers, he dispatched a telegram to the president of the Boer Republic, Paulus Kruger, congratulating him on "restoring peace with your own resources in the face of armed bands which have broken into your country." The people in England were deeply hurt by such tactlessness.

Four years later—in 1900—when a German contingent left for China to deal with the Boxer Rebellion he ex-horted them: "Anyone who falls into your hands falls to your sword! Just as the Huns under King Etzel created for themselves a respected name, the German name will be remembered in China for a thousand years." The world was shocked by the speech.

And in October 1908 in an interview to the London *Daily Telegraph* he blubbered indiscreetly that, while he was a friend of England, most Germans were not. And he told the interviewer that Germany's naval policy was directed against Japan, not against England, and also that it was he who had advised the British command how to defeat the Boers.

His military maneuvers, his blustering utterances about Germany's "mailed fist" and "shining armor" were to warn the world that the Germans were determined to keep their "place in the sun."

The kaiser boasted: "We are destined to great things and I am leading you to marvelous times." Great Britain, France, Russia took note of the boast. When war came they were allied against their common enemy — the kaiser's Germany.

45

VETERANS ARE MARCHING . . .

GERMANY, as the old Socialist leader Wilhelm Liebknecht told the English publicist Wickham Steed, is "an inverted pyramid. Its apex, firmly imbedded in the ground, is the spike atop the Prussian soldier's helmet. Everything rests on that. One day . . . it will topple over, smashing itself and much else in the process."

Under the kaiser's full-steam-ahead policy, militarism and militant nationalism ruled supreme. "Saber rattling" was the thing. The romantic idea of a world united under German supremacy enthralled the nation. In his first Reichstag speech Chancellor Bülow said, "We want our place in the sun," meaning a colonial empire for Germany and a strong navy to protect it.

Older men dreamed of past military glory, younger ones of adventure. For four decades they had lived in peace; now they itched for action—they prepared themselves for war.

MARCHING... MARCHING... MARCHING...

CHIMNEY SWEEPS ARE MARCHING . . .

THE KAISER
WITH HIS SIX SONS
IS MARCHING . . .

SERENITY AT THE BRANDENBURG GATE. The postman walks with his bicycle, the young man rides in his car.

PEACEFUL SUNDAY IN THE SIEGESALLEE with strollers looking at the statues of the German emperors.

TOASTING THE NEW YEAR. Stars of the German stage at a gala New Year's Eve celebration in Berlin empty their champagne glasses to a peaceful and prosperous 1910. From left to right: Hans Junkermann, Else von Rüttersheim, Mrs. Junkermann, Josef Giampietro, Phila Wolff, the celebrated Fritzi Massary, and Guido Thielscher.

THE LAST YEARS OF PEACE

48

Drawing by F. Matania
AMATEUR DANCE CONTESTS IN BADEN-BADEN.

THE OTHER SIDE OF THE COIN—GATHERING WOOD FOR THE FAMILY STOVE. A TYPICAL BERLIN SCENE.

BERLIN had grown into a metropolis. Horse-drawn buses had given way to electric trams. The newly opened subway took passengers from one part of the city to another. There were 7,000 automobiles in the city; twelve of them—all big Mercedes—belonged to the kaiser. They all had special horns, and when the Tatü-tata sounded no one could fail to notice that the emperor was riding by.

In the department stores—at Wertheim or at Tietz—one could buy anything, even the newly introduced tomatoes. At Aschinger a *Stulle* (sandwich) with a beer cost 20 pfennigs. There were twenty big theaters playing to full capacity nightly. Apartment houses with luxury dwellings shot up at the Kurfürstendamm. They were good years—with enough work, enough food, and plenty of amusement.

WALKING FOR HEALTH
IN BERLIN'S TIERGARTEN.

WORLD WAR I

NOBODY WANTED war—not Germany, not England, not Russia, not the French, not even the Austrians — yet war came. It came because of fears and suspicions between nations and because of the political ineptness of the diplomats.

The French feared that the sabre-rattling militarism of Germany was directed against them. England feared losing its supremacy on the seas and its prominence in world trade to the Germans. Austria feared the nationalistic movements in Serbia, Croatia, Bosnia, Czechoslovakia. Russia feared revolution at home and Austrian hegemony in the Balkans.

War came because of the German desire for world domination, because of the unbending attitude of the British, because of the revenge-seeking French, because of the blundering Austrians. And when it did come, people rejoiced. Each country believed that it would be victorious and that it would win the war quickly.

Germany had been preparing for "the day" ever since the turn of the century, and even before. Its meticulously conceived strategy was embodied in the Schlieffen Plan. General Count Alfred von Schlieffen, the chief of the German General Staff for fifteen years (from 1891 to 1906), evolved it during that period. He changed it, perfected it, elaborated on it, and embellished it right up to his death.

The main feature of his plan was a wide encircling sweep against France by the German army's right wing, which was to march through neutral Belgium. The German high command was aware that the violation of Belgium neutrality would bring Great Britain into the war, but thought that the strategic advantage in taking the short route to France was worth the gamble. Schlieffen's plan was daring and risky; its success depended on surprise and swiftness; within six weeks the war had to be won.

The plan was based on "crushing the enemy's flanks" and exterminating the French army by "attacking its rear." The bulk of the German forces — about seven-eighths of the entire

WAR IS DECLARED ON RUSSIA. On August 2, 1914, the day after Germany declared war on Russia, thousands listen to the war speeches in Munich's Odeonsplatz. In the crowd a young man, 25-year-old

THE AUSTRIAN ARCHDUKE FRANZ FERDINAND AND HIS WIFE WERE ASSASSINATED ON JUNE 28, 1914.

Adolf Hitler (see enlargement). He had come to Munich the year before to study painting and architecture. His mother had died at the end of 1907, and since her death the young man was at loose ends, eking out a living in Vienna by taking occasional jobs. His chief occupation was painting city scenes for framemakers and picture postcards for vendors. Upset with the Austrian city —it was, as he later wrote, "the saddest period of my life"— he moved to Bavaria, where, after war was declared on Russia and on France, he volunteered his services to his new country. From the beginning of the war till its end, he was at the front.

51

THE DAY WAR WAS DECLARED. On August 3, 1914, Kaiser Wilhelm II accepts the homage of his subjects from the balcony of his palace. "I see no parties any longer—I see only Germans," he orated.

army — was to pounce on France while one-eighth was to hold back the Russians until the war was decided in the west and troops could be transferred to the east.

The immediate reason for the outbreak of the war was the assassination of the Archduke Franz Ferdinand, the heir to the Austrian throne, by Bosnian nationalists at Sarajevo.

The Austrian government—encouraged by the kaiser — sent a ferocious, humiliating ultimatum to Serbia, charging them with being a party to the archduke's death. Though the Serbs were willing to accept the demands of the ultimatum, the politicians of the dual monarchy were resolved to punish them by war. Thus on July 28, 1914, exactly a month after the archduke's death, war was declared.

The English struggled manfully to contain the conflict and to settle the issues in a conference of the European states, but when Russia ordered general mobilization, Germany followed suit and all hopes for a peaceful settle-

"A STATE OF WAR EXISTS," ANNOUNCES AN OFFICER TO THE PEOPLE OF BERLIN ON THE LAST DAY OF JULY 1914.

Sieg Heil!
The people of
Berlin cheer
the declaration
of war.

OFF TO THE FRENCH FRONT. Seasoned German soldiers on their way to France. On the sides of their railway wagons they chalked such slogans as "Excursion to Paris"; "See you on the Boulevard"; "On for the Battle"; "The tip of my saber is itching."

FROM THE RANKS OF THE RESERVISTS came many of the volunteers, mature men with families who hastened to do their patriotic duty and to fight for the Fatherland.

ment vanished. On August 3 Germany and France declared war on each other; the next day Great Britain declared war against Germany. On August 6 the Austro-Hungarian monarchy declared war on Russia.

Europe was aflame; the armies of the nations were marching in Belgium, in France, in Russia, in Serbia.

A wave of patriotism in the belligerent countries sent the troops into battle with flowers and cheers. The Germans were particularly jubilant. They had been at peace since 1871. Their young men did not know what war was like; none of them had seen a battlefield. Life for them seemed dull when their fathers and grandfathers reminisced about glorious battles. They longed for heroic times, they longed to taste the danger of combat. Their philosophers and teachers imbued

1914, December:

A SCENE REPEATED IN EVERY GERMAN STATION. Wives and sweethearts in their Sunday best wave good-by to their men as the military band plays "Muss I' denn, Muss I' denn zu Städtle hinaus . . ." before the troop train departs for the French front.

them with the spirit of superiority. Convinced of the invincibility of their arms, they were confident of victory. Thus they welcomed war with all the pent-up passion of their frustrated souls. The kaiser and his government promised them that the war would be won by Christmas; they would hardly get their uniforms soiled. They remembered with pride their last three wars — in 1864, in 1866, and in 1871 — and how fast and easily they had won them. If they could do it three times, they could do it again.

Twenty-five-year-old Adolf Hitler was among the cheering multitude in Munich on that hot day in August when war began. He later recalled: "Overpowered by rapturous enthusiasm, I fell upon my knees and thanked heaven from an overflowing heart for granting me the good fortune of being

THERE WAS JUBILATION AND CHEERING. The people believed that they were fighting to defend their Fatherland. They also believed the war would be over quickly.

55

allowed to live in these times." Other young Germans felt the same.

On August 2 Germany sent a note to Belgium demanding free passage of German troops through Belgium territory, and a friendly neutrality. When Belgium refused the request, the German army marched into the country anyway. The Belgians fought the invaders bravely, slowing down their advance, but they could not succeed against the overwhelming number of the enemy, who pushed on with relentless fury, flattening the countryside with their gargantuan new guns.

Reaching French soil, the Germans' encircling right wing — the "fist" of the Schlieffen Plan — crashed into the British and the French around Mons and forced them into retreat.

While the Germans were rolling forward to the French capital, events in the east were proceeding on an equally grand scale. Along the whole front from the Baltic Sea to the Rumanian border the Russians were fighting Austrian and German forces. In the south against Austria the ten days' battle of Lemberg was raging, ending in a decisive victory for the Russians. The Austrians were pushed back.

"In the North the Russian armies, in a noble desire to take the pressure off the West, attacked the Germans in East Prussia, and gained the first bat-

THE ATTACK IN FRANCE...

1914, August:
WORLD WAR I: GERMAN COMPANY AT THE MARNE IN FULL-SCALE ATTACK.

tles," wrote Winston Churchill. "The effect of this Russian advance for which the Allies must ever be grateful, was to draw two army corps from the

German march on Paris." This move brought the Schlieffen Plan into jeopardy. The two army corps which the Germans withdrew from the front were their only reserves in the west. They were to fill any gap which might open in their advancing lines.

On August 20 General von Kluck marched with 40,000 troops into Brussels, taking the Belgian capital; the Belgian forces retreated to Antwerp.

Two days later in the battle in the Ardennes (August 22–24) Germany scored a great victory; it appeared that their steamroller could not be halted and that the French army was facing annihilation.

About the same time (August 23–31) the German Eighth Army in Russia under the command of General Hindenburg with General Ludendorff as his chief of staff totally destroyed two Russian corps and reduced two others to half strength. It was a tremendous victory — the victory at Tannenberg — and it made Hindenburg a national

MOVING INTO RUSSIA: GERMAN SUPPLY TRAIN AT THE EASTERN FRONT.

... AND THE RESULT

1914, September:
THE BURNING OF THE DEAD, KILLED DURING THE FIGHTING AT THE MARNE.

of his predecessor, realized that the defeat at the Marne meant that Germany could no longer hope for a quick victory, that it would be a long and tough war.

After the Marne defeat Moltke was replaced, but the battles under the direction of General Falkenhayn — at Ypres, at Verdun, at Armentières, at Langemarck — brought the decision no nearer.

The front became static. The soldiers dug themselves in. During the entire length of the war the lines did not move in either direction more than six miles. From their fixed positions the opponents shot at each other; they grappled in the long trenches; they killed each other wearily.

The whole of Europe became a battlefield, a wasteland of corpses. Armies were fighting in France, in Russia, in Poland, in Italy, in the Balkans; they were fighting not only on land, but in the air and at sea. German aviators bombed the English coast and the city of Paris. English submarines blockaded German harbors.

It was war on a scale the world had never seen before. During its four terrible years 9,998,000 men lost their lives in combat; 6,295,000 were heavily wounded, more than 14,000,000 were lightly wounded, about 6,000,000 were reported missing.

hero. The 125,000 Russian prisoners the Germans took pointed to a quick end of the war.

On the second of September the Germans crossed the Marne River. General Joffre, the commander of the French forces, told his army that "a body of troops which cannot advance must at all costs keep the ground it has acquired and be shot rather than retreat." Nearly four hundred divisions on both sides fought each other on a line two hundred miles from Paris to Verdun and round the corner from Verdun to the Vosges.

Luck deserted the Germans. A gap opened in their lines, and as their two reserve army corps had gone to the Russian front, they were not able to fill it. The French and the British recognized the opportunity, marched boldly into the gap, forcing the withdrawal of the German troops. Thus, the drive of the Germans came to a halt; the Schlieffen Plan fell apart in the reality of battle. The German army

had to pull back to a defensive position on the Aisne. Moltke, the chief of the German General Staff, who meekly revised and watered down the plans

AFTER A GERMAN ATTACK—THE RUSSIANS SUFFERED MANY LOSSES.

57

A CORPORAL IN THE WAR

HITLER WAS TWENTY-FIVE YEARS OLD when the war began. Until then he had led an aimless life. After he failed to gain admission to the Academy of Art, he loafed in Vienna, skidding into the depths of poverty. For a while he lived in a flophouse, then for several years in a home for men. In the spring of 1913 he left Vienna and "the saddest period of my life." In Munich, his next home, he continued his aimless existence.

After war broke out he petitioned the king to let him, an Austrian, fight in the Bavarian army. Assigned to the Sixteenth Bavarian Reserve Infantry Regiment, he was sent to the front.

He was wounded twice and temporarily blinded in a gas attack.

His superior officers considered him "an exceedingly brave, effective, and conscientious soldier," and though he never attained a rank higher than that of a lance corporal, he earned the Iron Cross First and Second Class and many other military medals. For him the four war years were "the greatest and most unforgettable time of my earthly existence . . . everything past receded to shallow nothingness. . . ." In the all-male world of soldiers, he felt safe.

The armistice found him in the Pasewalk military hospital in Pomerania, recovering from his gas poisoning and despondent at the defeat.

"The more I tried to achieve clarity on the monstrous event . . . the more

THE LEADERS OF THE GERMAN ARMY: General Paul von Hindenburg, who as a young lieutenant was present at the foundation of the Reich, and his chief of staff General Erich Ludendorff. Years later both were involved with the corporal at the right— Ludendorff joined him in the 1923 putsch, Hindenburg named him chancellor in 1933.

EMPEROR FRANZ JOSEF DIED ON NOVEMBER 21, 1916.

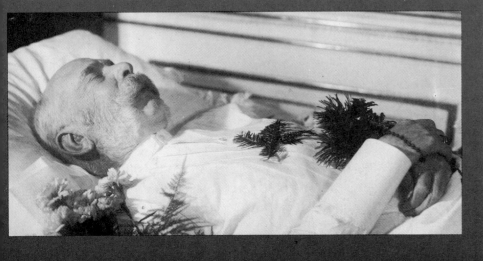

the shame of indignation and disgrace burned my brow," he noted later in *Mein Kampf.* "In these nights hatred grew in me, hatred for those responsible for this deed."

He made up his mind to go into politics. Almost thirty, he was to begin his life anew, this time with a goal.

LANCE CORPORAL ADOLF HITLER (right), WITH TWO OF HIS COMRADES.

THE END

AFTER THE TERRIBLE BLOODLETTING at Verdun, General Falkenhayn was replaced by the victorious generals on the eastern front, Hindenburg and Ludendorff.

The new high command endorsed the policy of unrestricted submarine warfare, convinced that the measure would bring England to her knees. Though Chancellor Bethmann-Hollweg was in fierce opposition to the policy, fearing that it would induce America's entry into the war, the will of the generals and admirals prevailed. On the first day of February 1917, Germany commenced its submarine campaign. A few weeks later, on April 6, the United States entered the war.

The German high command soon realized that the unrestricted warfare would not subdue England. Incited by the failure of the policy, representatives in the Reichstag sought a solution to bring the war to an end. Social Democratic and Progressive deputies joined the Center in a declaration for "a purely defensive war without any thought of conquest." The peace resolutions, as they became called, were proposed by the leading Center party member Matthias Erzberger and were adopted by the House. General Luden-

Illustrated London News, *February 3, 1917*

GERMANY DECLARED unrestricted submarine warfare. Survivors of the *Ivernia* scramble into their lifeboat after the English vessel was torpedoed by submarine in the Mediterranean in January 1917. In the disaster 150 people lost their lives.

Drawing by Norman Wilkinson in the Illustrated London News, *May 15, 1915*

THE SINKING OF THE *LUSITANIA*. Torpedoed by a German submarine off the coast of Ireland on May 7, 1915, the ship went down with 1,255 passengers aboard.

IN SIGHT

dorff, furiously opposing them, forced Bethmann-Hollweg's resignation. The new chancellor, Georg Michaelis, Ludendorff's puppet, announced himself in favor of the resolution as I understand it," which meant that he was ready to disregard it.

Now the two generals—Hindenburg and Ludendorff—became virtual dictators of the country; political power rested in them, not with the Reichstag. Determined to bring the war to a victorious conclusion on the battlefield and not through diplomatic negotiations, they refused to accept Pope Benedict's reasonable peace proposals.

In the fall of 1917 the Communists under Lenin took over the government of Russia. The commissars wanted peace and they were ready to accept it on any terms. In the spring of 1918 in Brest-Litovsk the German military forced a severe, annexationist treaty on the Russians, in sharp contrast to the Reichstag's peace resolutions.

After the war had been concluded in the east, German battalions were transferred to the western front in a hurry. Ludendorff hoped that his great spring offensive in France would secure victory. At first it seemed that the German steamroller would anni-

AMERICA ENTERS THE WAR. On April 6, 1917, after all his peace efforts had failed and after a number of American ships had been sunk by German submarines, President Woodrow Wilson reads America's war declaration to Congress.

THE YANKS ARE COMING! Members of Company E of the Michigan National Guard leave Pontiac in June 1917 to board ships for the battlefields of Europe.

61

WAR WAS IN EVERYBODY'S BLOOD. Children in a Berlin working-class district imitate their elders by playing war games. They march and parade, carrying flags.

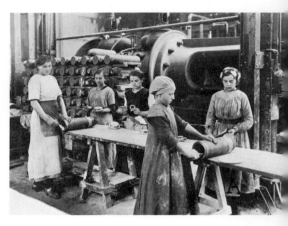

GERMAN WOMEN FILL SHELL CASINGS.

CAPTURED BY THE ENEMY.
Exhausted German prisoners of war catch up on lost sleep in a French detention camp.

THE ATTACK ON VERDUN in 1916 took the lives of many thousands, leaving the Casemate Gully looking like a landscape of the moon

LES SAUVAGES

Que te faut-il
ie plus, bon
vieux Dieu
allemand?

WILHELM THE BUTCHER.
A French cartoon on the kaiser.

hilate the French, but when on August 8 an Australian army corps under General Monash pierced the German front line, the day, in Ludendorff's words, became "the black day for the German army."

Fresh American troops poured onto the battlefield continuously. The hard-pressed Germans were forced to roll back their front to escape encirclement.

On September 28 Germany's allies — Austria-Hungary, Bulgaria, and Turkey—threw in the towel. Ludendorff and Hindenburg lost their nerve and insisted on an immediate armistice. The war had been lost. To negotiate with the enemy, Prince Max von Baden was appointed chancellor.

The high command hoped for an armistice which would give them time to reorganize the troops and prepare them for a fresh assault. But President Wilson in his note of October 23 dashed their hopes. He made it clear that he would not propose an armistice

GERMAN MEN ARE DEAD IN BATTLE.

HUNGER OVER THE LAND. Because of the British blockade, food grew scarce. German housewives had to stand in line all day long for a loaf of bread or a piece of meat.

AFTER THE SOMME OFFENSIVE, the French and the British armies captured 182,502 German soldiers and vast quantities of war material.

WAR LEADERS AT HEADQUARTERS. Hindenburg, Böhm-Ermolli, Ludendorff, Bardolf, and von Seeckt confer in Poland.

to the Allies which would allow the resumption of hostilities. Arrogantly, the generals called Wilson's statement "unacceptable."

Three days later Ludendorff was relieved of his duties. Putting on false whiskers and dark glasses, and dressed in civilian clothes, he fled to Sweden. On November 6 General Gröner, who succeeded him as quartermaster general, informed the chancellor that the army would have to surrender if an armistice could not be arranged within three days.

To Prince Max's urgent note President Wilson replied that the Allies were willing to enter peace negotia-

tions on the basis of the Fourteen Points, and that French marshal Foch would explain the armistice conditions to the generals. As there was no alternative, Wilson's proposals had to be accepted. Representatives were appointed to receive the armistice terms. The war—after four years of suffering and sacrifice—came to a close.

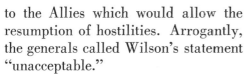

MARSHALL FOCH'S MESSAGE
bringing an end to the hostilities.

LABOR

INDUSTRIALIZATION brought with it the growth of labor. The first labor parties came into being when Ferdinand Lassalle founded the General German Workers' Association in 1863, and Wilhelm Liebknecht and August Bebel founded the Social Democratic Labor party in 1868. After unification, the two parties merged in 1875 as the Socialist Labor party. It called for legislative reforms and improvement of working conditions but, much to the annoyance of Marx, stayed silent about revolution and class struggle.

Between 1878 and 1890 Bismarckian legislation suppressed the socialists. When the party became legal again in 1891, its program, adopted in Erfurt, compromised between reformists and revolutionaries. It contained such reform proposals as an eight-hour working day, prohibition of child labor, factory inspection, right of unionization, and so on.

When years later Eduard Bernstein offered a series of reforms, the schism between reformists and radicals widened. In the Mannheim congress of 1906 (after the defeat of the Russian revolution), the radicals were blocked by the trade unionists.

But Karl Liebknecht, the leader of the radical wing, kept on agitating against militarism. For this he was imprisoned for a year and a half.

In the Jena congress of 1905 Friedrich Ebert was elected to the Executive. He reorganized and modernized the

FRIEDRICH EBERT, ONE OF THE SOCIAL DEMOCRATIC LEADERS. The industrious, shrewd, and honest Ebert was an early recruit to the socialist movement. A saddler, born in 1870 the son of a poor tailor, he was a gifted conciliator and became the leader of the majority Socialists in 1916. After the monarchy toppled he was selected for the presidency of the Republic.

HARD TIMES FORCED MEN (many old, many unfit for service) to work in the munitions factories. Their dissatisfaction at the beginning of 1918 erupted in a strike.

64

SPLITS

party, introducing such novel equipment as telephones and typewriters. Even before he became co-chairman—after Bebel's death in 1913—he wielded the power in the organization.

In August 1914 the Social Democratic Reichstag delegation, displaying national unity in defense of the state, voted unanimously for war credits and accepted the *Burgfrieden*, a political truce, for the duration of hostilities.

Liebknecht, who protested against the violation of Belgian neutrality, the annexationist war aim, and the social and political irresponsibility of the government, was assailed by the party leaders for failing in his duty both to his party and to his country.

The final break between the moderates and radicals came after the tumultuous Reichstag session on March 24, 1916, over the emergency budget, when those who disapproved the party's policies were charged with being agents of the enemy. Disbarred from the party they organized themselves into an Arbeitsgemeinschaft which a year later became the Independent Socialist party (U.S.P.D.). Soon the radical wing of the Independents—Liebknecht and his friends—split away; their Spartacist Bund became the Communist party of Germany.

The split of the Social Democrats into three factions—majority Socialists, Independents, and Communists—paved the way for Hitler's totalitarian dictatorship.

KARL LIEBKNECHT, ONE OF THE LEADERS OF THE SPARTACISTS. Liebknecht, an eloquent revolutionary, voted against war credits in August 1914. He was arrested during an anti-war demonstration in 1916 and imprisoned for two years. Released before the war ended, he headed the radical Spartacist Union, which, by the end of 1918, had become the Communist party.

HARD TIMES FORCED WOMEN to earn extra money to keep their households going. They made clothing in their homes, which they brought to collection stations.

REVOLUTION IN BERLIN

THEY CALLED IT a revolution. But was it really? There was no one—with the possible exception of Karl Liebknecht and Rosa Luxemburg on the extreme left—ready to lead the masses, ready to formulate their aims, ready to outline a new order in place of the old.

Imperial Germany had ceased to exist not because it had been overthrown by revolutionaries, but because its army had been beaten, because its resources and its people were exhausted. The kaiser had to abdicate, and "the military masters of the mo-

narchical autocrats" had to depart, because President Wilson and the Allies refused to deal with them. And the military leaders clamored for an armistice to forestall the army's collapse.

On November 8, a day before the upheaval in Berlin, the good-natured Bavarian king searched for his boxes of cigars before moving out of his palace in Munich, while the witty Saxon king told his subjects in his inimitable Saxon dialect: "Now do your shit by yourselves!" ("*Macht euren Dreck alleene!*")

On November 9, with the armistice terms already in the hands of the German negotiators to be signed within seventy-two hours, Prince Max von Baden, the imperial chancellor, still had received no word from the kaiser. So at noon, waiting no longer for a decision, he announced the abdication of Wilhelm II and handed the government over to Friedrich Ebert, the leader of the largest party in the Reichstag, the Social Democrats. "Germany's fate now depends upon your conscience," Prince Max told Ebert,

1918, November 9:   *Photo: Willi Ruge*
SOLDIERS BACK FROM THE FRONT WAVE A RED FLAG AT BRANDENBURG GATE. THE PEOPLE SEEM SURPRISED.

1918:
ON NOVEMBER 9 AT TWO O'CLOCK IN THE AFTERNOON: The Social Democrat Philipp Scheidemann announces the Democratic Republic from a balcony of the Reichstag in Berlin.

1918:
ON NOVEMBER 9 AT FOUR O'CLOCK IN THE AFTERNOON: The Spartacist leader Karl Liebknecht announces a German Soviet Republic from the balcony of the kaiser's deserted palace.

and Ebert replied: "I have lost two sons for this country!"

By then the streets of Berlin were swarming with people who had left their jobs to demonstrate against the war and to demand "peace and bread." They marched through the streets and filled Unter den Linden, shouting slogans and waving flags, cutting the imperial cockade from soldiers' caps and slashing the insignia from officers' tunics—venting their pent-up hatred of Prussian militarism.

By evening the demonstrations subsided and Berlin had gone to bed. Next morning the papers carried the news—known already to everyone—that the imperial government had resigned and the Social Democrats had taken over.

BATTALIONS OF SAILORS MOVE INTO THE PALACE OF KAISER WILHELM.

THE MONARCHY TOPPLES

1918, November 11:
THE NEW OCCUPANTS. Workers' and Soldiers' Council members back from war make themselves at home in the Reichstag.

below right:
THE KAISER'S ABDICATION DOCUMENT rescinding all his rights to the German crown.

1918, November 10:
THE KAISER FLEES. In the early morning hours Wilhelm II waits at the Dutch border for the special train which will carry him into exile. He never saw his homeland again.

1918, November 9:
ON THE DAY OF THE REVOLUTION THE EMPEROR'S RETAINERS LEAVE THE PALACE WITH THEIR BELONGINGS.

IN HIS NOTE of October 23, 1918, President Wilson had declared that if the monarchical autocrats and military masters were to remain at Germany's helm, America would ask "not for peace negotiations, but surrender."

Still hoping to save his throne, the kaiser conferred with his generals, ready to move against his rebellious subjects and subdue them. He had to be told that the army was no longer behind him, and that the country demanded his abdication.

The Social Democrats had no plans to abolish the monarchy; they would have served happily under the old state form. All they asked was the abdication of the kaiser. "I hate revolution like sin," exclaimed Ebert, and he was peeved when his colleague Scheidemann declared the Republic in an impromptu speech. He admonished Scheidemann for making such a far-reaching announcement without prior consultation.

On November 9 the monarchy ceased to exist. Though the kaiser still tried to maneuver himself out of his predicament and refused to sign his abdication, events caught up with him. He had to go.

During the early hours of the next morning, his private train took him to Holland, never to return to his homeland. Ludendorff had already flown to Sweden, wearing false whiskers.

Thus the Hohenzollern monarchy ended—not with a bang, but with a whimper.

1918, November:

THE ARMISTICE WAS SIGNED, THE TROOPS LEFT THE TRENCHES AND RUSHED HOME AS FAST AS THEY COULD.

To MAINTAIN ORDER Ebert needed the help of the army. He reached an understanding with General Wilhelm Gröner which turned out to be a fatal one for the Republic, but one which at that time hardly could be avoided.

To bring the troops home in an orderly way, the high command asked the government's support for the officer corps so discipline could be maintained. It further asked for transport and provisions for the troops still at the front, and the promise of a firm stand against the spread of Bolshevism.

In return the officer corps promised to support the new government and not to take up arms against it. Field Marshal Hindenburg was to remain at his post and supervise the return of the troops.

However, without waiting for their orders, the exhausted soldiers began to stream home. They were bewildered and could not understand why they had lost the war. For years they had been made to believe that they were invincible. Trusting in victory, they were unprepared for defeat.

Returning from the battlefield, they found the homeland in chaos, its social institutions shattered, order and discipline gone. Had they made their sacrifices for this?

THE HEROIC DAYS ARE OVER

HOMEWARD BOUND—OVER THE RHINE BRIDGE AT KOBLENZ.

EXHAUSTED ERMAN TROOPS N THEIR WAY UT OF BELGIUM.

THE SECRETARY OF WAR GREETS THE SOLDIERS. The politicians Molkenbuhr, Scheidemann, and Wels stand on the right of General Scheuch; to his left, General Lequis.

BENEATH *"FRIEDE, FREIHEIT,"* THE ARMY ENTERS BERLIN.

1918, DECEMBER 10:

EBERT GREETS the returning troops. The head of the government told them: "You have not been beaten on the battlefield," a statement of which he was reminded for the rest of his life.

MARCHING THROUGH THE BRANDENBURG GATE IN 1918 AS THEY DID AFTER THE FRANCO-PRUSSIAN WAR IN 1871.

RETURN FROM THE WAR

A MONTH AFTER the armistice Berlin welcomed the return of the troops, and in the time-honored tradition they marched through the Brandenburg Gate. Even though this time they brought defeat, Unter den Linden resounded with cheers and hurrahs and bands played as if it were a victory celebration. Government dignitaries made speeches from a specially erected platform. Carried away by the occasion, Ebert said that the Germans had not been beaten—a phrase his enemies later used to great advantage.

No German wanted to believe in defeat. The people could not comprehend that all their sacrifices had been in vain. They looked for a scapegoat—and soon found one: the "November criminals." It was the new Republican government that had sold them out, that was responsible for the defeat—not the kaiser and his generals. And the people believed the blatant lie.

THE OPENING MEETING of the Workers' and Soldiers' Council in Berlin in which 450 deputies took part for the first time.

Sitting on the government benches: The Socialist party leaders Emil Barth, Ebert, Dr. Ludwig Haase, and Philipp Scheidemann.

WORKERS' COUNCIL

THE WORKERS' and Soldiers' Council —the new Republic's first parliament —did not represent the nation; at first its members came only from the Berlin area. Only when their great congress convened in mid-December was the whole country represented in it.

The majority Socialists won the

1918, November 25:
AT THE CONFERENCE OF GERMAN STATES in the Berlin Reichs Chancellery, representatives of the several states discussed proposals for a constitution.

1918, December 16–19:

VOTING FOR PARLIAMENTARY DEMOCRACY. The majority Socialists won a great victory in the meetings as 400 delegates sup- ported a constitutional national assembly, while only 50 opposed it. The Independents then withdrew, splitting the labor movement.

Zentralbild, Berlin

On the left of Friedrich Ebert, who addresses the delegates, are Emil Barth, Otto Lands- berg, Dr. Ludwig Haase; on his left, Wilhelm Dittmann and Kurt Baake.

election while many radicals—among them Karl Liebknecht and Rosa Lux- emburg—could not even be elected.

The cabinet (now called the Coun- cil of the People's Representatives) was formed by three majority Social- ists (Ebert, Scheidemann, Landsberg) and three Independents (Haase, Ditt- mann, Barth). The Socialists propa- gated "peace, security, order," the Independents the principle of "a social republic" in which workers would hold the power—a soviet republic.

The moderate view prevailed in the congress as the motion for electing a national assembly by democratic means carried overwhelmingly. There- upon the Independents took their sup- porters to the streets, expecting to achieve victory through arms.

75

FIGHTING AT

On November 9, 1918, a contingent of 3,000 sailors moved into the kaiser's palace to protect the new government. It was a motley crew—more intent on looting than on revolution. Hardly settled, they stole everything they could lay their hands on—silver, paintings, china, and fixtures.

When they were ordered to leave the palace, they refused. After a quibble over their back pay, a group of them moved to the chancellery, surrounded it, and seized the city's military commander, the Social Democrat Otto Wels, and two of his associates, keeping them captive.

Friedrich Ebert, the head of the new government, turned to Supreme Military Headquarters, and Quartermaster General Gröner, General Ludendorff's successor, was willing to dispatch troops to subdue the rebellious navymen.

On Christmas Day 1918, a division under the command of General Lequis took up position outside the palace and began bombarding it. Plaster fell

1918, December:
ARMED CIVILIANS ARRIVE AT THE KAISER'S PALACE TO RESTORE ORDER.

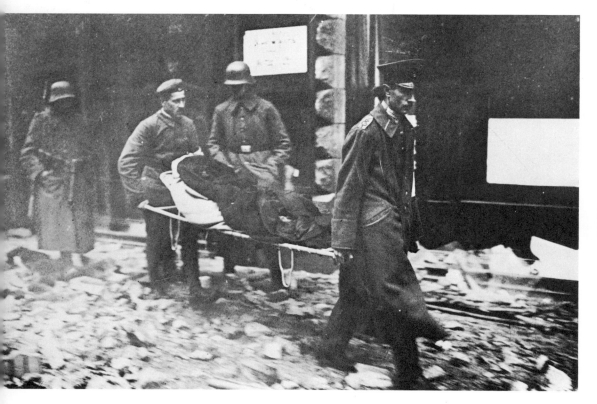

A CASUALTY IN THE CHRISTMAS DAY FIGHTING IS CARRIED TO SAFETY.

MACHINE GUNNERS AT BEGAS FOUNTAIN

A DESTROYED PILLAR AT THE MARSTALL.

THE PALACE

1919, December:
GOVERNMENT TROOPS AT THE PALACE SET UP THEIR MACHINE GUN NEST.

to the pavement, all the windows were shattered, the walls of the building split. The defenders were forced to capitulate and release their captives.

The fighting at the palace had far-reaching political consequences. The left wing of the Social Democrats—the Spartacists and the Independent Socialists—resented the government action of calling in old army troops against the sailors. In the end the Independents severed their connections with the majority Socialists—refusing to be associated with the Social Democratic "murderers." The Spartacists, who were ill at ease about their temporary alliance with the Independents, broke away from them and formed their own organization, calling it the Communist party of Germany.

The unity of labor was in ruins. The three political organizations to which most working people belonged—the majority Socialists, the Independents, and the Communists—faced each other as enemies.

SPARTACISTS CARRY A WHITE FLAG ON THEIR WAY TO NEGOTIATE.

THE FAÇADE AFTER THE BOMBARDMENT.

HTING AT THE MARSTALL WAS PROLONGED.

BROTHER AGAINST BROTHER

1919, January:
THE STREETS OF BERLIN TURN INTO A BATTLEFIELD. The Spartacist workers under Karl Liebknecht and the government troops called out by the Social Democratic government fought each other with bitterness. Both factions called a general strike.

A BERLIN STREET SCENE IN THE

THE RADICALS in the ranks of labor attacked the Social Democrats for calling out old reactionary army troops against the revolutionary sailors. The three representatives of the left-wing Independents left the cabinet and were replaced by more conservative men.

Pathé Newsreel

FIRST WEEK OF JANUARY 1919. IN THE SAVAGE FIGHTING THOUSANDS OF WORKERS LOST THEIR LIVES.

The government then demanded the resignations of other Independents holding lesser posts. When Emil Eichhorn, chief of the Berlin police—a highly respected Independent Socialist and a close friend of the late Socialist leader August Bebel—refused to resign, he was summarily dismissed. Thereupon his enraged supporters moved into the police presidium and called their supporters for a massive demonstration against "the dictatorial rule of Ebert and Scheidemann."

On January 5 the Independents and the Communists took to the streets of Berlin, determined to force the government of the majority Socialists into submission. They were well supplied with money and weapons from the Soviet embassy. Adolf Joffe, who represented the Russians in Berlin, was a

1919, January:

IN THE NEWSPAPER DISTRICT the Spartacists and the government troops were battling each other. By mid-January the opposition of the Communist forces was broken.

friend of Trotsky and, as such, a firm believer in world revolution. He fomented the radical movement, hoping to transform Germany into a Soviet state. The Spartacists—now calling themselves Communists—were in the forefront of the upheavals. They asked for a dictatorship of the proletariat and a close tie with the Russian Communist government. Taking over the leading newspaper offices in the city—*Ullstein, Mosse, Scherl,* even the Social Democratic *Vorwärts*—they issued their own publications.

The hard-pressed Ebert government once more had to turn to the army for help. Gustav Noske, a pillar of the middle-of-the-road Social Democrats and now a member of the cabinet, organized the resistance. Accepting his appointment as supreme commander, he said cockily: "Someone must be the bloodhound; and I will not shrink from the responsibility." He approved the formation of Freikorps, to be manned by veterans and drifters from the old army and led by former officers.

The battle between the Communists and the troops fighting for the government began, and it raged for seven days—the "bloody Spartacus week" —from January 6 to 12. In the fighting the Freikorps took savage vengeance on "the Red traitors," forcing them out of the police presidium and killing 156 Communists. Many of the defenders at the *Vorwärts* were massacred by a Potsdam regiment as they walked out of the building to surren-

FUNERAL PROCESSIONS IN THE CAPITAL became a common occurrence during the month of December. Those who lost their lives in the street fighting were buried with solemn ceremonies and many thousands of their comrades followed the coffins.

ROSA LUXEMBURG, another of the Spartacist leaders, was brutally clubbed to death by members of the old army.

1918, December 6:
AT THE FUNERAL OF REVOLUTIONARY WORKERS killed in the first days of the uprising, Spartacist leader Karl Liebknecht speaks. Within a few weeks he was murdered.

der. In the encounters a thousand revolutionaries lost their lives.

The fighting was hardly over when a brutal act of Freikorps officers stirred passions anew. In the evening of January 15 they abducted and murdered the two Communist leaders: Karl Liebknecht and Rosa Luxemburg—a vile and senseless act. Both Liebknecht and Luxemburg were against the armed uprising, both had urged their supporters to take part in the forthcoming election for the national assembly rather than boycott it.

These first political murders in the new Republic paved the way for countless others—from then on murder and violence became an accepted practice of domestic policy.

The Communist uprising spread to the Ruhr, and to the cities of Leipzig, Hamburg, and Bremen. It returned to Berlin, where once more a general strike was called, and once more the Freikorps moved against the workers. "Butcher" Noske ordered that anyone with a weapon in his hand be shot on sight, and the Freikorps men willingly obeyed his words.

The fightings widened the gulf between the parties of the workers. Social Democrats and Communists grew into bitter adversaries, hating each other more than their common reactionary enemies. Their antagonism, which never healed, undermined the future of the Republic.

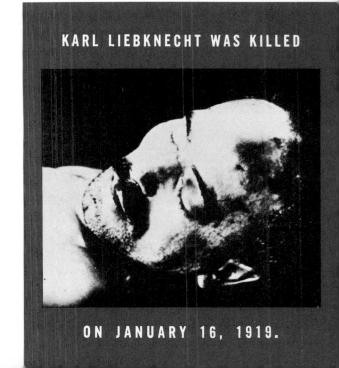

KARL LIEBKNECHT WAS KILLED

ON JANUARY 16, 1919.

1919, January 19:

AFTER A LIFE UNDER A MONARCHY GERMANS CHOSE A NATIONAL ASSEMBLY UNDER THE SYMBOLS OF THE OLD ORDER

OVER THIRTY million people—half the country's population—went to the polls on the Republic's first voting day. Everyone over twenty was eligible to cast a ballot, and for the first time in German history, women were allowed to vote.

The result was an overwhelming victory for the Social Democrats; they received over 11.5 million votes and won 163 of the national assembly's 421 seats. Next came the two Catholic parties with almost 6 million votes. (The Centrum, marked with Z on the graph on page 85, was to be represented by 73 delegates; their southern brethren of the Bavarian People's Party—BVP=Bayerische Volks-Partei —by 18.) The Democrats (D) made an extremely strong showing with 5.5 million votes, which gave them 75 seats. The Nationalists (DNVP =Deutschnationale Volks-Partei) received less than 3 million votes, and had 44 seats,

FIRST VOTING
FOR THE
REPUBLIC

THE LEADER OF THE SOCIAL DEMOCRATIC PARTY, Friedrich Ebert, and his wife on their way to the polling place on January 19, 1919. The national assembly elected him the first president of the German Republic.

THE CRUCIFIX AND THE KAISER.

while the Independents (USP=Unabhängige Sozialdemokratische Partei) got 2.3 million votes and 22 seats. The German People's Party (DVP= Deutsche Volks-Partei) was the greatest sufferer with only 1.6 million votes and 19 seats. The smaller rightist parties (KlRP=Kleine Rechts Parteien)

FOR THE FIRST TIME women were allowed to vote.

ELECTION PROPAGANDA IN BERLIN. Veterans of the war roamed the city's streets distributing political leaflets from their army trucks to the interested citizens.

DEMOCRATIC PARTY SUPPORTERS march in the streets with their brass band.

DEMONSTRATING AGAINST THE VOTE. The Communists urged their supporters not to vote. As their propaganda made little sense to the workers, they did not follow it.

COMMUNIST POSTER showing Liebknecht, slain before the election.

got 3, and the smaller middle parties (KlMP=Kleine Mittel Parteien) got 4.

The election constituted a triumph for political democracy. The three great parties supporting the Republic—the Social Democrats, Center, and Democrats—gathered over three-quarters of all the votes cast and were represented by 311 deputies.

If at this time the Western democracies had offered a helping hand to their defeated enemy; if the statesmen of England, France, and America had had a fairer vision of the future; if they had been prepared to offer magnanimous peace terms; if they had been willing to initiate liberal trade policies to aid the starving populace

of the new Germany and to put the economy on its feet, the future of Europe would have been promising indeed. There would have been peace and tranquillity for a long time to come. But the Allied statesmen—the French Clemenceau, the English Lloyd George, and the Italian Orlando—who wielded the power in the drafting of

THE POLLING PLACE. Voters take one more glance at a candidate's literature.

SOON TO BE CHANCELLOR. Philipp Scheidemann, one of the leaders of the Social Democrats, and his wife cast their votes at a polling place in Steglitz, a suburb of Berlin.

NATIONALIST POSTER recalling Frederick the Great's Prussian spirit.

GETTING THE PEOPLE OUT TO VOTE. The Social Democratic party had money and a good political organization. Their victory at the polls was never in doubt.

the peace treaty, were not magnanimous, but vengeful. And they were able to force President Wilson to give in to their fateful policies. The "big four" at Versailles made critical blunders. Their harsh demands, their greed, their moral righteousness, their determination to keep the Germans under their thumbs and "make them pay" for

their deeds in the war paid ghastly dividends. Their unforgiving attitude helped pave the way for Adolf Hitler and his cruel National Socialist dictatorship—and for the most horrible war the world has ever seen.

But this is hindsight. Had these men been able to peer into the future, they would have acted in a different way.

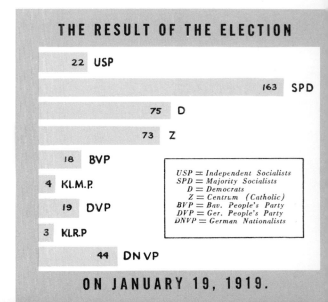

THE RESULT OF THE ELECTION

22 USP
163 SPD
75 D
73 Z
18 BVP
4 Kl.M.P.
19 DVP
3 Kl.R.P
44 DNVP

USP = Independent Socialists
SPD = Majority Socialists
D = Democrats
Z = Centrum (Catholic)
BVP = Bav. People's Party
DVP = Ger. People's Party
DNVP = German Nationalists

ON JANUARY 19, 1919.

THE WEIMAR PARLIAMENT

THREE LEADING POLITICIANS. Social Democrat Philipp Scheidemann, the Weimar government's first chancellor, with Count Johann-Heinrich Bernstorff, former German ambassador in Washington, and Dr. Hugo Preuss, author of the new constitution.

THE COUNTRY'S FIRST National Constituent Assembly met in Weimar, the city of Goethe and Schiller.

In his opening address Friedrich Ebert, the head of the new government,

THE NATIONAL THEATER IN WEIMAR, where the first national assembly met. The crowd around the Goethe-Schiller monument waits for the opening of the session.

THE NEW PARLIAMENT. On February 6, 1919, Friedrich Ebert addressed the first national assembly. On the government

advocated a return to parliamentary methods in order to deal with the economic and social changes resulting from Germany's defeat in the war.

He emphasized that the war had not been lost because of the revolution, nor could the Republic be blamed for the armistice; the generals had led the armies to defeat, and Prince Max von Baden's government was forced to ask for the armistice.

Ebert protested Allied plans to impose harsh and severe peace terms on

THE MEETING IS IN PROGRESS. The representatives of the newly elected national assembly are seated in the orchestra of the Weimar National Theater while the press and the spectators are in the balcony.

bench from right to left: Philipp Scheidemann, Dr. Otto Landsberg, Rudolf Wissel, and Prussian premier Paul Hirsch. On the right, the first man on the aisle is Count von Brockdorff-Rantzau, who was to represent Germany at the peace conference.

Germany and issued a warning: "The German people cannot be made the wage slaves of other countries for twenty, forty, or sixty years." He proposed cooperation and expressed the new regime's friendly and peaceful intentions toward all other nations. He insisted that the peace terms be based on President Wilson's Fourteen Points and urged Germany's admission into the League of Nations.

On February 11, acting on the provisional constitution, the delegates in the assembly made Ebert president of the Reich. A new government came into being under the chancellorship of Philipp Scheidemann. His cabinet consisted of members of the three largest parties—the Social Democrats, Democrats, and Center—the parties of the Weimar Coalition. The opposition was composed of the Nationalists and the Independent Socialists.

With the formation of the first parliamentary cabinet, the machinery of the government began to roll.

FRIEDRICH EBERT (x) on the balcony following his election to the presidency on February 11, 1919.

1919, May 1:
THE THREE-WEEK-OLD COMMUNIST GOVERNMENT ENDED WHEN GOVERNMENT TROOPS ENTERED THE CITY.

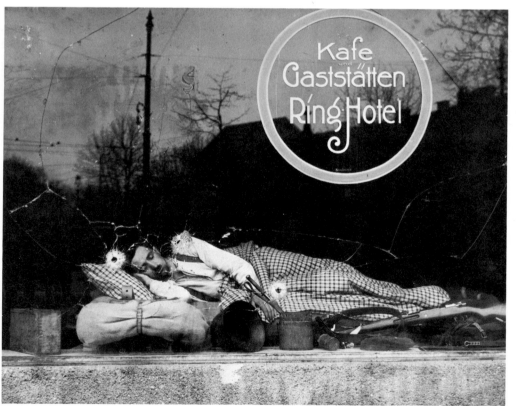

1919, May 2:
NOT A WINDOW DECORATION. An exhausted soldier of the government troops, who were brought to Munich to subdue the Communists, takes a nap in the window of a hostelry.

SOVIET IN

EVEN BEFORE the upheaval in Berlin, there had been a revolution in Munich. On November 7 the Bavarian king was deposed and journalist Kurt Eisner became prime minister. He was an odd choice—an honest and decent man but with no talent for political leadership. He lost his support rapidly. In the first Diet election on January 12, 1919, he and his followers could only secure 3 seats, while the conservative Bavarian People's Party received 66.

On February 21, while on his way to the Landtag opening to hand in his resignation, Eisner was shot by the young Nationalist officer Count Arco-Valley. The assassination (only a few days after the murders of Karl Lieb-

THE LAST BATTLES. A WOMAN PEERS OVER THE BARRICADES WONDERING IF IT IS SAFE TO RUSH HOME.

BAVARIA

knecht and Rosa Luxemburg in Berlin) inflamed the populace; a Worker-Soldier Peasant Central Committee assumed power and proclaimed a state of siege in Munich. On March 17, when the Diet was allowed to reconvene, the Social Democrat Johannes Hoffmann was chosen minister president; but four days later, after receiving the news that a Communist government had come to power in Hungary, a group of radical *literati* formed a Communist government and proclaimed the Bavarian Soviet Republic. Hoffmann and his ministers fled, and the city was taken by the Communists.

For a few days the romantic young revolutionary poet Ernst Toller head-

1919, February:
THE HEAD OF THE BAVARIAN GOVERNMENT. The assassination of Kurt Eisner (in center) by the young Count Arco-Valley paved the way for the Bavarian Soviet Republic.

1919, May 2:

ARRESTED COMMUNISTS are led across Munich's Max Joseph Platz by a lone government soldier. Both sides committed brutalities: the Communists murdered hostages, the "liberators" murdered citizens who, they believed, sympathized with the Communists.

ed the government; but in less than a week Russian-bred Communists had ousted him and taken over. Led by the twenty-three-year-old sailor Rudolf Egelhofer, the revolutionary army—workers, drifters, jobless—turned into an undisciplined mob. Banks were raided, homes ransacked, property confiscated.

From its exile in Bamberg the Hoffmann government called for opposition to the Communist regime.

On their march toward Munich troops of the army clashed with Communists in Dachau and suffered defeat. Hoffmann now asked the Berlin government for Freikorps and they were hurriedly dispatched. On their way they committed incredible atrocities, shooting everyone who opposed them, killing fifty-two Russian war prisoners in their

COMMUNISTS DESTROYED THE POLICE PRESIDIUM FILES.

GYMNASIUM WALL WHERE THE HOSTAGES WERE SHOT.

1919, May:

THE HOME GUARD TAKES OVER. Armed members of the home guard patrol the streets of the city in an effort to restore order.

COMMUNIST FRITZ SEIDEL was caught and sentenced to death for ordering the execution of civilian hostages without trial.

camp, and murdering a group of medics. In retaliation the Communists shot hostage members of the nationalistic, anti-Semitic Thule Society.

On May Day 1919, the "liberating" troops entered Munich from all directions, killing many of the Reds as they surrendered. Hundreds of Communist combatants were slain; twenty-two members of the Catholic St. Joseph's Club were massacred on a whim.

Munich long remembered those bloody and violent days. The rule of the Reds evoked hatred for Communism, and because many of the Communist leaders were Jews, the flame of anti-Semitism burned high. Bavaria took a turn to the right—a situation which Corporal Adolf Hitler, who remained quietly in a Munich barracks during the upheaval, exploited later.

FREIKORPS WERDENFELS TROOPS MOVE INTO MUNICH.

LT. COL. FAUPEL SALUTES THE LIBERATION TROOPS.

THE PEACE TERMS

THIS WAS CLEMENCEAU'S hour for which he had waited forty-seven years. As a young man he had witnessed his country's collapse and Germany's triumph in 1870. The time for his revenge had come. After he addressed the conference the thick volume of peace terms was handed to the German representatives. They were not permitted to respond to the terms or to debate them—they were allowed to reply to them in writing only. The drafting of the treaty was done by the victors without German participation.

The chief aim of the "peacemakers" was to crush German militarism so that it could never rise again. Thus the German army had to be reduced to 100,000 men, the general staff to be dissolved, all war-making capability curtailed. Germany was not to own military airplanes, armored cars, submarines. It had drastically to reduce its navy and its merchant fleet.

As to territorial requests, in the west, the Germans were to surrender Alsace-Lorraine to France and to demilitarize the Rhine. The French were to occupy the Saar province with its valuable mines for fifteen years; they were also to occupy the land west of the Rhine. In the east, Germany was to renounce Upper Silesia to Poland (this provision was later modified), and also West Prussia and most of Posen. Danzig was to be set up as a free city, the port of Memel incorporated into Lithuania. All German colonies in Africa had to be relinquished.

The terms were not as harsh as expected—though Germany was to lose some 70,000 square kilometers of territory together with six million inhabitants, the treaty's provisions did not break up the country itself; after Russia it still remained the largest nation in Europe.

Remembering well how Bismarck forced France to pay five billion francs in reparations after the 1870 war, the seventy-eight-year-old Clemenceau insisted that Germany pay for all war damages it had caused. A year later—in 1920—the Allied Reparation Commission set the amount of reparations at 132 billion gold marks.

Photo: ABC

LEAVING BERLIN FOR VERSAILLES. The leader of the German delegation, Count Ulrich von Brockdorff-Rantzau (facing the camera in center) at the Potsdamer Station before his departure.

Photo: Henri Manuel

THE GERMANS IN VERSAILLES—a picture taken through a window—listen to Georges Clemenceau. After the Frenchman's speech the draft of the treaty was handed to the Germans.

1919, May 7:

THE SIX GERMAN DELEGATES as they leave their hotel for the Trianon Palace in Versailles on May 7, 1919. From left to right, Robert Leinert, Social Democratic president of the Prussian Landtag; Dr. Carl Melchior, a partner in the Max Warburg Bank of Hamburg and the delegation's financial expert; John Giesberts, postmaster-general and leader of the Christian Workers' Movement; Count Ulrich von Brockdorff-Rantzau, foreign minister, who headed the delegation; Dr. Otto Landsberg, minister of justice; Dr. Walter Schücking, a Democratic member of the Reichstag and a specialist on international law. The delegation's adviser, Dr. Walter Simons, ministerial director of the foreign office, is not in the picture.

Though the German delegation had no official knowledge of the treaty's provisions — which were negotiated by the Allies in secret sessions — they learned about its contents through journalistic and political channels and were prepared for it.

THE SIGNING OF THE TREATY

THE COPY OF THE TREATY IS TAKEN TO THE HALL.

Painting by William Orpen

HEAD TABLE AT THE VERSAILLES CONFERENCE.

1919, June 28:
IN THE HALL OF MIRRORS AT

To ALL GERMAN counterproposals, to all suggestion for changes, Clemenceau turned a deaf ear. He insisted that the Germans sign the treaty.

In the national assembly in Berlin, all parties argued against the signing. But what else was there to do? Matthias Erzberger, the leading member of the Center party, remonstrated with

VERSAILLES, WHERE THE EMPIRE WAS PROCLAIMED IN 1871, GERMAN DELEGATES SIGN A TREATY OF DEFEAT.

his colleagues that even though the treaty's provisions were hard, they must be accepted.

On June 23, only a few hours before the expiration of the deadline, the assembly voted for acceptance, with the German Nationalists, the German People's Party, with some members of the Center party and the Democrats in opposition up to the bitter end.

The ceremonial signing of the treaty took place in the same Hall of Mirrors at Versailles where the Bismarckian German Reich was proclaimed in 1871. France had her *revanche*. Alsace-Lorraine was hers again. It was a happy day for Clemenceau—*"Une belle journée,"* he exclaimed.

SIGNATURES UNDER THE TREATY:
For the Americans: President Woodrow Wilson, Robert Lansing, and Henry White. For the Germans: Müller and Dr. Bell.

95

1919, May 12:

"WHAT HAND WOULD NOT WITHER that binds itself and us in these fetters," orated Chancellor Philipp Scheidemann before the national assembly in the Berlin University. "This treaty in the opinion of the government cannot be accepted." Opposed to its provisions, Scheidemann resigned; Gustav Bauer's government, which followed him, reluctantly accepted the "dictated peace."

BERLIN'S STUDENT FRATERNITIES PROTEST THE "DISGRACEFUL PEACE."

AGAINST THE TREATY

THE TREATY'S provisions—particularly Article 231, the war guilt clause placing the blame for the war on Germany, and Article 228, the clause calling for punishment of Germans "for acts against the laws and customs of war"—caused great excitement in Germany. Meetings of protest were held in every city and hamlet; the nation went into mourning; theaters and movies

1919, June:

"NOTHING BUT THE FOURTEEN POINTS," reads the banner at Berlin's victory column, referring to President Wilson's proposals. At the time Wilson submitted his Fourteen Points for consideration, he said: "There shall be no annexations, no contributions, no punitive damages." But at the peace conference his proposals had been changed. The Germans felt they had been betrayed.

were closed. The Germans felt deceived because the terms sharply contradicted Wilson's Fourteen Points; they had laid down their arms because they believed Wilson's promises—conveniently forgetting that there was nothing else they could have done since they were beaten and their own supreme command insisted on an armistice.

For Foreign Minister Scheidemann the terms were "unfulfillable, unbearable, and ruinous"; therefore he would not sign them. In a bitter address he told the national assembly: "What hand would not wither that binds itself and us in these fetters."

Hindenburg, still supreme commander, suggested "an honorable defeat [rather] than a shameful peace," a high-sounding phrase, which, if followed, would have led the nation not only to chaos but to dismemberment.

PROTESTING THE LOSS OF THE GERMAN-SPEAKING ALSACE-LORRAINE.

THE WEIMAR CONSTITUTION

THE NATIONAL ASSEMBLY met in Weimar on February 6, 1919. Five days later it elected Friedrich Ebert as provisional president, and on February 24 Dr. Hugo Preuss introduced his draft of the new constitution.

Preuss, a brilliant scholar, a liberal of leftist conviction, and an admirer of Baron Stein and his reforms in Prussia, was a professor of constitutional law at the Commercial University of Berlin. The Nationalists eyed him with suspicion, not only because he was a liberal, but also because he was a Jew. In his book *The German Nation and Its Politics*, published just after the beginning of the war, he implied that the war would force Germany away from the monarchy and toward democracy. During the war years he argued for constitutional changes and reforms—forwarding a memorandum of his thoughts to Chancellor Bethmann-Hollweg in 1917.

A democratic constitution for Germany had to solve the problem of "balancing the powers of the central government with those of its constituent members"—a problem which had been with the country ever since its beginning. Bismarck seemed to have found the answer—he believed the German princes were "indispensable links" between people and state—but with the collapse of the monarchy, the Bismarckian ideas went overboard. What kind of role should the state governments play in a democratic Republic? They were just as conscious of their prerogatives as the princes had been, if not more so. Bavaria held onto her blue-white colors; Prussia would not consider giving up any of her hegemony.

Preuss favored a strong central government. He maintained that it would be anachronistic to let Prussia keep her separate power status within the future German Republic. When his first draft of the Constitution was made public early in January 1919, the storm broke. All parties, from right to left, strongly criticized Preuss's suggestion for a unitary government.

The assembly referred the draft to a committee, where it was discussed with meticulous care. Each one of the 181 articles was read and debated twice; thus five months passed before the committee could complete its task. All issues were debated with great fervor. The article prohibiting formal orders and titles brought an avalanche of protest. To give up the titles? No longer to be called Herr Geheimrat or Frau Regierungsrat? The article about the colors of the flag aroused deep feelings. The liberals favored adoption of the black, red, and gold colors of the 1848 revolution, the rightists were for the black, white, and red flag of the old German Reich. In the end a compromise was made with black, red, and gold as the flag of the Reich, and black, white, and red the colors of the merchant marine.

The preamble to the proposed constitution—vaguely leaning on the words of the American constitution—stated: "The German people, united in all their branches, inspired by the determination to renew and strengthen its Reich in liberty and justice, to preserve peace both at home and abroad, and to foster social progress, have adopted the following constitution."

The Reich was to be a republic, its political authority vested in the people. The legislature was to be bicameral, with a Reichstag elected by proportional representation, and a Reichsrat, or council, representing the "lands "—the states which formed the German Reich. The ultimate expression of popular will and the supreme legislative power would be with the Reichstag. While representation was to be proportional, the voting would be done by parties. Preuss conceived the powers of the president to resemble those of the French head of state rather than those of the American. A supreme court was to be created.

The constitution was modeled on the parliamentary institutions of Western Europe as well as on the American constitution. (Unfortunately, no attention was paid to the fact that the existence of two strong national parties in America contributed to that constitution's success.)

Preuss's conception was a democratic and centralized German Reich. It was to be a unitary federal state, its members to be the "lands" (no longer called the "states"). National defense was to be under the exclusive jurisdiction of the federal government; but the lands were to retain control over the administration of the courts, the maintenance of law and order, local administration, and education. The finances of the Republic were to be centralized, relieving the lands of their former economic leverage in national politics. A National Economic Council was to be formed to review governmental drafts of social and economic legislation.

The right to vote was to be given to everyone over twenty—men and women alike. (This turned out to be no blessing for democracy. When Hitler was drumming for support, the German women were the first to give him their vote, even though he made no secret of his belief that their place was in the kitchen.)

The final draft of the constitution was adopted on August 11—which became Constitution Day—with 262 favorable votes by the Social Democrats, Center party, and Democrats. Oppos-

Article 1.

The German Federation is a republic. Supreme power emanates from the people.

Article 22.

The representatives are elected by the universal, equal, direct, and secret suffrage of all men and women over twenty years of age in accordance with the principle of proportional representation . . .

Article 48.

If a state fails to perform the duties imposed upon it by the federal constitution or by federal law, the President of the Federation may enforce performance with the aid of the armed forces.

If public order and security are seriously disturbed or endangered within the Federation, the President . . . may take all necessary steps for their restoration . . . with the aid of the armed forces. For the said purpose he may suspend for the time being, either wholly or in part, the fundamental rights described in Articles 114, 115, 117, 118, 123, 124, and 153.

Article 109.

All Germans are equal before the law. Men and women have in principle the same political rights and duties.

Titles may be conferred only when descriptive of an office or calling; academic degrees are not hereby affected.

Orders and decorations may not be conferred by the state.

Article 114.

Personal freedom is inviolable. No restraint or deprivation of personal liberty by the public power is admissible, unless authorized by law.

Article 117.

The secrecy of correspondence, as well as the secrecy of postal, telegraphic, and telephonic communications is inviolable . . .

Article 119.

Marriage, as being the basis of family life and the fundamental condition for the preservation and increase of the nation, is under the special protection of the constitution. It rests upon the equality of rights of the two sexes.

A FEW OF THE 181 ARTICLES OF THE WEIMAR CONSTITUTION, WHICH HAD BEEN ADOPTED ON AUGUST 11, 1919.

ing it were 75 representatives of the Nationalists, the German People's Party, and the left-wing Independent Socialists.

The main fault of the document, as hindsight showed, was its far too positive attitude; born in the revolutionary days, it did not provide for future contingencies. Thus Article 48, which empowered the president to permit the chancellor to rule by emergency decrees, was adopted with no safeguard against future abuse. In later years, when Hindenburg had allowed Brüning and Papen to rule by such decrees, he could not deny them to Hitler. And Hitler—after he was allowed to govern without a parliamentary majority—not only circumvented the words of the constitution, but its entire meaning.

DRUGGIST FROM LINZ.

BROKER "HANNES."

LOCKSMITH FROM COLOGNE.

ART DEALER SAM SALZ.

GERMAN

WHAT IS A GERMAN? Isn't he like any other human being? Hath not a German eyes? Hath not a German hands, organs, dimensions, senses, passions?

In the twenties August Sander immortalized his compatriots from all walks of life in photographs which are striking revelations of their character. The subjects who faced his camera grew up under the reign of Kaiser Wilhelm II, lived through the World War and the revolution, and were now settled in the Republic. Their faces display that "Deutschland, Deutschland

Photographs by August Sander taken in the twenties

PASTRY COOK FRANZ BREMER.

TEACHER FROM WESTERWALD.

PEOPLE

über Alles" look, a confidence in the superiority of the German race. As citizens of the Weimar Republic, some of them had already rallied behind the Austrian corporal who harangued them about national pride and unity and told them that their army had not suffered defeat in the war, but had been betrayed by the politicians and Socialists at home.

No nation likes to be reminded of its failures. People erase humiliations from memory, finding scapegoats to take the blame for their defeats.

STUDENT FROM NÜRNBERG

DEPUTY JOHANNES SCHEERER.

101

THE LEFT FIGHTS ON

1919, Summer:
THE CARCASS OF A HORSE, killed during a street battle between the Communists and government troops, is pounced upon by the starving people of the strife-torn city.

STREET FIGHTING BETWEEN THE

THE PARTY of the Social Democrats was the workingman's party—its members were law-abiding petty bourgeois, not revolutionaries. They were for better working conditions, for higher wages, and the eight-hour day—not for class warfare and the dictatorship of

POTSDAMER PLATZ
DURING THE TRANSPORTATION STRIKE
IN JULY 1919.

GOVERNMENT TROOPS AND RADICAL WORKERS CONTINUED EVEN AFTER THE ADOPTION OF THE CONSTITUTION.

the proletariat. Only the left-wing Spartacists and Independents kept the flame of revolution burning.

One of the revolutionary issues before the country was the proposed Factory Council Law. It was strongly opposed by management—which did not want council representatives to sit on the boards of their companies or to open their books to them. The Independent Socialists were against the law as well, fearing that the councils might turn into company unions. The streets of Berlin saw demonstrations and clashes. On the day of the bill's second reading in the Reichstag, forty-two workers were killed in a confrontation with police. The government declared a national emergency and once more "Butcher" Noske called out army troops against the workers.

103

1921:

AN AIRPLANE CEMETERY IN A SUBURB OF BERLIN. The Versailles treaty did not allow the Germans to keep their military aircraft; they had to be destroyed, every single one of them. The only airplanes permitted were those for civilian purposes.

NO MORE WAR!

THE RIGID MILITARY stipulations of the peace treaty were difficult to enforce. The Germans rebelled against the reduction of their army to 100,000 men and the ban on all kinds of war weap-

THE ARMY HAD BEEN RESTRICTED TO 100,000 MEN.

UNIVERSAL MILITARY SERVICE WAS ABOLISHED.

GIVEN TO THE FLAMES. Both fighter planes and Red Cross aircraft were burned. The Allied inspection committees supervised the execution of the treaty's provisions.

ons. And when they could not convince the Allies to modify their terms, they turned to Soviet Russia. By a secret agreement the Soviets allowed the Germans to train pilots and build aircraft and tanks inside Russia; in exchange the Germans were to reorganize the outdated Red Army. Both nations were satisfied with the arrangement—both benefited by it.

THE TREATY FORBADE SUBMARINES AND ALSO TANKS. ALL RIFLES AND GUNS HAD TO BE SURRENDERED.

GENERAL HINDENBURG AFTER HIS TESTIMONY on November 18, 1920, before the national assembly's investigating committee which was attempting to find out why Germany lost the war. Refusing to answer questions, Hindenburg read a prepared statement to the committee in which he defended the army and denounced the political parties for betraying and deserting the military leadership. He referred to the fictitious words of an English general who was supposed to have said the German army had not lost the war on the battlefield but had been stabbed in the back. That the statement had no basis in fact did not bother the right-wing politicians—they repeated it over and over again until the "stab in the back" legend was believed by millions of Germans.

"STAB IN THE BACK"

THE NATIONAL ASSEMBLY formed a committee to investigate the causes of the defeat and to establish the responsibility for it.

When General Hindenburg appeared before the committee, he declared that according to an English general the German army had not lost the war but had been stabbed in the back. Who this English general was, he would not say —and never did. Subsequently, the names of Sir Frederick Maurice and Sir Neil Malcolm were mentioned.

That the allegation should have been made by the same Hindenburg who on August 14, 1918, admitted that the war could not be won, and who on October 25, 1918, announced that the only alternative to an armistice would be the heroic downfall of the whole nation was surprising indeed. During the war he never with one word suggested that his army had been "stabbed in the back." It was a full year after the defeat before he came up with the phrase—much to the joy of the Nationalists, who promptly adopted it as a slogan in their attacks on the Republican government, the "November criminals."

A FATEFUL TRIAL

As TIME WENT ON the animosity between the ardent Nationalist Karl Helfferich and the Catholic Center representative Matthias Erzberger grew in intensity. Helfferich venomously attacked Erzberger, the man who offered a peace resolution in the Reichstag in 1917, who signed the Allied peace terms at Compiègne in 1919 at the request of the high command, and who became Helfferich's successor.

Their antagonism led to the celebrated libel suit early in 1920. Erzberger was forced to resign from the cabinet, his political career seemingly at end. But the Nationalists were still not satisfied. A year later, when Erzberger tried to resume his political activity, he was murdered by two officers of the Nationalists' terrorist right-wing gang: the Organization Consul. The man whom the Nationalists blamed for Germany's surrender received his "punishment" at last.

MATTHIAS ERZBERGER
(1875–1921), the finance minister in the Republic, sued for libel after he was attacked by his antagonist Dr. Helfferich in a newspaper article. The court accepted most of Helfferich's accusations; Erzberger resigned. Scarcely a year later he was murdered.

DR. KARL HELFFERICH
(1872–1924), the finance minister in the monarchy and archenemy of Erzberger, who called him "the least responsible of all ministers of finance." His response in the *Kreuzzeitung* led to the suit and a Pyrrhic victory. Three years later he was killed in a train crash.

TO KEEP ALIVE

Food was scarce, jobs scarcer. The Allied blockade was lifted only slowly and gradually; thus little food came from outside the country. The war had destroyed Germany's production

BERLINERS SEARCHING FOR COAL.

capacity and the misery was intensified by the severe winter.

Money bought less; a year after the war's end the mark was worth only one-fifth of what it had been before 1914.

The rapidly mounting inflation played havoc with people's savings. Those who kept their money in institutions to provide for necessities, sickness, or old age, were stymied to see their little hard-earned capital shrunk to nothing. As the value of the mark dwindled, as the price of a pound of butter or a loaf of bread rose into astronomic sums, the small investors saw their savings forfeited; they were left without means, without reserves.

Soon the entire middle class—small investors, pensioners—was reduced to abject poverty. To keep themselves going the people from the cities scoured

the countryside for food and firewood; they sold their belongings—the family silver, their jewelry, and even old tin cans. They could hardly think or talk of anything but food. Some lucky families kept pigs in their pantries to be slaughtered as the need arose. Others raised chickens in their gardens.

Most of the men and women were suffering from hunger. If a store offered dog biscuits a long line formed outside to procure them. People ate whatever they could find. Horsemeat became a delicacy, potato a luxury.

Germany had become a vast starvation camp—and there was no relief in sight. It seemed that the miserable war years would never come to an end.

The people endured their suffering —there was nothing else to do. But a deep-seated resentment welled up in

MIDDLE-CLASS WOMEN GATHER FIREWOOD IN THE COUNTRY—TO BARTER FOR LIFE'S NECESSITIES IN BERLIN.

Photo: Willi Ruge

THE SIGHT OF MUTILATED WAR VETERANS BEGGING ON THE STREETS OF THE CAPITAL BECAME A COMMON ONE.

their souls against the government which would not or could not help them. They remembered the old days. Under the kaiser there was enough to eat—and there was order, not perpetual fighting in the streets. It was diffi- cult for the country to come to terms with defeat—to accept that the war had been lost, and that it was the kaiser and his generals who were responsible for conditions, and not the demo- cratic government of the new Republic. The nationalist organizations, preparing for the day when they would be ready to take their revenge, fanned the discontent, kept the people's dis- satisfaction burning, and lured them into their ranks.

THE KAPP PUTSCH

THE REPUBLIC was still in its infancy —only sixteen months old; yet it was surrounded by enemies not only abroad, but at home as well. Rightist politicians, Freikorps leaders, and Reichswehr officers felt the time had come to overthrow the government. From outside came pressure for the reduction of the army to 100,000 men, as stipulated in the peace treaty—and a demand for bringing judgments against the "war criminals," from the kaiser and his generals down to hundreds of lesser officers.

The army was alarmed. What would happen to them if the government acceded to some of the Allies' requests —as it was bound to do—and dismissed 40,000 men and 20,000 officers? Where could they get jobs?

The men in the Freikorps were also uneasy. The government was ready to disband them—not only were they costly, but they were enemies of the

WALTHER VON LUETTWITZ, commander of the troops in the Berlin area, was one of the many disgruntled generals who tried to set up a military dictatorship.

BERLIN WAS IN AN UPROAR.

1920, March 15:
"STOP! OR YOU WILL BE SHOT," reads the sign at an intersection in the city.

THE FLAG OF THE MONARCHY is unfurled by the rebelling soldiers.

ARTILLERY EMPLACEMENT at Unter den Linden not far from Brandenburg Gate.

CAPTAIN HERMANN EHRHARDT, the notorious Freikorps leader whose brigade played a vital role in subduing the Bavarian Communists, was another putschist.

GENERAL VON SEECKT the chief of the army (right) with General Blomberg (left)

110

1920, March 15:   *Photograph by Wolfgang Weber*

FIGHTING IN THE GROSSE FRANKFURTER STRASSE.

BARRICADES IN THE WILHELMSTRASSE.

Republic. War Minister Gustav Noske ordered General Luettwitz, the commander of the troops in the Berlin area, to dissolve the Freikorps under his command. One of these was the celebrated Ehrhardt Brigade, which had fought against the Poles in Upper Silesia, against the Communists in Berlin, and which had a deep-seated antagonism for the Social Democratic government and the Republic. Its members dreamed of a glorious national army and the restoration of old times. Apprehensive about losing their jobs, they readied for a putsch—to bring the government down.

The incident which sparked the uprising was the judgment in the Helfferich-Erzberger trial announced on March 12—a victory for the old regime and a sharp defeat for the Republic. The forces of reaction—not too intelligent and not too well-prepared—thought that all they had to do was to make a move and the government would collapse.

Thus on the evening of the day the judgment became known, the troops of Luettwitz and Ehrhardt moved toward Berlin from the barracks at Döberitz, some twenty-five miles from the city.

The Ebert government turned to the chief of the army for help, but General Seeckt is supposed to have replied: "Reichswehr does not fire on Reichswehr." Though the general's official biographer noted this remark, those who knew Seeckt deny he ever made such a statement. But the fact remains that the Reichswehr did not move against the "invaders."

The government, without protection and apprehensive of being captured by the putschists and kept as hostages, fled Berlin, and from Dresden called for a general strike.

On the morning of March 13 the putschists' military formation reached the government district in the center of the city. Without resistance the chancellery and other offices were taken over by the troops under General Luettwitz. Posters on the walls of buildings announced that the Social Democratic government of Ebert had been deposed, and that the new chancellor of the Reich was Dr. Wolfgang

1920, March 17:   *Ufa Newsreel*

THE FINAL DEED OF THE PUTSCHISTS. On March 17, the last of the four-day Kapp putsch when "National Chancellor Kapp" threw in the sponge, and when Ehrhardt's brigade was given orders to move out of Berlin, the retreating troops turned their machine guns on the jeering crowd at the Brandenburg Gate, killing a dozen innocent people. This senseless massacre marked the end of the putsch. The ambitions of the right-wingers were thwarted by the general strike of the working class.

Kapp, the provincial director of East Prussia—a mediocre Nationalist politician.

The putschists believed such an announcement would suffice—and that the government would topple. Expecting the support of the populace, they had no other plans. Because it was a Saturday, no typists were in the chancellery—thus no orders could be issued until Kapp's daughter arrived and began to pound them out on a typewriter. There were no rubber stamps because the bureaucrats in the ministries had hidden them—and how could one issue orders without rubber stamps? The officials of the Reichsbank refused to hand out money to the new officials without the presentation of authorized signatures.

The Ebert government's call for a general strike was answered by the workers; the strength of the trade unions asserted itself. Life in the city came to a standstill. Streetcars ceased to run, transportation came to a halt—there was no electricity, and the water supply of Berlin began to give out.

Although the Reichswehr remained invisible, the aloof attitude of General Seeckt boded ill for the putschists. Thus, without a shot being fired, the putsch collapsed. In the afternoon of the seventeenth—four days after the Freikorps had marched into the city—

they moved back to their barracks at Döberitz, singing along the way:

"The Ehrhardt Brigade smashes everything to bits,
Watch out, you worker son-of-a-bitch!"

Before the brigade left Berlin, there was a bloody incident at the Brandenburg Gate. Taunted by youngsters, the frustrated Freikorpsmen fired into the crowd, leaving on the pavement a number of dead. They also left behind the working people's hatred of them, a hatred which was readily reciprocated. This animosity between the reactionary nationalistic military forces and the supporters of a democratic state form lasted as long as the Republic.

113

1920, APRIL: ARMED WORKERS MOVE INTO THE BATTLE IN THE RUHR.

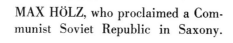

MAX HÖLZ, who proclaimed a Communist Soviet Republic in Saxony.

HOME GUARD MEMBERS IN THE RUHR DISTRICT AT RIFLE PRACTICE.

THE REDS STRIKE BACK

THE UPROAR OVER the Kapp putsch spread to the Ruhr and to the Saxon Vogtland. Armed bands of workers were ready not only to fight the expected right-wing coup, but to bring about a radical revolution. Some of the industrial cities of the Ruhr were taken over. In retaliation for the upheavals, the French moved into Germany and occupied a number of towns.

IN THE ELECTION OF JUNE 6, 1920, the governmental coalition suffered a severe defeat. Its votes dropped from 19 million to 11 million, while the rightist parties gained from 5.5 to 9.1 million votes, and the Communists from 2.1 to 3.3 million votes.

Chancellor Hermann Müller, who resigned after the Weimar Coalition lost its majority in the Reichstag, was asked to form a new cabinet but failed when the Independents refused to cooperate. After a long crisis Centrist Fehrenbach became chancellor.

A SWING TO THE RIGHT

PROPAGANDA POSTERS OF THE COMPETING POLITICAL PARTIES.

THE PARTIES OF THE right cried for a new election, hoping that the result would increase their representation in the first Reichstag. It did. With lawlessness, inflation, and unemployment on the increase, the voters grew disillusioned with the new Republic.

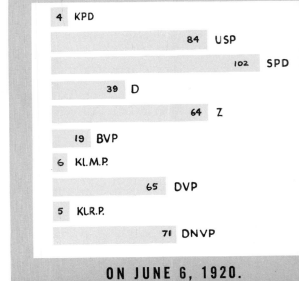

VOTING FOR THE 1st REICHSTAG

4	KPD	
	84	USP
	102	SPD
39	D	
	64	Z
19	BVP	
6	Kl.M.P.	
	65	DVP
5	Kl.R.P.	
	71	DNVP

ON JUNE 6, 1920.

THE REPARATIONS ISSUE

A YEAR AFTER the signing of the peace, an international conference was called to Spa to discuss German disarmament, German coal deliveries, and other related issues. For the first time the Germans were asked to sit with French and British representatives as equal partners.

The conference began under a cloud of suspicion. The German representatives—General Seeckt and Defense Minister Gessler—asked for a larger German armed force than stipulated in the Versailles treaty—an army of 200,000, twice the number allowed. When Lloyd George refused to consider their motion, the German delegates requested fifteen additional months during which they promised to reduce the army to 100,000. The Allies retorted that the Germans, besides their regular army, also had a vast number of armed men in their home guards and their military police; therefore they must adhere to their obligations.

On the other major issue before the conference—German coal deliveries to France—there was a heated argument. Hugo Stinnes, Germany's leading industrialist and now a member of its delegation, a man not known for tact or humility, called the Allies "insane conquerors," and berated them for their exorbitant demands. He warned that if the French would occupy the Ruhr all German coal deliveries to them would cease instantly. His blustering speech almost wrecked the conference. Both the French and the British delegates reacted with mounting anger; they sent for their respective army commanders, Marshal Foch and General Wilson, to join them at Spa and to plan the occupation of more German areas.

At home Walter Simons, the German foreign minister, pleaded for acceptance of the Spa protocols. The Nationalists in the Reichstag launched a full-scale attack against the government and hailed Stinnes for his courage in telling off the French. That Stinnes's bombastic outburst produced no practical results was not taken into consideration. Germans still lived in a never-never land; they still did not accept the fact that they had lost the war.

The reparation issue was not on the official agenda at Spa. According to the peace treaty, the date for announcing the exact sum which Germany was to pay was still ten months away—May 1, 1921. Before that date France was to receive goods from the Germans in value to 20 billion gold marks.

There was much discussion of creating a provisional reparation plan until the final figures could be determined. The chief of the commerce division of the French Foreign Office (Mr. Seydoux) proposed a three-billion gold mark annual payment for the next five years. But as the politicians of France wanted more, Seydoux's plan was abandoned. In their discussions in Paris on January 24, 1921, the British and French agreed to demand from Germany an annual sum increasing from two to six billion gold marks over a forty-two-year period. The debate over the reparation payments continued unabated during the entire fourteen years of the Weimar Republic.

THE FIRST INTERNATIONAL CONFERENCE AT SPA TO WHICH GERMAN REPRESENTATIVES WERE INVITED.

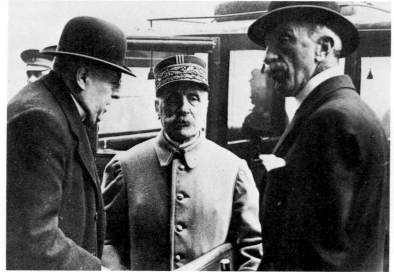

1920, July 5–16:
ALLIED MILITARY CHIEFS AT SPA. Marshal Ferdinand Foch and Sir Henry Wilson, commanding general of the English.

GERMAN REPRESENTATIVES AT SPA. Finance Minister Wirth, Chancellor Fehrenbach, and Foreign Minister Simons.

1921, March:

THE FATE OF UPPER SILESIA. Many patriotic native-born Silesians (*heimattreue Oberschlesier*) who lived in Germany returned to their homeland to take part in the plebiscite. Among them were many Jews.

Originally the Versailles peace treaty decided to give the industrially rich province to Poland. But when the Germans protested, the provision was changed to a plebiscite. In the voting on March 21, 1921, about 700,000 people voted for keeping Upper Silesia German, but 479,000 cast their ballots for Polish rule. The decision to partition the land was a crippling blow to Germany.

PLEBISCITE IN SILESIA

THE SITUATION in Upper Silesia was a vexing one. Poland desired its mines, Germany was determined to keep them. In the plebiscite a decisive majority voted to remain with Germany; because of this the German government asked for the whole of Upper Silesia. After the Allied plebiscite commission arrived to draw up a boundary line, Polish volunteer troops organized by the lawyer Korfanty invaded the disputed areas. The Germans promptly sent "volunteer troops" against them. Although these Freikorps won victories over the Poles, the final decision about the disposition of the province remained with the League of Nations, which then set up a committee of four neutrals from Belgium, Brazil, China, and Spain to draw up the border.

The issue was complicated by the Allied ultimatum on May 5, which demanded positive answers from the Germans about their plans regarding reparation payments, disarmament, and the trial of war criminals. The Fehrenbach government resigned, and the new government under Joseph Wirth promised a policy of fulfillment.

Some days later the Germans and the Poles entered into an agreement which guaranteed full civil rights for the next fifteen years to everyone living in Upper Silesia. This agreement settled the future of the province.

ON NOVEMBER 5, 1921, THE REMAINS OF KING LUDWIG OF BAVARIA AND HIS WIFE ARE INTERRED IN MUNICH

THE BURIAL OF THE EMPRESS. On April 19, 1921, the remains of the former Empress Augusta Victoria were taken to her grave in Potsdam. Her sons, the Princes Eitel Friedrich (with his wife), August Wilhelm, Adalbert, and Oscar, follow the coffin.

IN THE FUNERAL PROCESSION, which turned into a great nationalistic demonstration and show against the Republic, the two top generals, Hindenburg and Ludendorff, walked behind the hearse with Admiral von Tirpitz and General von Heeringen.

IS THIS A REPUBLIC?

CUSTOMS CHANGE slowly. Though Germany was now a Republic, the mores of the monarchy remained ingrained in the minds and hearts of the people. They yearned for the glitter and the gold, for the pomp and ostentatious display—for the good old days.

During the first years of the Republic (and even after, for that matter) colorful receptions were still held by the Prussian aristocracy in Potsdam. Former imperial officers—resplendent in their gaudy uniforms, medals, and ribbons—were cheered and acclaimed by the populace. And royal funerals became opportunities for propagandistic protestations against the Republican regime.

FIELD MARSHAL AUGUST VON MACKENSEN IN THE FUNERAL PROCESSION.

WITH IMPRESSIVE MILITARY POMP.

MANY PATRIOTIC ORGANIZATIONS, particularly the student corps in full regalia with banners flying, came out in force to accompany the empress on her last journey.

1920, August 7:

THE BUDDING LEADER OF THE BAVARIAN NAZIS, thirty-one-year-old Adolf Hitler, was a Munich delegate at the Austrian National Socialist meeting in Salzburg in the summer of 1920. The idea and name of National Socialism came not from Germany, but from Austria, where nationalistic working bunds were in existence at the end of the nineteenth century. At Salzburg the name "German National Socialist Party of Austria" was adopted. Hitler did not like to be reminded that the movement had started in Austria; no Nazi publication in Germany was allowed to carry the above photograph, showing Hitler (x) at the outset of his career.

A NEW POLITICAL PARTY

As MUNICH was engulfed in revolution, Corporal Hitler stayed in his barracks. After the upheavals he became an "educational officer" in the army, whose duty was to check on groups undesirable to the military. It was a year later, in September 1919, that he attended a small meeting of the German Workers' Party and shortly thereafter joined them.

On February 24 of the following year, the first mass meeting of the new party was held, at which Hitler enunciated the National Socialists' aims: a twenty-five-point hodgepodge of vile racism, extreme nationalism, brutal

PARTY MEMBER FIVE—A FAKE. Hitler's number was 555—by eliminating the final two digits it became number 5.

anti-Semitism, and economic phantasmagoria. The meeting was followed by others, with attendance growing.

Almost single-handedly Hitler built the party. His propaganda sense, his organizational ability and speaking talent made the National Socialist German Workers' Party—its new name—a force in German politics. A newspaper—the *Völkische Beobachter*—was bought; party emblems were designed, bearing the swastika; troops—which later became the S.A.—were organized, the slogan "Germany awake" was adopted, as were the techniques of foreign propaganda.

120

RATHENAU MURDERED

THE NEW CHANCELLOR—Joseph Wirth—accepted the ultimatum of the Allies and was willing to meet its conditions. He hoped that a "policy of fulfillment" would convince the world of Germany's honorable intentions and that solutions to the vexing problems of reparations could be reached through negotiations.

Wirth named Walther Rathenau as his foreign minister. Rathenau—a liberal intellectual, son of the founder of Germany's General Electric Company (AEG), and a political thinker of the highest order—accepted the call with hesitation, knowing of the difficulties ahead. The Nationalists loathed his liberalism, and many people opposed him not only because he came from the intellectual elite, but also because he was born a Jew.

Soon after joining the cabinet, Rathenau concluded an agreement with the French about payments in kind to French civilians who had suffered losses in the war. Though the accord—called the Wiesbaden agreement—was widely criticized, it seemed a step in the right direction.

Germany's economic difficulties were enormous. Inflationary trends hindered the country's reparation payments, and as the Allies were doing their level best to shut Germany out of world trade, foreign exchange was hard to arrange. The relation of the mark to the dollar widened. By the fall of 1921 the exchange rate, which before the war stood at 4.20 marks to the dollar, had jumped to 200 marks.

In November 1921 the full Reparation Commission came to Berlin to make on-the-spot observations of economic conditions. Germany asked for postponement of its reparation payments due in January and February of the following year. Grudgingly the Allies granted the request at their meeting in Cannes but set stringent conditions.

The time had come to discuss the issues dispassionately and to attempt to find a solution. The French and the British consented to an economic conference to be held in Genoa. For the first time representatives of Germany and Russia—the two nations defeated in the war—were invited to participate as equal partners with Britain and France.

Rathenau represented Germany with Chancellor Wirth and others from the cabinet. The conference split into four negotiating groups—each of them focusing attention on a single problem. But more significant than the official meetings were the private conversations between the conferees. Rathenau, apprehensive that Lloyd George, the English premier, would make a pact with Russia detrimental to Germany,

WALTHER RATHENAU.

was overjoyed when Russian foreign minister Chicherin approached him for a private meeting. Rapprochement between Germany and Russia had been under consideration for some time. Now it seemed that the harvest of the conversations would be reaped.

On Easter Sunday, April 16, the Russian and German delegates met in secret in Rapallo—a nearby town on the Italian Riviera—and within a few hours they reached an agreement. The significant achievements of the Treaty of Rapallo, as the agreement became known, were threefold. First, the renunciation of Germany's and Russia's war claims against each other; second, they were to give each other in the commercial sphere the rights of the most favored nation; and third, they were to resume diplomatic relations.

When news of the Rapallo treaty reached Genoa, the French and the British delegates were dismayed, but there was little they could do about it. It was their bungling diplomacy that had driven Germany and Russia into each other's arms.

In Germany public opinion was sharply divided. The parties of the right were against the pact; they had no desire to make friends with the Communists—and most Social Democrats felt the same way.

The racist press ranted; its vulgar ditties assailed Chancellor Wirth and his foreign minister. The *Schwarzwälder Volkswacht* printed the "poem":

"Go and get at Joseph Wirth,
Break his head until it *'klirrt.'*
Kill off Walther Rathenau,
That goddamned no good
Jewish sow."

Other Nationalist papers wrote in similar fashion. Their insidious attacks brought results—two months after the Treaty of Rapallo, Rathenau was assassinated in Berlin. His killers were two young Nationalists, blond-haired and blue-eyed, the type so attractive to him in private life.

After the assassination President Hindenburg signed a decree under Article 48 of the constitution "for the protection of the Republic," and Chancellor Wirth called on all Germans to cleanse themselves of "this atmosphere of murder, rape, and poison." In an emotion-laden speech he told the Reichstag—with his eyes resting on the benches of the right: "There stands the enemy, and there can be no doubt —the enemy stands on the right."

THE MARCH ON ROME

1922, November 1:
THE MARCH ON ROME. On October 30, Benito Mussolini formed his government, which brought Fascism to Italy. His regime lasted for twenty-one years—until 1943.

MUSSOLINI IN ROME. He is on his way to swear allegiance to King Victor Emmanuel.

BENITO MUSSOLINI (named for the Mexican revolutionary Benito Juarez) was born in 1883, the son of a Socialist blacksmith. Brought up in a Catholic seminary, he was expelled for stabbing a fellow pupil. At nineteen he went to Switzerland to avoid military service at home. Arrested for begging in Lausanne, he was deported from one canton after another for using a forged passport. Dirty and unkempt, hungry and penniless, he slept under bridges.

Returning to Italy, he did his military duty, took up journalism, and became an organizer of the Socialist party. During the war when he veered away from the Socialists' policy of neutrality, he was expelled from the party and organized the *Fasci di Azione Rivoluzionaria* (revolutionary action squadron), a group supporting the war.

After war's end the revolutionary spirit in Italy revived, with strikes and factory seizures raising the specter of Bolshevism. Mussolini's squadrons acted to protect the property of landowners and industrialists; they attacked Socialist centers, murdering their political antagonists. The industrialists and big landowners began to open their coffers and gave Mussolini money as long as it was spent on weakening the Socialists. At first public support of the Fascists was scant. However, the poet D'Annunzio's march into Fiume in the fall of 1919 strengthened the nationalist spirit.

The liberal government of Giolitti thought it opportune to use Mussolini's Fascists against the workers; Fascist candidates were put on the ballot and elected. As a legislator Mussolini showed his real colors: an opportunist with no firm convictions who at times supported the Catholics, at other times the liberals.

Recurring strikes and civil disorders strengthened his position and weakened the governing coalition. And

1922, November 1:
THE KING MEETS HIS NEW PRIME MINISTER, BENITO MUSSOLINI, AT THE TOMB OF THE UNKNOWN SOLDIER.

while three cabinets toppled, Mussolini became a force to be reckoned with, demanding that the government "be given to us or we shall descend on Rome and take it."

An eloquent speaker, he preached discipline, order, and unity. He justified violence as moral when employed for the greatness of Italy.

Fearing that a civil war might cost him his throne, King Victor Emmanuel asked him to form the new govern-

ment. But by then his disheveled Blackshirts were already on the march toward the capital. Mussolini did not join them—he made his "march" to Rome in a comfortable sleeping car.

At the outset the Mussolini government was moderate with many non-Fascists in the cabinet. "Order" in the country was soon restored, the upheavals in the streets suppressed, and the trains ran on time. The changes impressed even Winston Churchill. But

gradually the real face of Fascism emerged: brutality, authoritarianism, dictatorship. On January 3, 1925, Mussolini declared himself a dictator.

In Munich Adolf Hitler patterned himself on the Italian leader, copying his gestures, copying the Fascist salute, dressing his followers, not in black shirts, but in brown. And just as Mussolini marched on Rome, Hitler expected to lead his supporters on a march to Berlin.

1921, January:
THE GERMAN PEOPLE WERE UNITED AS NEVER BEFORE IN THEIR PROTEST AGAINST THE RUHR OCCUPATION BY

THE FRENCH OCCUPY THE

THE ENGLISH AND THE AMERICANS urged the French to be generous to the Germans and to accept reduced reparation payments. But as they themselves would not reduce the loans which they had given to France, that country insisted on full payments from Germany.

At the end of December 1922, when the split between the diplomats of Great Britain and France had widened, the joint Reparation Commission declared Germany in default on coal and wood deliveries. This entitled France to impose sanctions. Disregarding all warnings, French and Belgian troops

marched into the Ruhr on January 11, 1923—a disastrous decision.

The news of the occupation united all Germans. A policy of passive resistance was initiated, bringing production and transportation in the Ruhr to a virtual standstill. German workers would not obey the orders of the

COMING: French troops were moving into the city of Mainz on January 11, 1923.

GOING: German railroad workers who refused to cooperate with the French were ordered to leave their homes and move out of the occupied territory. The trainmen's passive resistance sabotaged train schedules; the number of wrecks and accidents mounted.

A GERMAN PROPAGANDA PHOTOGRAPH DEPICTING FRENCH BEHAVIOR.

THE FRENCH AND BELGIAN FORCES.

RUHR

French; German partisans committed acts of sabotage, blowing up trains, wrecking factories.

The confrontation of the wartime adversaries, unwilling and unable to resolve their differences in a peaceful manner, brought Germany and France to the brink of disaster.

125

NAZI DEMONSTRATIONS IN MUNICH. Two weeks after the Ruhr occupation on January 28, 1923, Adolf Hitler ordered the members of his fledgling National Socialist party to don their newly designed uniforms and carry their fresh standards in a parade on the Marsfeld. This was the Nazis' first party day. Mocking Chancellor Cuno's plea for a united front against the French, Hitler cried: "No! Not down with France, but down with the traitors to the Fatherland—down with the November criminals!"

THE FIRST PARTY DAY

1923, January 28:
FOR THE FIRST TIME THE SWASTIKA BANNERS WERE ON DISPLAY.

As MUSSOLINI HAD MARCHED on Rome, so Hitler wanted to march on Berlin. His call for a party day—the first of its kind—was the initial step.

The Munich authorities, fearing a clash between the Nazi and the Socialist troops, forbade the demonstration. But when Hitler retorted he would hold it anyway, the police backed down, cutting the twelve announced meetings to six and ordering the observances to be held indoors.

Disregarding the orders, Hitler told his 6,000 storm troopers to present their standards in the open. And—on a cold, snowy January day—they did.

RE YOU FOR or
e you against?
rgo Lion, the
fer-thin star of the
lde Bühne cabaret
Berlin, sings the
ty: "Are you for or
you against? Are
a against or are
for? And why
you against and
y are you for?"
e audience under-
od her meaning.

Photo by Riese

PHILOSOPHERS OF NAZISM

THE CHIEF INGREDIENTS of the Nazis' theories—racial superiority, reactionary nationalism, savage anti-Semitism, German mythology—derived from the thinkers of the nineteenth century: Fichte, who preached the superiority of Germans; Hegel, who advocated supremacy of the state over the individual; Treitschke, for whom war was a "theoretical necessity"; Nietzsche with his superman; Wagner with his mystic world of German sagas.

The race theories which held Hitler in thrall were formulated by the Frenchman Gobineau, adopted by the English H. S. Chamberlain, vulgarized by the German Eckart and the Austrian "Jörg Lanz von Liebenfels," whose *Ostara* publications on the superiority of the blond, blue-eyed Aryans became Hitler's favorite reading.

DIETRICH ECKART (1868–1923) was one of the spiritual founders of National Socialism. A journalist, a poet, a dramatist, a great talker, a great eater, a great drinker, he was a typical Bavarian character who hated Jews, Communists, and liberals. Early in 1920 he made Hitler's acquaintance and became the young budding politician's teacher, mentor, protector.

RICHARD WAGNER (1813–1883), the idol of Adolf Hitler. "Whoever wanted to grasp the idea of National Socialism," Hitler once said, "must first know Wagner."

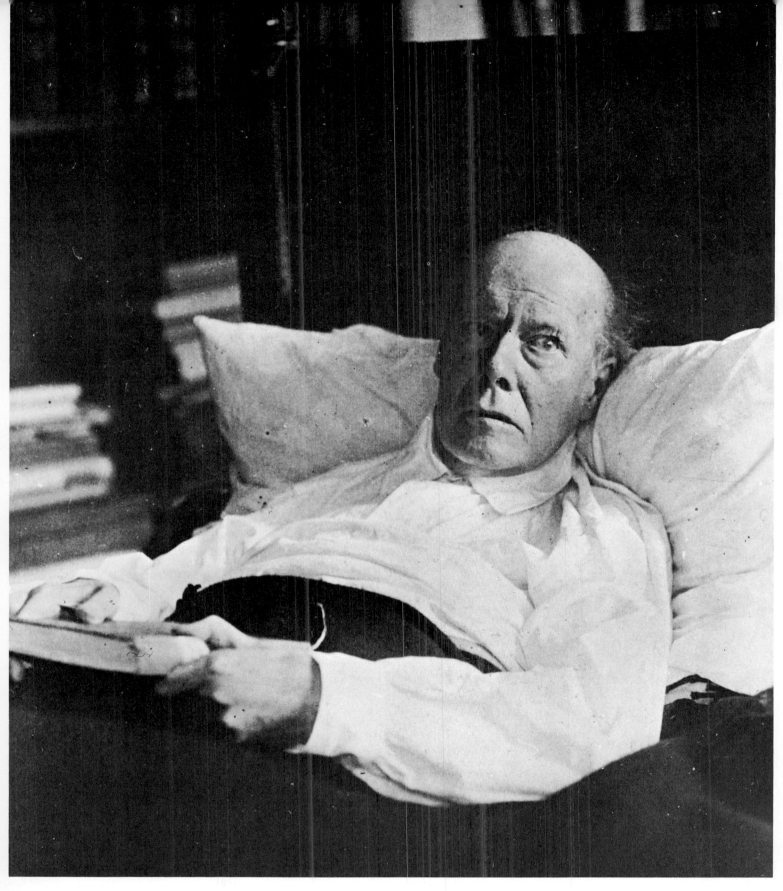

HOUSTON STEWART CHAMBERLAIN (1855–1927), the patron saint of National Socialism, was born in England but became a German citizen. A neurotic psychopath with a brilliant mind, he was a disciple of the French diplomat Arthur de Gobineau, whose racist theories in his *Essay on the Inequality of the Human Race* permeated Chamberlain's thinking.

In his *Foundation of the Nineteenth Century*, published in 1899, Chamberlain proclaimed that the Teutons, pre-eminently the Germans, should be masters of the world because of their racial superiority. The book, which was a resounding success in Germany, also extolled the most despicable anti-Semitism, arguing that Jesus was not a Jew, but probably an Aryan. Kaiser Wilhelm became the author's friend and was given advice by him.

In 1882, at the age of twenty-seven, Chamberlain made the acquaintance of Richard Wagner and his wife and fell under their spell. Another twenty-seven years later he settled in Bayreuth after divorcing his wife in order to marry the Wagners' daughter Eva. He met Hitler in 1923 and felt that the young man was destined by God to lead the German people. Although the renegade Englishman died six years before the Nazis came to power, his racial and anti-Semitic theories became the fundamental tenets and basic philosophies of the Third Reich.

INFLATION

How **CAN ONE** describe those incredible times? In the morning a newspaper cost 50,000 marks—in the evening, 100,000. The price of a single pair of shoelaces would have bought an entire shoestore with all its inventory a few weeks before. Beggars threw away 100,000-mark notes as they could buy nothing with them.

INFLATION MONEY FILLS EVERY NOOK AND CRANNY.

HOW IS THE DOLLAR? A Berlin bank window with the latest quotations in the summer of 1923. At the beginning of the year the American dollar was worth 7,525 marks. By August the exchange rate had risen to over a million, and by the first week in October a single dollar cost 250 million paper marks. In November the rate rose to 600 milliard marks, in December to the astronomical figure of 4,210,500,000,000. It was then that the Rentenmark came into being. The mark was devalued; instead of 4.2 billion marks per dollar, the exchange rate became simply 4.20 marks.

IN NOVEMBER 1923 A BILLION-MARK WAS WORTH 25 AMERICAN CENTS—NOT ENOUGH FOR A POUND OF BUTTER.

ON PAYDAY MESSENGERS FROM FACTORIES CARRY LARGE SACKS FULL OF PAPER MONEY TO MEET PAYROLLS.

At first, inflation mounted gradually, but after Rathenau's murder the tempo accelerated. In June 1922 the exchange rate between the dollar and mark was 350; three months later it had dipped to 1,300, and by the end of the year to 7,000. And finally, with passive resistance, the mark's value plummeted into nothingness.

The government spent 40 million gold marks a day to support the passive resistance movement in the Ruhr. Such sums could not be raised by added taxation, nor were any other new sources of revenue in the offing. Thus the government resorted to the expedient of printing money. By August 1923 the Reichsbank was issuing 46 billion fresh marks every day.

In that apocalyptic year of 1923 the value of the dollar rose from 7,500 marks in January to 4,200,000,-000 marks in November.

OUTSIDE A BERLIN BANK. Every conceivable kind of container—wicker baskets, traveling bags, linen satchels, and briefcases—is used to carry money from place to place.

131

THE PEOPLE SUFFER

THE INFLATION hit the country like a tornado, leaving devastation in its wake. The year 1923, when the value of the mark tumbled, was a nightmare. The price of a loaf of bread, a bottle of milk rose to milliards. Wages could not keep step with the skyrocketing prices. A salary of a billion was not enough to pay for the bare necessities.

Workers, wage earners demanded their wages and salaries two or even three times a week. On paydays wives waited at the factory gates or outside the offices to rush with their husbands' earnings to the nearest store, where they bought anything they could lay their hands on, whether they needed it or not. Goods did not depreciate as fast as currency and they could be sold in the future without much loss.

It was a topsy-turvy, incomprehensible world. Savings dwindled to nothing. Pensions grew worthless. Investments lost their value. Older people were bewildered. They did not know how to keep their hard-earned savings. Families exchanged their heirlooms for bread and butter.

I remember the time vividly. Twice a week I received my salary, all in cash. As soon as I got the money I raced to the bank and invested my earnings in stocks, in Norddeutscher Lloyd, in Hapag, and in other industrial enterprises. I bought dollar notes with the inflated marks, paying milliards, and even billions for a single dollar. I thought I was clever; I believed I would be able to hold on to my earnings. But when the inflation was over and the mark became stabilized, I took stock — all my savings amounted to $103. And I was one of the lucky ones. I at least had a hundred dollars to my name, while others had not even a penny.

Yet there were some who made money—the speculators, those who bought goods and sold them at substantial profits, those who dealt in food, those who dealt in real estate, paying for it later, those who speculated on time. Foreigners streamed into Germany and lived in princely fashion on a few dollars.

Nightclubs, cabarets, theaters, places of amusement were filled to the brim—not only with *schiebers* and speculators, but with those who despaired at the senselessness of life and were ready to spend all they possessed on an evening of pleasure. As money had little value, why not at least have a few hours of enjoyment from it? Young girls from good homes sold their bodies for a meal, young men numbed themselves with cocaine and morphine.

Opponents of the government blamed the Jews for fostering the inflation, yet the greatest inflation profiteer was not a Jew but Hugo Stinnes,

REDUCED TO BEGGING.

TIN CANS ARE SOLD BY MIDDLE-CLASS WOMEN WHO NEEDED EVERY PFENNIG TO KEEP THEIR FAMILIES GOING.

Germany's most prominent industrialist. He acquired mines, factories, real estate until he had amassed about 25 per cent of all the nation's industry. At one time he owned well over 1000 different enterprises.

When in 1924 the country returned to normal conditions, the poverty of the masses, their suffering, was beyond belief. They were an easy prey to the agitation of the opposition. They swelled the ranks of the Communists and the right-wing radicals.

A NIGHTLONG QUEUE FOR MEAT.

THE MILITARY EXACTNESS OF THE TILLER GIRLS, A SUGARY SUBSTITUTE FOR PRUSSIAN MILITARISM, STIRRED

FOR CENTURIES Prussian militarism was hammered into the German mind, soul, and body until it became part of the nation's make-up. For the Germans militarism was a cover for their ambitions and desires—it set them apart from others, it gave them a feeling of superiority and strength. And now that the Republic had shed the trappings —all the parades, all the ceremonies, all the martial music, all the snappy uniforms—life seemed dreary and empty.

The drab disorderliness of their civilian existence made the people yearn for the old times, when they marched to the tunes of military bands. To bring those memories to life—whether consciously or not—variety shows offered troops of dancing girls, twenty-four, thirty, thirty-six of them, dressed

MILITARISM ON THE STAGE

AUDIENCES TO WILD ENTHUSIASM.

alike, raising their legs in unison, moving with military exactness. The audiences who came to see them cheered and applauded—the bouncing Tiller girls brought something back into their lives which they had sorely missed—glamour, precision, order.

GERMAN DAY IN NÜRNBERG

On September 2, the anniversary of the German victory at Sedan in 1871, groups of nationalistic organizations met in Nürnberg to celebrate. Their show turned into a massive demonstration against the Republic.

Large delegations from patriotic leagues paraded through the streets of the medieval city, none larger or more militarily precise than the contingents of the National Socialists. General Ludendorff, back from his exile, attended in full regalia; Adolf Hitler, the young Nazi leader, in a trenchcoat with a stick.

1923, September 2:
THE RIGHT-WING ORGANIZATIONS IN

The paramilitary organizations of Bavaria issued a manifesto calling for the overthrow of the Republican government and for the annulment of the Versailles treaty. The bund's military leader was Hermann Kriebel, while Adolf Hitler was its political head. In a meeting Hitler threatened that before long "the dice will roll" and that "what is in the making today will be greater than the World War" —an oblique forewarning of a national putsch. Old veterans of former wars with medals clinging to their black tailcoats and officers in their colorful uniforms of the monarchy cheered the young demagogue, who made it clear that the day of reckoning was near.

A YOUNG MAN IN A RAINCOAT. Thirty-four-year-old Adolf Hitler, the leader of the rapidly growing National Socialist party, which had its headquarters in Munich, watches the parade. Hitler at this time of his career sought the support of the old conservatives.

136

NÜRNBERG CELEBRATE THE FIFTY-THIRD ANNIVERSARY OF THE GERMAN VICTORY OVER THE FRENCH AT SEDAN.

GENERAL LUDENDORFF, the loser of the First World War for Germany. After the revolution he fled to Sweden in disguise; on his return he became the instant hero of the National Socialists.

THE DIGNITARIES WATCH THE PARADE of the Nazi storm troopers. Adolf Hitler stands next to Julius Streicher, the anti-Semitic editor of the Jew-baiting publication *Der Stürmer*.

137

STRESEMANN TURNS THE TIDE

COUNT KUNO WESTARP, leader of the German Nationalists, opposed the decision to cease resisting the French.

CHANCELLOR CUNO, a man with a chronic nervous condition, could not master the nation's great problems: Ruhr occupation, passive resistance, inflation, unemployment. The country looked for a strong leader and found him in Gustav Stresemann.

The son of a Berlin innkeeper, Stresemann had the Berliner sense of humor. He saw the ironies of life and could laugh at himself.

During the war when he became the leader of the National Liberals, he was an avid supporter of the monarchy. A thorough-going nationalist and annexationist, he followed his predecessor Ernst Bassermann's maxim, "Where a drop of German blood has flowed there we remain." Thus he was for colonialism and he endorsed the crass annexationist treaty of Brest-Litovsk, which shocked the world and revealed what Germany would do if it won the war.

But after the defeat, Stresemann realized that the monarchy could not be restored, and his practical sense led him to work within the framework of the Republic even though he remained a close friend of the crown prince. Always a pragmatist—his critics called him an opportunist—he was one of the most outstanding political figures in the Weimar Republic.

Upon becoming chancellor in August 1923 he recognized that the pas-

GUSTAV STRESEMANN (1878–1929) formed a cabinet in August 1923 with the parties of the Weimar Coalition. He ended passive resistance in the Rhineland and sought rapprochement with France.

sive resistance policy was draining the country's finances to exhaustion. As there was no way to increase revenues, and as money for expenditures was needed, the Reichsbank was forced to print more and more bank notes. With enormous quantities of paper money in circulation, the value of the mark dwindled to nothing.

Stresemann was determined to stop the unworkable policy. On September 26, 1923, he issued a proclamation calling for the end of passive resistance. "To preserve the life of the nation and the state, we are confronted with the bitter necessity of ceasing our struggle," it said. A few weeks later the Rentenmark was introduced and the currency was stabilized.

But the cauldron of political passions was boiling. Only a day before the proclamation, Bavaria declared a state of emergency. The national government in Berlin responded with a declaration of emergency throughout the entire Reich, and named Otto Gessler, the defense minister (and not General Seeckt), to deal with the situation. And while in Bavaria Hitler and his Nazis kept the political storm brewing, in Saxony and Thuringia the leftists created upheavals.

Stresemann showed a firm hand both against the right and the left. He wanted to form a cabinet with a broad parliamentary base from the Social Democrats to his own German People's Party like the old Weimar Coalition. He started on a new path, the path of reconciliation with the country's former adversaries.

The augury for it was promising. In France the *revanche*-seeking Poincaré was soon to bow out and the liberal-minded Herriot and Briand to take over. In England the mounting strength of the Labour party held out hope for the return of peaceful times.

1923, December:
THE POLICE CLEAR THE MULACKSTRASSE AFTER AN UPHEAVAL IN THE WORKINGMEN'S DISTRICT OF BERLIN.

TROUBLES EVERYWHERE

THE YEAR 1923 was a sad one for the Republic. There were troubles everywhere: passive resistance and a separatist movement in the Rhineland, Communists in the governments of Saxony and Thuringia, a nationalist state commissioner general in Bavaria. Inflation and unemployment brought suffering to millions.

The fabric of the country was ripping apart: conditions were chaotic. The government had to fight on many fronts.

The fertile ground of dissension gave Adolf Hitler and his supporters the opportunity to assert themselves. Hitler dreamed of capturing "Marxist and Jewish Berlin" and taking over the national government—doing what Benito Mussolini and his Fascists had done a year earlier in Rome.

A WOMAN LOOTER IN FREIBURG IS CHASED AWAY BY THE MILITARY.

BEHIND THE BARRICADES. Heinrich Himmler, who later became Munich police president, head of the S.S. and the Gestapo, with his comrades before the Munich war office.

THE HITLER STOSSTRUPP. These early supporters constituted the Nazis' paramili-

AT THE ODEONSPLATZ after the battle, mounted policemen ride with their bayonets lowered. Order was quickly restored, as the populace of Munich was not with the Nazis.

AT THE FELDHERRNHALLE the demonstrators clashed with police troops who

THE PUTSCH

THE MUNICH BEER HALL PUTSCH is often called Hitler's great failure, but in reality it marked the ascent of his political career; from that defeat he learned to avoid similar mistakes in the future.

In October 1923 he thought the time ripe to seize the Bavarian government and march into Berlin.

The upheaval erupted on October 8. That evening Nazis invaded a political meeting in the Bürgerbräu cellar. "The national revolution has begun," cried Hitler. The members of the govern-

tary organization. After the abortive putsch they formed the nucleus of the S.S. and S.A.

IN FRONT OF THE TOWN HALL on Marienplatz a Nazi speaker exhorts his audience to join in the march. Those who sympathized with the Nazis followed their troops.

pened fire; 16 Nazis died. General Ludendorff (center) was among the marchers.

THE OBERLAND BUND parades the streets with swastika armbands and flags. Though the Munich putsch was squelched, it threw the national spotlight on the Nazi movement.

ment who were present were forced to promise to join a new cabinet. "I have four shots in my pistol—three for my collaborators if they abandon me, the last for myself," shouted Hitler.

In the following confusion Kahr, the commissioner general of Bavaria,

escaped and, back in his office, he vowed immediate action against the "treachery and deceit of ambitious scoundrels." In Berlin the government appointed General Seeckt to deal with the Bavarian situation.

Opposed by the legitimate govern-

ment in Bavaria, by the national government in Berlin, and by the Reichswehr, Hitler's putsch had no chance. Still, next morning he marched his troops into the heart of Munich. The police opened fire. Sixteen men lost their lives.

THE OPENING MEETING. In the big hall of the former Infantry School in Munich's Blutenburgstrasse, the process began on February 26, 1924, lasting till March 27. County Court Director Georg Neithardt presided; next to him an assistant and three lay judges.

THE TRIAL IN MUNICH

THREE LAY JUDGES AND AN ALTERNATE. Insurance inspector Christian Zimmermann, insurance clerk Philipp Hermann, tobacconist Max Brauneis (alternate), and merchant Leonhard Beck.

THE DEFENDANTS. Lt. Heinz Pernet, Dr. Friedrich Weber, Wilhelm Frick, Lt. Col. Hermann Kriebel, Gen. Ludendorff, Hitler, Lt. Wilhelm Brückner, Capt. Ernst Röhm, and Lt. Robert Wagner.

LATE IN FEBRUARY 1924 Hitler and nine others were defendants before the Munich People's Court, charged with fomenting and organizing a putsch against the government. During the twenty-four-day trial he dominated the proceedings, turning the courtroom into a propaganda forum. He acknowledged being the instigator of the putsch and said that he should be honored for this and not blamed. He warned that the army he had organized would grow at a rapid rate and that "the scattered bands will become battalions; the battalions, regiments; the regiments, divisions." In his summing-up he exclaimed that "the old cockade will be rescued from the filth; and the old banners will be unfurled again," which in simple words meant the restoration of the old regime and provocation of war with France in revenge for the defeat of 1918.

Compared to Hitler, the other defendants paled into insignificance. General Ludendorff cut a pitiful figure, ranting against "international Jewry" and against the Catholic church.

The sentences turned out to be exceptionally mild. Hitler, Kriebel, Pöhner, and Weber got five years in a fortress but were eligible for probation after six months. The other five—Brückner, Röhm, Pernet, Wagner, and Frick—received one and a half years with probation. Ludendorff went free.

THE CHIEF DEFENDANTS during a break in the proceedings of the trial. In the group on the left: General Ludendorff, resplendent in his colorful uniform, chats with Dr. Friedrich Weber, while Hitler and the general's stepson, Lieutenant Heinz Pernet, listen to his words. On the right, the bemedalled Lieutenant Wilhelm Brückner, one of the leaders in the Nazis' paramilitary organization, watches the group. Later Brückner became Hitler's inseparable companion and was his bodyguard until the end of the regime.

OUTSIDE THE BUILDING Ernst Pöhner, also a defendant, greets General Ludendorff and his lawyer, Walter Lütgebrune. At right, holding a sheaf of documents, is Lt. Pernet, Ludendorff's stepson.

ACQUITTED. On April 1, 1924, the 59-year-old General Ludendorff in full regalia leaves the court building after the sentence was handed down The judges would not convict the general of treason.

143

FILM—THE NEW ART FORM

THE DECADE AFTER the war was the golden age of the silent film. The studios outside Berlin were working day and night. "The simplicity of the German cinema then indicated that the intelligence and artistry, the creative imagination and craftsmanship, so essential to the production of a unified work of art, lay in the studios of Neubabelsberg and Staaken," wrote Paul Rotha of this period.

The German government—hoping for foreign exchange—encouraged the movie industry with laws and money. The *Kontingent law* required distributors to take one home-made film for every American, thus forcing the companies to make German films.

The production boom started soon after the war. In 1919 Ernst Lubitsch directed *Madame Dubarry*, and a year later *Anna Boleyn*, two spectacular productions with big mass scenes. At about the same time, Robert Wiene was completing his expressionistic *The Cabinet of Dr. Caligari*.

Pola Negri, following her phenomenal success as Madame Dubarry, also starred in the Lubitsch films *Sumurun* and *Flame*. Paul Wegener made an indelible impression with his creation of the *Golem*, the legendary figure of Jewish folklore. Otto Gebühr played —no, he became—*Fridericus Rex*, the revered Prussian emperor; Emil Jan-

A DELIGHTFUL LUBITSCH COMEDY: *The Daughters of Kohlhiesel*, in which Henny Porten portrayed both daughters.

THE NIBELUNGEN SAGA was filmed by Fritz Lang in 1923–1924 with Paul Richter portraying Siegfried.

THE CABINET OF DR. CALIGARI, the pathbreaking expressionistic film with Werner Krauss and Conrad Veidt, was based on a script by Carl Mayer and Hans Janowitz and directed by Robert Wiene in 1920. It was a hit.

THE "FLUID" CAMERA during the filming of *Metropolis* in 1926. From a moving platform, cameraman Karl Freund captures Gustav Fröhlich (left), with Fritz Lang (behind him) directing the scene. Both Freund and Lang later emigrated to the U.S.

A SCENE FROM THE PHENOMENALLY SUCCESSFUL 1925 UFA CULTURE FILM, *THE WAYS TO STRENGTH AND BEAUTY*.
By the middle of the twenties the art of film-making reached its peak. In 1925 Emil Jannings offered *Tartuffe*, the young and little-known Greta Garbo had a supporting role in G. W. Pabst's *The Joyless Street*, Conrad Veidt starred in *Orlac's Hands*. It was also the year of Sergei Eisenstein's *Panzerkreuzer Potemkin*, of Charlie Chaplin's *The Gold Rush*, and of E. A. Dupont's *Variety*.

nings played the male leads in *Madame Dubarry* and *Anna Boleyn* and also appeared under the direction of Fred W. Murnau in *The Last Laugh* and under Paul Czinner in *Nju*, the story of a love triangle, with Elizabeth Bergner and Conrad Veidt.

In 1923 Fritz Lang began his *Nibelungen Saga*, Ludwig Berger made *Cinderella*, and Karl Grune *The Street*.

One of the first great writers for the film was Carl Mayer, the coauthor of *Caligari*, who experimented with telling a story without titles. His scripts for *The Last Laugh, Tartuffe, Hinter-*

treppe were outstanding examples of the new art form: his crisp, single-word sentences introduced a new style.

In the middle of the decade G. W. Pabst directed *The Joyless Street*, Greta Garbo's first German film (with Werner Krauss and Asta Nielsen), E. A. Dupont produced *Variety* (with Emil Jannings and Lia de Putty), Fritz Lang his monumental *Metropolis* (with Brigitte Helm and Gustav Fröhlich), Heinrich Galeen *The Student from Prague* (with Conrad Veidt and Elizza La Porta).

G. W. Pabst's classic story of the

French revolution, *Loves of Jeanne Ney*, made in 1927, was based on the novel by Ilya Ehrenburg, who later became the chief propagandist of Soviet Russia. In the same year Walther Ruttmann came out with his documentary, *Berlin, Symphony of a City*, for which Carl Mayer wrote the script. And two years later in 1929 the Viennese-American Joseph von Sternberg produced *The Blue Angel*.

The feverish pace of artistic activity slackened as the Nazis rose to power and as actors and directors left to live and work in foreign countries.

145

VOTING FOR
THE SECOND REICHSTAG

THE CONFERENCE of economic experts under the chairmanship of the American general Charles Dawes met in Paris at the end of January 1924. They had been asked by the Reparation Commission to find a solution to the reparations problems and to propose a plan acceptable to creditor and debtor nations alike. They were not looking for a political, but an economic, solution; their deliberations were based on the assumption that "the fiscal and economic unity of Germany would be restored," in other words, that the Allied occupation of the Ruhr would come to an end.

The Dawes commission's principal proposals centered on "productive guarantees," assuring creditors that they would receive their due. They suggested, among other things, the transfer of German railways from the government to a private corporation; a first mortgage on German industrial plants and property; a Reichsbank independent of the government. The Reich was to pledge its tariff receipts and four of its large tax receipts. An Allied agent would be appointed to supervise the plan's execution.

As to payments: the commission proposed that after a period of four years, during which Germany was to pay lower sums, the yearly rates would rise to 2.4 billion marks. The experts left the final and exact sum of reparations open; it was to depend on the recovery of the German economy.

To be able to pay the first rate, Germany was to receive an international loan (principally from the United States) of 800 million gold

POLICE CHASING DEMONSTRATORS on Unter den Linden during the campaign.

marks; this loan would also help maintain the stability of the mark.

The commission submitted its recommendations to the various interested governments on April 9; by then the Reichstag had already been dissolved. The dissolution came because the Social Democrats asked for changes in the emergency decrees, and when the government did not accede to the demand, they insisted on voting on the issue. It was one of their blunders—they should have known that a new election would not benefit them.

The principal issue of the election became the Dawes Plan. Both the Na-

tionalists and the Communists attacked it violently—mainly because some of its provisions interfered with Germany's sovereignty. They harangued against "a new Versailles," and against "the enslavement of the German people."

A week before the election the Marx-Stresemann government declared its willingness to go along with the Dawes commission's recommendations principally because they offered a peaceful solution to the problems. They pleaded for acceptance of the plan so "we can free our brothers in the Rhine and the Ruhr" and replace "an oppressive military force with principles and claims based upon economic reasons."

Twenty-three parties put up candidates in the election. The fragmentation of the middle benefited the far left and far right. The Communists—who in the interim had garnered the votes of the Independents—elected 62 delegates (primarily they had only 4), and the Nazis won 32 seats. It was the first time that the National Socialists had participated in a Reichstag election. As the NSDAP was still banned, the Nazi candidates had to campaign under different labels.

The result showed a decline of the middle parties; the Social Democrats lost 71 seats; from 171 in the first Reichstag, they dropped to 100; the German People's Party—the party of Stresemann—lost 20; the Democrats lost 11.

By the time the ballots were counted —on May 4—Hitler had been sentenced for his part in the abortive Munich putsch and was serving his term in the fortress of Landsberg.

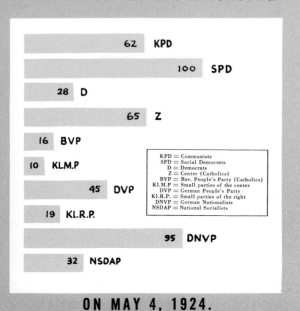

VOTING FOR THE 2nd REICHSTAG

62	KPD
100	SPD
28	D
65	Z
16	BVP
10	Kl.M.P
45	DVP
19	Kl.R.P.
95	DNVP
32	NSDAP

KPD = Communists
SPD = Social Democrats
D = Democrats
Z = Center (Catholics)
BVP = Bav. People's Party (Catholics)
Kl.M.P = Small parties of the center
DVP = German People's Party
Kl.R.P. = Small parties of the right
DNVP = German Nationalists
NSDAP = National Socialists

ON MAY 4, 1924.

1924, December 7:

ELECTION DAY SCENES BEFORE THE POLLING PLACES OF THE CAPITAL.

VOTING FOR THE THIRD REICHSTAG

THE RECOMMENDATIONS of the Dawes report were not binding to any of the powers. To translate them into a treaty, an international conference was called to London for the middle of July 1924.

Chancellor Marx and Foreign Minister Stresemann arrived in the English capital on August 5, when the conference was already in full swing. They were received with friendly demonstrations by the Londoners.

Prime Minister Herriot, leader of the radical party in France, knew that if he could not reach an agreement with the German liberals, the old German conservative reactionaries would return to power, and he would have far greater difficulty dealing with them than with the Marx-Stresemann government. In his private and secret talks with the German foreign minister, Herriot agreed to end the occupation of the Ruhr. All French forces were to be withdrawn within a year; Dortmund was to be freed right away.

By the middle of August the negotiators had reached an accord, and on the sixteenth of that month Stresemann signed the agreement. His harder task

—submitting bills to implement the accord and steering them through the Reichstag—lay ahead of him.

During the debates about the bills the Nationalists played cheap politics; they accused Stresemann of selling out the country and demanded that before the bills were adopted, the war guilt clause of the Versailles treaty should be annulled. Though they must have realized that the legislation proposed by Stresemann was in Germany's best interest, they refused to share responsibility for it, playing both ends against the middle. When the final passage of the bills came up for a vote, half of the Nationalists voted with the government, the other half against it. Through this political maneuver the bills became law and the Nationalists could not be accused that their intransigence blocked the freeing of the Ruhr—one of the chief practical results of the bills' acceptance.

After the voting, Chancellor Marx tried to broaden his political base so he could govern with a parliamentary majority. When the Nationalists refused to be lured into the coalition,

Marx dissolved the Reichstag.

By the time of the new election—on December 7, 1924—the beneficial results of the Dawes Plan were being felt, and conditions in the country had improved. Because of this, the parties on the far right and far left—the National Socialists and the Communists —lost much of their former support. The Nazis lost 18, the Communists 17 seats. And while the radical parties suffered defeat, the moderates made spectacular gains; the Social Democrats added 31 delegates to their strength, the German People's Party 5, and the Democrats 4. It looked as if the Nazis, with only 14 delegates in the Reichstag, had shot their bolt.

The new government, in the euphoria of the victory, pardoned Hitler. Even the most astute politicians—in and out of Germany—regarded him as a man of the past. He was released from prison and left Landsberg in time to spend Christmas at home.

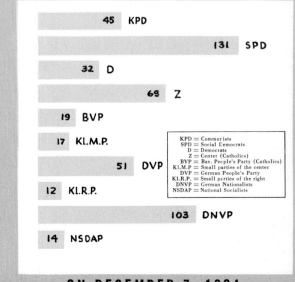

VOTING FOR THE 3rd REICHSTAG

45	KPD
131	SPD
32	D
69	Z
19	BVP
17	Kl.M.P.
51	DVP
12	Kl.R.P.
103	DNVP
14	NSDAP

KPD = Communists
SPD = Social Democrats
D = Democrats
Z = Center (Catholics)
BVP = Bav. People's Party (Catholics)
Kl.M.P = Small parties of the center
DVP = German People's Party
Kl.R.P. = Small parties of the right
DNVP = German Nationalists
NSDAP = National Socialists

ON DECEMBER 7, 1924.

IN PRISON

HIS TWO HUNDRED and sixty-four days in the Landsberg fortress held no hardship for him. The days passed pleasantly. He was given a comfortable sunny room on the first floor of the prison, he wore his own clothes—Bavarian shorts with Tyrolean jackets or workingmen's coveralls—he was permitted to have newspapers and to receive visitors. Food and sweets, flowers and presents came in constantly. Of his female admirers Winifred Wagner sent imposing flower arrangements, Frau Bechstein consoled him with delicacies of the season. On his thirty-fifth birthday his quarters looked more like a flower shop than a prison cell. Letters and cards arrived by the thousands.

To while away the time he began to dictate his thoughts, first to his loyal batman Emil Maurice, then to Rudolf Hess, who returned from Austria to serve his sentence close to him. Thus the book—*Mein Kampf*—began to take shape.

HITLER'S 35TH BIRTHDAY PICTURE.

1924, Summer:

HITLER'S PRISON CELL was a comfortable room. On the wall next to some pictures, a laurel wreath. He could have visitors, he could confer with his friends, he could dictate his memoirs.

Photographs by Heinrich Hoffmann

Seated next to Hitler is Lt. Col. Hermann Kriebel, military leader of the Kampfbund; standing behind Hitler is Emil Maurice, who acted not only as his secretary but also as his valet.

149

RISONER HITLER IN LANDSBERG FORTRESS.
ntenced to five years, he served only eight and a half months.

NUDES AND JAZZ

BERLIN, "the great Babylonian whore," was in the throes of pleasure madness. Moral scruples were dropped, sex barriers were down. Transvestism was fashionable, promiscuity was *comme il faut*, the sniffing of cocaine routine. "I don't sleep with just one, I sleep with the whole damn crew—because that's the modern thing to do," sang the diseuse Ilse Bois.

On the Kurfürstendamm prostitutes paraded, fifteen-year-olds brazenly offered themselves to passers-by, middle-aged housewives took young boys to their rooms. To escape their misery and emptiness, people indulged in pleasures of the flesh and of the senses.

THE WRITER BERTOLT BRECHT PERFORMS in a Munich cabaret. He blows the recorder in a sketch by the celebrated comedian Karl Valentin (sitting next to Brecht in bowler hat). The lady in the top hat is Liesl Karlstadt, Valentin's perpetual partner.

THE SCANDALOUS ANITA BERBER.

JAZZ AT THE HALLER REVUE.

IN BERLIN'S SCALA VARIETY.

150

YES, WE HAVE NO BANANAS
Josephine Baker, the toast of the twentie

THE PRESIDENT DIES

FRIEDRICH EBERT was a jovial, decent, and honest man. Born in 1871 the son of a Catholic tailor, he started out life as a journeyman saddler, eventually becoming chairman of the saddlers' union in Bremen. As a moderate trade unionist who cared more for party organization than for social theories, he was well liked by all who got to know him. He was not yet thirty when he was elected to the Bremen city council, where he became leader of the Social Democratic faction. From then on his political rise was fast.

In 1904 he was cochairman of his party's convention; a year later he was named secretary to the Social Democratic central committee in Berlin. He reorganized the party's machinery; in the 1912 election the Social Democrats increased their delegate strength from 43 to 110. As a Reichstag deputy Ebert's prestige grew.

During the last year of the war he became chairman of the central committee, one of the most influential political posts in the Reichstag. On November 9, 1918, as leader of the majority party, he was handed the chancellorship, and on February 11, 1919, the national assembly in Weimar elected him provisional president.

As the country's first president Ebert tried to serve the interests of all. A conciliatory man who believed in compromise, from the outset he was caught in a crossfire of explosive attacks. He lost the support of his party's left wing when he called out troops against the workers in the early days of the revolution, and he was assailed by Nationalist groups when Reichswehr troops beat down the Kapp putsch.

The people, used to the glittering uniforms of the kaiser, could not ad-

just to having a civilian as head of state. "The Germans do not want a president in a top hat," wrote Lord d'Abernon, the British ambassador in Berlin. "He has to wear a uniform and a chestful of medals. When they see as their leader a man who wears a top hat and who looks as though he might have been a neighbor, then each thinks to himself, 'I could do that too.'"

The attacks on the "saddlers' apprentice"—as Ebert was called by his enemies—continued until his death. In 1922 on a visit to Munich a man called him a traitor and Ebert brought suit; but when he was asked to appear in person before a Bavarian court, he withdrew it to spare himself a humiliating cross-examination. This encouraged his opponents to further attacks. "Come now, Mr. Ebert, prove that you really are not a traitor," wrote a Nationalist scribbler in a provincial news-

LEADER OF THE SOCIAL DEMOCRATS. Friedrich Ebert and Philipp Scheidemann politicking in the days before the First War.

PRESIDENT. Friedrich Ebert in 1922 reviews the honor guard. Behind him are General von Seeckt and Chancellor Joseph Wirth.

EBERT DIED ON THE LAST DAY OF FEBRUARY 1925. His remains were taken to Heidelberg for burial. Only 54 years old, he had been president for six years. Even in death Ebert was violently attacked by the Communists, who charged him with being putty in the hands of big business and with allowing the industrialists to exploit workers and government to their own interest.

paper. Once more Ebert was forced to file suit—one of the one hundred and fifty he did file—against his accuser. The suit ended dismally. In December 1924 a Magdeburg judge ruled against the president, declaring that he had committed treason by supporting the strikers in 1918. Such absurdities could and did happen in the Republic: a Nationalist judge, a holdover from the monarchy, could declare the president of the Republic a traitor. Ebert was deeply wounded by the "judgment"; he was a patriotic man who had lost two of his sons in the war.

About the same time the Magdeburg decision was handed down, the Barmat affair burst upon the country, implicating Social Democratic politicians with financial wrongdoing and undermining Ebert's stature.

Businessman and entrepreneur Julius Barmat, a Russian Jew living in Holland, sold vast quantities of food to Germany during the lean years of the war. In the early years of the Republic, he continued his operations, enlarging and diversifying his enterprises. But with the end of inflation his overextended empire collapsed. On the last day of 1924 Barmat and his associates were arrested; their liabilities were set at roughly ten million marks, not an unusually large sum, but as Barmat was a Jew who had obtained loans with the help of his Social Democratic friends, the Nationalists made political capital of the affair. They accused Ebert of helping Barmat with a permanent German visa, and they tried to implicate the president in other wrongdoing. By then Ebert was gravely ill. Because he had made up his mind to be available if called to testify before the investigating committee, he refused to enter a hospital. When he did, it was too late. His appendix ruptured, causing peritonitis, and within a few days he died, "literally scourged to death by the shameful prosecution."

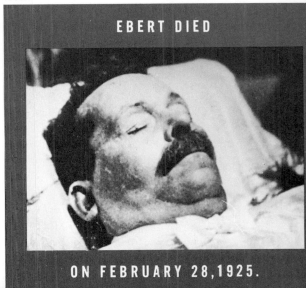

EBERT DIED

ON FEBRUARY 28, 1925.

ELECTING A PRESIDENT

FOR THE FIRST TIME Germany was electing a president. (Friedrich Ebert, the country's first chief executive, had not been elected by popular vote, but selected by members of the national assembly.)

All major parties offered candidates. Prussian prime minister Otto Braun was the choice of the Social Democrats, ex-Chancellor Wilhelm Marx ran under the banner of the Center party; Dr. Karl Jarres, former mayor of Duisburg and minister in earlier cabinets, was the candidate of the Nationalists; Bavarian premier Heinrich Held of the Bavarian Catholics; General Erich Ludendorff of the National Socialists. The Democrats chose Dr. Willy Hugo Hellpach, state president of Baden, and the Communists their Reichstag deputy, Ernst Thälmann.

In the voting on March 29, 1925, none of the seven candidates attained a majority. Jarres led the field with 10.7 million votes, followed by Braun with 7.8 million. Marx received almost 4 million, Thälmann 1.8 million, Hellpach 1.5 million, Held nearly 1 million, while General Ludendorff could only muster 200,000 votes.

So a second election had to be held in which a simple plurality was sufficient.

Both the middle parties and the Nationalists searched for a strong man with whom they would be sure to win. After protracted arguments the middle parties rallied behind the Catholic Wilhelm Marx while the parties of the right chose General Hindenburg, the seventy-seven-year-old war hero. Though Hindenburg had never been

1925, March 29:

CLEANING UP THE CITY AFTER THE ELECTION. Tons of debris, the leftover propaganda leaflets of the various political parties, are swept from the streets of Berlin.

FOR WILHELM MARX, the man of action.

FOR THÄLMANN, the Communist leader.

FOR HINDENBURG, the Nationalist.

154

FIELD MARSHAL PAUL VON HINDENBURG, supported by all the parties of the right, became president with 14,655,766 votes.

WILHELM MARX was supported by the Centrists, the Democrats, and the Social Democrats but received only 13,751,615 votes.

in politics, he was persuaded by his old friend Admiral Tirpitz to allow his name to be put in nomination so victory for the conservatives and the Nationalists could be assured.

The presidential candidacy of one of the kaiser's most famous generals only six years after the war alarmed the world. Would the Germans never learn? asked the French in dismay. Hadn't they had enough of saber-rattling Prussian generals?

As expected, Hindenburg won in

ERNST THÄLMANN, the Communist, got 1,931,151 votes. Had the Communists supported Marx, Hindenburg would have lost.

the second trial with 14.5 million votes against Marx's 13.7 and Thälmann's 1.9 million. If the Bavarian People's Party had remained loyal to the Catholic Marx, or if the Communists had not put up a candidate of their own, Hindenburg could not have become president.

His triumph was a victory for the monarchists, the Nationalists, the militarists. His great figure overshadowed that of the Republic. Would he—once in office—help to overthrow it?

155

THE NEW PRESIDENT

HINDENBURG, or to give his full name, Paul Ludwig Hans von Beneckendorff und von Hindenburg, came from a military family with a soldierly tradition going back as far as the thirteenth century.

Born in 1847, he fought in the war against Austria before he was twenty.

After forty years in the army he retired with the rank of general in 1911, because he saw "no prospect of a war." But when war did come three years later, he was named to command the Eighth Army in East Prussia, where two Russian armies were moving against the German heartland. In a gigantic battle the Russians suffered defeat; the victory of the Germans was reported from Tannenberg, where their forebears, the Teutons, had been subdued by the Poles in 1410. Though Hindenburg had no hand in planning the battle, he was given credit for the victory. In 1916 he became chief of the general staff, with Ludendorff as his quartermaster general. The two directed the armies in the west as well as the politicians at home.

With the end of the war Hindenburg's career seemed to come to an end. He retired to Hannover, where he wrote his memoirs, reiterating his contention that the Germans had not been beaten in the field, but "stabbed in the back."

Shrewd and ambitious, a monarchist and a militarist, he was now back in power—as the civilian president of the democratic Republic.

1925, Summer:

PRESIDENT VON HINDENBURG FACES A BATTERY OF PHOTOGRAPHERS IN THE PRESIDENTIAL PALACE GARDEN.

A BOOK IS BORN

THE FIRST ANNOUNCEMENT of Hitler's book in 1924 had the long cumbersome title *Four and a Half Years of Struggle Against Lies, Stupidity and Cowardice*. But Max Amann, Hitler's wartime comrade and now manager of the party's publishing house, reduced it to two words: *Mein Kampf* (My Struggle).

1925, Summer:
AN EDITORIAL CONFERENCE in a coffee house. During his imprisonment in Landsberg, Hitler first dictated the first half of a book to Emil Maurice, then to Rudolf Hess. After his release the anti-Semitic Father Bernhard Staempfle of the *Miesbacher-Anzeiger* and later Josef Czerny, a

EDITORIAL COMMENT: At an adjoining table at the Café Heck, the sharp-tongued literary critic Anton Kuh with Stefan Lorant, editor of the *Münchner Illustrierte Presse*.

HITLER WAS NOT a writer. His literary style was drab, his argumentation unconvincing, his logic woolly. He took his ideas from newspapers, pamphlets, and racist magazines, his phrases from plays and operas. He was not a reader either—in his many thousands of pho-

158

Photograph by Heinrich Hoffmann

journalist on the *Völkischer Beobachter,* rewrote, revised, and edited the manuscript, pruning the author's verbosity, clarifying his thoughts, making the text comprehensible to readers. Many discussions about the work took place in Munich's lovely English Garden at the Café Heck. The book's main purpose was to convince the world that Hitler was the sole founder and builder of the National Socialist movement. Those who played vital parts in the rise of the party—Ernst Röhm, Hermann Esser, Julius Streicher, Gregor Strasser—were not even mentioned. The volume, finally titled *Mein Kampf,* was published in the fall of 1925. It made little stir and sold only 9,473 copies. Sales got worse the following year —only 6,913—and in 1927 only 5,607. As Hitler climbed the ladder, the sales figures increased. From 1933 on, when he became chancellor, a great many millions of copies of the book were sold.

tographs, not a single one shows him with a book. He himself said: "I never read a novel. That kind of reading annoys me." He had no library, either in his youth or later. He was a half-educated man with a vulgar mind, a tortured scribbler whose sentences never seemed to come to an end. And yet he produced a book which influenced the lives of millions.

Mein Kampf begins in an autobiographical vein, then changes into a collection of half-baked theories on "nation and race," "philosophy and party," "conception of the folkish state," but it has a brilliant chapter on "propaganda and organization."

When the book was published, the public hardly noticed it. Even Hitler's most ardent admirers were heard to say that it was unreadable and a bore.

159

1925:

AT THE FIRST SESSION OF THE LOCARNO CONFERENCE on October 16, 1925, a protocol was signed by the representatives of Germany, France, Belgium, Great Britain, and Italy which guaranteed the frontiers fixed by the Versailles treaty. For Germany it meant the final loss of Alsace-Lorraine.

The participants seated around the table: in front, the Germans: Chancellor Hans Luther; Foreign Minister Gustav Stresemann; Karl von Schubert, state secretary of the foreign office. Next to them on the left, the Italians: Count Dino Grandi (with short beard), also Benito Mussolini. Then the British led by the monocled foreign secretary Sir Austen Chamberlain. Opposite the Germans, the French with Foreign Minister Aristide Briand in the center. On the right, Eduard Beneš of Czechoslovakia, Émile Vandervelde of Belgium, and Grabski, the Polish prime minister.

WORKING FOR PEACE

STRESEMANN sought political reconciliation with France and an international agreement with other nations, so Germany could have a peaceful development. His efforts were successful. The meeting of the seven nations in Locarno led to a mutual security pact and an easing of tension in Europe. Germany accepted the finality of her western borders (the Rhine was to be demilitarized) and was willing to submit the question of her eastern border to arbitration.

The spirit of Locarno was the spirit of mutual trust, proving, in Erich Eyck's words, "that two nations which had been enemies for centuries could be reconciled and united in the common work of peace." It led to Germany's admission to the League of Nations.

A HARMLESS NEWS PHOTO . . .
of German representative Stresemann joking with international newsmen in Locarno.

.. BECOMES A VICIOUS CARICATURE.
German artist Frohne turned the picture into a vile attack on the foreign secretary.

A POSTCARD FROM LOCARNO signed by the chief delegates. "The treaty of Locarno could be the beginning of a great and new European development—and I hope that it will," wrote Stresemann. Briand added his signature and Chamberlain wrote at the bottom, "And so say all of us."

SIGNING OF THE LOCARNO TREATIES IN LONDON. The agreements were initialed by the Locarno negotiators on October 16, Austen Chamberlain's sixty-second birthday. On November 22 President Hindenburg affixed his signature to the four Reichstag-voted Locarno laws in Berlin; the next day Chancellor Luther and Foreign Minister Stresemann journeyed to London to sign the documents in the British foreign office.

ROCKING THE REPUBLIC

TO EXPROPRIATE THE PRINCES' PROPERTIES. The Communists and Social Democrats suggested confiscating the properties of the princes without any compensation.

After the Reichstag had declined to pass a bill to that effect, a petition was submitted to that body signed by 12.5 million people, three times the 10 per cent of all qualified voters needed for its acceptance. However, when on May 6, 1926, the Reichstag rejected the petition by a vote of 236 to 142, the Communists and Social Democrats prepared for a referendum. If more than half of the 40 million eligible voters were to cast their votes for their proposal, expropriation without compensation would become law. On June 20 the referendum was held. The Socialist parties' 14,455,184 yes vote was 4.5 million votes short.

A PRESIDENTIAL ORDER ABOUT THE FLAG was issued by President Hindenburg on May 5, 1926. It was a great political blunder creating a crisis which led to the downfall of Chancellor Luther and his cabinet.

The decision on the new flag for the Republic was reached after a compromise. While the new colors—black, red, and gold—became the official ones, the old imperial colors with black, white, and red (with the new colors in the upper corner) remained the merchant flag to be flown by all ships.

Those who remained faithful to the flag of the monarchy, particularly German citizens living abroad, put so much pressure on the government that Hindenburg (himself loyal to the old flag) issued a directive that in the future all German legations and consulates must display both flags—the black, red, and gold and also the black, white, and red.

IN THE SPRING of 1926 two issues stirred passions and created further division; one was the expropriation of the princes' property, the other was the colors of the flag. The Nationalists agitated against expropriation; the Social Democrats and Communists were for it, arguing that the princes had received their property from the people and—since their power was taken from them—it should be returned to the people. Quite naturally, the princes fought back. In some southern states they were able to settle with the new governments, while in others, like Prussia, they could not. The Reichstag refused to pass an expropriation law, and when it was tested through a referendum, there were not enough votes to make it a law by popular will. The result was a victory for the conservative Nationalists—and a defeat for the Republic.

The other issue which broke at about the same time was the president's directive about the flag. Hindenburg, who grew up and served under the monarchy's colors, had no fondness for the Republic's flag. Supported by the Nationalists at home and Germans living in foreign countries, he ordered German legations and consulates to display the merchant design of the black-white-red alongside the nation's official standard. The act stirred up political passions and led to the resignation of the cabinet. Chancellor Luther could not understand why such a minor issue could bring about his cabinet's downfall. It did not dawn on him that the black, red, and gold was the symbol of the Republic which he as chancellor was supposed to represent.

GERMANY IN THE LEAGUE OF NATIONS. Germany's foreign minister Gustav Stresemann accepted his nation's admittance to the League: "The safest foundation for peace is a policy of mutual understanding and mutual respect between nations." Briand replied: "We cannot expect to solve our problems by brutal, violent and bloody means." The hope of the world for peace brightened.

GENEVA

THE TREATIES of Locarno led to Germany's entry into the League of Nations. On February 10, 1926, Stresemann asked the secretary-general of the League for Germany's admittance. His request stirred up a hornet's nest in the assembly. If Germany was granted a permanent seat, other powers felt they deserved permanent seats as well. After a protracted debate Germany was finally admitted. On September 9 Stresemann addressed the League and Briand responded with a memorable speech. Germany and France talked to each other as friends.

RELAXING. Stresemann—following a meeting of the League of Nations—sips his drink in Geneva's renowned Café Bavaria, the meeting place of politicians and newspapermen.

HITLER ADDRESSES A MEETING at the party's office in Munich, Schellingstrasse 50. At the speaker's table from left to right: Philip Bouhler, executive secretary of the party; Arthur Ziegler; Alfred Rosenberg; Walter Buch, chairman of the Uschla; Franz Xavier Schwarz, treasurer of the party; Adolf Hitler; Gregor Strasser; Heinrich Himmler; and

FOR THE FIRST TIME since his release, Hitler speaks on February 27, 1925. "No Jews are admitted," says the announcement.

REORGANIZING THI

WHILE HITLER WAS IN PRISON Nationalist and *völkisch* politicians fought for the leadership of the Nazis. But once released Hitler picked up the reins. Speaking in the Bürgerbräu cellar (on "Germany's future and our movement"), he declared: "I lead the movement alone—and nobody can make any conditions for me. . . ." Because of his intemperate speech, Bavaria forbade him to address open meetings for the next two years. Some of the other states followed the Bavarian example and barred Hitler from

THE PARTY CHIEF WITH HIS PROMINENT LIEUTENANTS:

OTTO STRASSER, with his brother Gregor one of Hitler's early supporters, agitated for nationalization of big industries and estates. When they challenged Hitler they were forced out of the party. Otto survived, Gregor was killed in 1934.

JULIUS STREICHER, the vulgar sex fiend and pornographic anti-Semite, brought his Franconian followers early into the Nazi party, for which Hitler remained eternally grateful to him. In the Nürnberg trial Streicher was sentenced to death by hanging.

at the end of the table, Karl Fiehler. After his release from prison, Hitler set himself the task of reorganizing the party and he did this with extraordinary success.

PARTY

speaking in public. During these years of silence, Hitler reorganized the party.

When the ban was lifted he took up where he had left off. In August 1927 twenty thousand National Socialists met in Nürnberg to greet their undisputed leader.

NAZI CHIEFTAINS MEET over a mug in Munich's Hofbräuhaus. From left to right: Gregor Strasser, Christian Weber, Hitler, Franz Xavier Schwarz, Max Amann, Ulrich Graf. With their backs to the camera in the foreground: Karl Fiehler and Julius Schaub.

VOTING FOR THE FOURTH REICHSTAG

THE RIGHTIST COALITION of the Nationalists, Stresemann's German People's Party, and the Catholic Center, was an unstable alliance. The Nationalists vehemently attacked Stresemann's foreign policy, ready to leave the government. But the actual break between factions came over a domestic issue—whether there should be common schools with instruction in different faiths, or secular, nondenominational ones. As no agreement could be reached, Chancellor Marx dissolved the Reichstag and called for new elections.

In the ensuing campaign the Social Democrats made an issue of the government's request for 9 million marks to begin construction of a small armed cruiser. Financial scandals in the defense ministry, particularly the investment of ministry funds in the Phoebus Film Company which went bankrupt, forced Defense Minister Otto Gessler out of office. He was replaced by Wilhelm Gröner, who campaigned for the Panzerkreuzer. The Social Democrats retorted: *Keine Panzerkreuzer, sondern Kinderspeisung* ("No armed

cruiser, rather food for children").

The election was a victory for the Social Democrats. They increased their strength from 131 to 153. Both Nationalists and the German People's Party lost (the Nationalist seats decreased from 103 to 73; the German People's Party from 51 to 45). But a more significant sign was the Nazis' loss of 100,000 votes.

Herman Müller, the Social Democrat, became chancellor and once more he formed a "great coalition" cabinet, hoping to bring order in the chaos.

1928, May 20:
WHETHER TO BUILD PANZERKREUZERS DOMINATED THE MAY ELECTION.

A POSTER OF THE NATIONALISTS demanding more power for the president.

VOTING FOR THE 4th REICHSTAG ON MAY 20, 1928.

	Seats
KPD	54
SPD	153
D	25
Z	62
BVP	16
Kl.M.P.	31
DVP	45
Kl.R.P.	20
DNVP	73
NSDAP	12

THE ABBREVIATIONS ON THE CHART

KPD *(Kommunistische Partei Deutschlands)* = the Party of the Communists
SPD *(Socialdemokratische Partei Deutschlands)* = Social Democrats
D *(Demokratische Partei)* = Democrats
Z *(Zentrum)* = the Party of the Catholics
BVP *(Bayrische Volks Partei)* = Bavarian People's Party (Catholic)
Kl.MP *(Kleine Mittel Parteien)* = Small Parties of the Center
DVP *(Deutsche Volks Partei)* = German People's Party (the party of industry)
Kl.RP *(Kleine Rechts Parteien)* = Small Right-Wing Parties
DNVP *(Deutschnationale Volks Partei)* = German Nationalists People's Party
NSDAP *(National Socialistische Deutsche Arbeiter Partei)* = National Socialists

THE POSTERS OF THE COMMUNISTS.

FIVE O'CLOCK TEA AT THE HOTEL ESPLANADE, ONE OF THE MOST MODERN AND ELEGANT HOSTELRIES IN BERLIN.

THÉ DANSANT

THE "GOLDEN TWENTIES" were golden only to those with money and to tourists who came to Berlin for enjoyment. The hotels were superb, the food exquisite; theater and films had never been better. The girls were beautiful, the men elegant. Any pleasure could be bought; nothing was forbidden. But most Germans could not afford these luxuries, they hardly had enough to feed themselves. And Hitler was in the wings. The reckoning was near.

EVERYBODY WAS DANCING. The twenties were the years of the dance craze. Afternoon dancing, particularly at the capital's internationally famous Hotel Adlon, was a pastime which Berlin society and foreign visitors constantly enjoyed. In the center of the dance floor, facing the camera, the popular owners of the hotel, Louis and Hedda Adlon.

167

THE "BAVARIAN"

Photographs by Heinrich Hoffmann

THE BAVARIAN GENTLEMAN. In the twenties Hitler wore such outfits to show that he wanted to be considered a native.

LEDERHOSEN. Gregor Strasser, Ernst Röhm, Hermann Göring, and Wilhelm Brückner—only Hitler wears a business suit.

THOUGH HITLER was born Austrian, his most ardent wish was to be taken for a Bavarian. In the years he lived in Munich (and at the front with Bavarian comrades), he mastered the Bavarian dialect, and in clothing and manner he tried to appear as a Bavarian.

A true Bavarian is a unique human being—no one is like him. ("Watch out," the Bavarian would say, "he did not compare us with animals, but with human beings—he is up to something!") The dialect he speaks is unfathomable, hardly understandable to outsiders, as strange to the ears as Chinese. The speech of a Bavarian is earthy, his expressions are coarse, but what he says—and how he says it—is funny. A Bavarian joke: "It is raining hard," remarks a Munich beer drinker; and his colleague retorts: "Outside?"

The world of a Bavarian is a close-knit one—his job, his family, his beer, and his *Weisswurst* (sausage)—perhaps not in that order. While one does not think of Bavaria as a land of artists, it has produced writers (Ludwig Thoma, Max Halbe, Oskar Maria Graf), composers (Richard Strauss, Hans Pfitzner), comedians (Karl Valentin, Weiss Ferdl), painters, architects, and poets. Thomas Mann, Lion Feuchtwanger, Bruno Walter all lived and worked in Munich, as did the incomparable circle of men who drafted the cartoons for *Simplicissimus*, Olaf Gulbransson, Thomas Theodor Heine, Karl Arnold, and others.

The Bavarian mentality is best expressed by the quatrain under Arnold's cartoon of a beer-drinking man (with swastikas on his eyelids):

"I want my peace and a revolution.
We must have order and a Jewish pogrom
And a dictator to show the *sauband*'
How to rebuild our Deutschland."

Hitler wanted to be a Bavarian with all his heart, with or without lederhosen.

HITLER IN LEDERHOSEN.
Portrait by Heinrich Hoffmann from 1928.

WRITERS,

Courtesy: Carl Zuckmayer

CARL ZUCKMAYER (1896–), author of *Der fröhliche Weinberg* (1925), *Schinderhannes* (1927), *Der Hauptmann von Köpenick* (1931), and numerous other successful plays, with his friend Emil Jannings, male star of *The Blue Angel* (1929), for which Zuckmayer wrote the script. During the second war Zuckmayer lived in the United States.

Courtesy: Liesl Frank Lustig

EMIL LUDWIG (1881–1948), who wrote biographies of Goethe, Bismarck, Wilhelm II, Napoleon, Abraham Lincoln, Franklin Delano Roosevelt, and Sigmund Freud.

Author's collection

ERNST TOLLER (1893–1939), dramatist and poet, who for a few days in 1919 headed the Bavarian Communist government, with his friend Stefan Lorant. Toller served five years in prison, where he spent his time writing plays and a book of poetry.

Courtesy: Mary Tucholsky

KURT TUCHOLSKY (1890–1935), at right, political polemicist, leading liberal journalist, and poet, wrote under various pseudonyms. Despondent over Hitler's Germany, he committed suicide in Sweden.

170

POETS

—were joined by a host of younger talent, among them Arnolt Bronnen, Walter Hasenclever, Georg Kaiser, Alfred Döblin, Hans Fallada, etc.

Courtesy: Frances Thanash

ERICH MARIA REMARQUE (1898–1970) and wife. The 31-year-old Berlin editor became famous in 1929 with his anti-war novel *All Quiet on the Western Front*.

Courtesy: Liesl Frank Lustig

THOMAS MANN (1875–1955) with his wife, Katja, in 1924 at the time of the publication of *The Magic Mountain*, when he was already a renowned author. He had established his name at the beginning of the century with his family chronicle, *Buddenbrooks*. In 1927 he received the Nobel Prize for Literature. In 1933 he fled from Germany.

Courtesy: Liesl Frank Lustig

THE POET KLABUND (1890–1928) with Bruno Frank (1887–1945), the playwright, novelist, and movie scriptwriter, on a vacation in 1925. Frank, Fritzi Massary's son-in-law, spent his last years in the U.S.

Courtesy: Helene Weigel-Brecht

BERTOLT BRECHT (1898–1956) in his Berlin home in 1928, the year the *Threepenny Opera*, with music by Kurt Weill, was first given. Ten years before, in 1918, he established his reputation with his play *Baal*, which earned him the Kleist Prize.

REPARATIONS

1928:

RATIFICATION OF THE KELLOGG PEACE PACT. President Coolidge endorses the pact. Next to him, Frank B. Kellogg and Secretary of the Treasury Andrew Mellon.

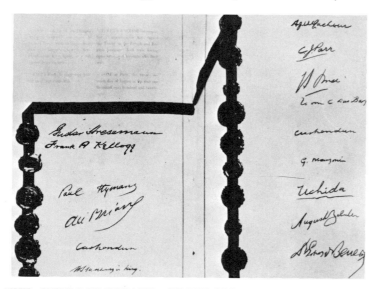

THE KELLOGG-BRIAND PROTOCOL condemned "recourse to war for the solution of international controversies."

1929, February:

THE YOUNG PLAN was debated at the Paris Reparations Conference. Left to right: the Americans Owen D. Young and J. P. Morgan with Sir Josiah Stamp of Great Britain.

THE TWO MAIN OBJECTIVES of Stresemann's foreign policy were the evacuation of the Rhineland and the lowering of the reparation payments. In Stresemann's belief, Germany had fulfilled the requirements set at Versailles by signing the London agreement; therefore the troops occupying the Rhineland must be removed. And to achieve the second objective he persuaded the French and the English to form a committee of experts—with two representatives from each of the countries involved—to come up with an acceptable proposal about reparations.

This conference of experts met in Paris on February 9, 1929 under the chairmanship of the American Owen D. Young. (The other American delegate was J. P. Morgan, the banker.) Hjalmar Schacht and Albert Vögler, industrialists of the far right, were the German representatives, with Ludwig Kastl, director of the bund of German industry, and Carl Melchior, the Hamburg banker, as alternates.

The Germans suggested an annual payment of 1.6 billion marks if two conditions could be met: one, Germany should be given raw materials from colonial sources, and two, Germany should be compensated for agricultural products it had lost in the east during the war. In blunt terms they were asking for the return of their colonies and for the abolition of the Polish corridor. Since these were political rather than economic issues, they should not have been discussed at the conference. The demands of the two nationalistic German delegates almost wrecked the meeting, which was saved only by the compromise proposal of Chairman Young.

After much bargaining, the experts signed the agreement on June 7, 1929, obligating Germany to pay an average of 1.99 billion marks a year for thirty-seven years, and lesser payments for another twenty-two years covering the inter-Allied war debt. The annual payments were to be in two parts, one unconditional (660 million marks),

REVISED

which had to be paid; while the other payments could be postponed.

The conditions were far less stringent than those of the Dawes Plan (which they were to supplant). There would be no foreign control and thus no interference with German sovereignty; there would be no reparation agent, no cost of living index, no economic uncertainties. It was a sizable reduction of Germany's former obligations.

Nevertheless, when the plan's provisions became public, the Nationalist press raged against Stresemann, denouncing his policies. Hugenberg spearheaded the attacks in his newspapers, and he orated: "It is better for all Germans to live together as proletarians until the hour of freedom strikes than for some of us to exploit our own people by becoming the agents and beneficiaries of foreign capital." Though the meaning of his words was not clear, the Nationalists applauded his ranting wholeheartedly.

In the debate on the Young Plan, the Reichstag voted down all no confidence motions brought against Stresemann, and endorsed German participation in the forthcoming international conference at The Hague, which was to legalize the plan.

The Hague conference turned out to be a triumph for Stresemann. Desperately ill, he gained conditions more favorable to his country. His strength spent, he died two months later, on October 3, 1929.

The acceptance of the Young Plan's provisions constituted another step in the effort to normalize relations between the former enemies. If the politicians had known that their petty wrangling over reparation payments would later be used as the Nazis' most effective propaganda weapon against the democratic governments, perhaps they would have acted differently. If the issue had been solved amicably so that Europe could have developed in a peaceful manner, much suffering would have been avoided. But the in-

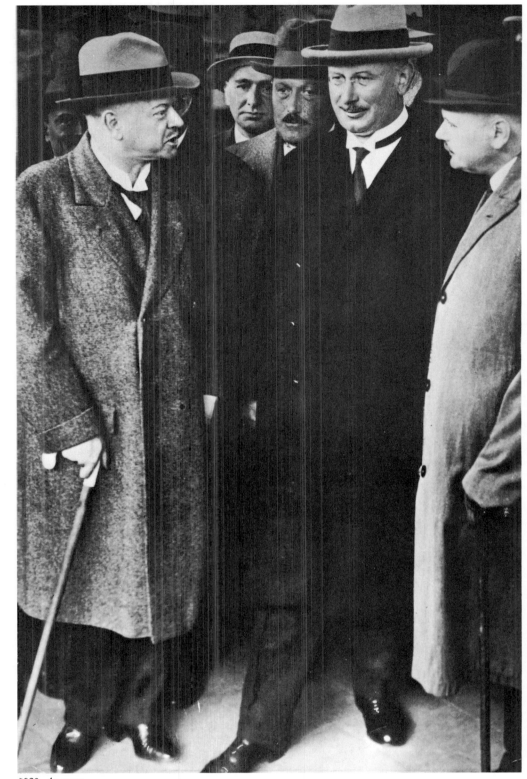

1929, August:
THE AILING STRESEMANN at The Hague with the Dutch foreign minister van Blokland. After protracted debate, France, Belgium, and Britain promised to withdraw their troops from the Rhineland and restore full sovereignty of the area to Germany.

transigent and short-sighted attitude of the victors played into the hands of the German nationalistic forces, who in the ensuing years united the discontented and the jobless in a struggle against "enslavement."

By 1933, when Hitler took over, the German reparation debt had been whittled down from the hundred and thirty-two billion originally set to a mere three billion marks.

GUSTAV STRESEMANN DIED

ON OCTOBER 3, 1929.

AGAINST THE YOUNG PLAN

1930, January: *Photographs by Dr. Erich Salomon*

THE HAGUE CONFERENCE continued into the new year of 1930. Julius Curtius (in center with cigar), Stresemann's successor as German foreign secretary, discusses the issues with the French statesmen. In this midnight conference at the Anjema restaurant, the actors from left to right are: German finance minister Paul Moldenhauer; French minister Louis Loucheur; French premier André Tardieu; and French minister Henri Cheron.

THE EXHAUSTED DELEGATES IN THE EARLY HOURS OF MORNING.

EVEN BEFORE the conference at The Hague convened to legalize the recommendations of the financial experts, a national committee was organized in Berlin to promote a referendum against the Young Plan. The head of the committee was Hugenberg and he was assisted by Seldte, the Stahlhelm leader, and by Class of the Pan-German group. They were to rally all the nationalist forces in united opposition to the Young Plan.

The Nationalists—who until then had kept a respectable distance from the Nazis—now asked Hitler to join them in the fight, and Hitler seized the opportunity. To be allied with the Nationalists gave him respectability and also much sought publicity. The newspapers owned by Hugenberg, the wire service owned by Hugenberg, the Ufa newsreels owned by Hugenberg all now carried the Nazi leader's speeches and the Nazi leader's pictures. Almost overnight he became known to millions who had not heard or seen him before. He moved around the country, addressing rallies, stirring up resentment against the Young Plan. The spotlight was on him. And as the campaign progressed it was Hitler more than Hugenberg who became the driving force behind the "National Committee for the German Referendum."

The committee's draft for a "freedom law" proposed annulment of Article 231 of the Versailles treaty (the war guilt clause), and also annulment of Articles 429 and 430 (concerning Allied occupation of Germany). And

1929, July 9:

OPPOSING THE YOUNG PLAN. Alfred Hugenberg advocated a people's referendum (*Volksbegehren*) against the Young Plan. To stir up the masses, he asked Hitler to join him in the crusade. The campaign and the publicity given to Hitler in the Hugenberg papers not only gave him the desired respectability, but made his name a familiar one all over Germany.

it would forbid the national government to assume new obligations or to sign "treaties with foreign powers."

According to the constitution, a referendum could be submitted to the voters if one-tenth of the national electorate petitioned for it. Hugenberg and Hitler collected the necessary signatures with ease.

But when the proposed law "against the enslavement of the German nation" was voted upon, only 6 million voters favored it. (Support of the majority of voters—21 million—was needed to make it a law.) The national opposition's proposals were soundly rejected. The majority of Germans would have none of the demagoguery of Hugenberg and Hitler.

1929, October 25:

A DAY AFTER BLACK THURSDAY IN AMERICA, Hitler spoke against the Young Plan in Munich's Circus Krone. But not enough votes could be amassed against acceptance of the plan. It was adopted by the Reichstag and signed by Hindenburg.

HITLER SPOKE IN TOWN AFTER TOWN ON BEHALF OF NATIONAL SOCIALISM—HERE IN MUNICH'S BÜRGERBRÄU.

THE RISE

HE HAD BOUNDLESS energy and a gift for organization, and he was a demagogue who could give voice to the grievances, frustrations, and resentments of his audience. A master manipulator of mass emotion, he could enthrall meetings by sputtering words of abuse, screaming hysterically, and banging the table with his fists.

Photographs by Heinrich Hoffmann

HIS AUDIENCES WERE MAINLY FROM THE MIDDLE CLASS, PEOPLE WHO HAD LOST THEIR MONEY IN INFLATION.

OF THE DRUMMER

What he said was usually the same: attacks on the "November criminals" and on the Versailles treaty; attacks on the Jews, whom he charged with being "responsible for the misery of Germany." A typical example of that theme from one of Hitler's early speeches: "A Jew will never become poor. He blows himself up and if you don't believe me, please look at some of our resorts; there you find two categories: the Germans who go there to take some fresh air and recover after their hard work, and the Jew who goes there to get rid of his fat. Go to the mountains—whom will you find there but Jews in their brown leather boots and new rucksacks. They would sit where the train brought them—like flies on a cadaver."

His German was poor; what he said was muddled and confused, he used clichés, but he was able to transfer his own excitement to the masses. His voice did not have a pleasant sound; it was thin—but carried far.

He was perhaps the best orator of his time. "He had neither scruples nor inhibitions," said Alan Bullock, characterizing him. "He was a man without roots, with neither home nor family; a man who admitted no loyalties, was bound by no traditions, and felt respect neither for God nor man."

177

A STAR IS BORN

Maria Magdalena Dietrich, the daughter of a Prussian cavalry officer, was born in Berlin on December 27, 1901. Forty-two years younger than the kaiser and twelve years younger than Adolf Hitler, she grew up in the last years of the Wilhelminic era. At war's end she was almost seventeen. She studied to become a musician, a violinist, but a burning ambition pushed her toward the stage.

VON STERNBERG DISCUSSES A SHOT WITH MARLENE.

"WHEN THE BEST FRIEND WITH HER BEST FRIEND . . ." sang Margo Lion and the budding young actress Marlene Dietrich in the revue *Es liegt in der Luft* (It is in the Air) in the Berlin Komödie.

THE DIRECTOR EXPLAINS A SCENE to the cast of *The Blue Angel*. Marlene Dietrich is flanked by Kurt Gerron and Emil Jannings.

1930, April 1:

MARLENE LEAVES FOR HOLLYWOOD. Many friends and admirers came to the Lehrter railway station—from which Bismarck had left Berlin 40 years before (see page 35)—to say farewell to the new movie star of *The Blue Angel* as she departed for America.

She went from theater to theater, from one film office to another, asking for a part. Her first film test was made when she was twenty by the writer of these lines. Soon she was playing small parts on the stage and in films. In 1924 she married the dashing assistant director Rudolf Sieber; a year later a daughter was born to them. Marlene—her first name by then—appeared in a number of mediocre films without distinguishing herself; she also sang in revues, driven by an indomitable will to make a career as an actress. Her break came in 1929 with the part of Lola in *The Blue Angel*.

The film's success brought her a contract from Hollywood, where she became a leading movie star and a legend in her own time.

Photographs from the author's collection

179

HARD TIMES

Photograph by Eric Andres

THE LONG LINE OF UNEMPLOYED BEFORE THE LABOR OFFICE IN HAMBURG

IN THE SEVERE winter of 1928–29, unemployment rose to over 2.5 million. The National Office for Unemployment Insurance, founded two years before, was unable to cope with the situation. And the government, itself in financial distress, had no funds to come to its aid. Expenditures had to be curtailed, relief payments limited, and taxes had to be increased. Chancellor Brüning preached auster-

EATING A MIDDAY MEAL OUTSIDE A SOUP KITCHEN—A SCENE WHICH WAS REPEATED IN THOUSANDS OF PLACES.

1929, Summer:

IN BERLIN—A LONG LINE OF PEOPLE QUEUE UP BEFORE A PAWNSHOP—TO EXCHANGE BELONGINGS FOR CASH.

ity. But how much more austerity could the nation endure? At the beginning of 1931 there were almost five million people without jobs. Brüning had to admit that "we have reached the limits of the privation we can impose upon our people."

Those without income pawned their possessions. Family ties drew closer; people in the country sent food to their relatives in the city.

I remember visiting the Schrippenkirche in Berlin on a Sunday morning in August 1930. Men in their Sunday best lined up before the "service." Inside the church they sat at large tables and were served coffee and buns. They ate in silence, looking bitter and grim. Seeing a tear rolling down a man's face, I asked him whether I could help. "We don't need anyone. We will help ourselves," he replied curtly. And he turned back his lapel. On the inside was pinned the swastika emblem.

1931:

MEN WERE IDLE. The number of unemployed grew to five million in 1930. The world economic crisis hit Germany hard. Able-bodied men who had worked all their lives had nothing to do. In their frustration they turned to Hitler, who promised to change conditions.

FOR LAW AND ORDER—*RECHT UND GESETZ!* Tired of the conditions brought about by the loss of the war and the revolu-tion, tired of the lack of discipline and the constant fighting in the streets, the masses yearned for more peaceful times.

THE CRY FOR LAW AND

THE PEOPLE were tired of the fighting in the streets, of the constant battles between Nazis and Communists; they were tired of labor demonstrations, of police raids against black marketeers, of strikes and work stoppages. They yearned for some kind of authority— for someone who would tell them what to do. They cried out for law and or-der. To them order meant a uniformity in their lives, while law meant punish-ment for those who deviated from the

ROBBED OF HIS CLOTHES.

ARREST OF A BLACK MARKETEER.

AND BEFORE LONG THEY GOT "LAW AND ORDER"—NAZI REGIMENTATION.

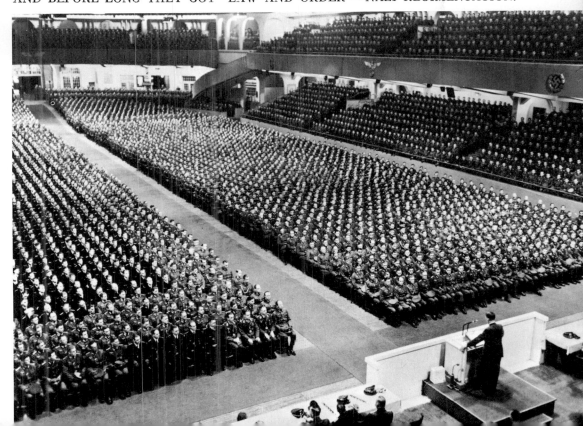

They wanted order, not upheavals. What they got was uniformity and regimentation.

ORDER

uniformity. Adolf Hitler felt their frustration and knew how to woo them, what to offer them: strong leadership and respect for law and order.

Photograph by Dr. Erich Salomon

MEETING OF THE BRÜNING CABINET in the garden of the chancellery on a hot summer day in 1930. From left to right, Dr. Wachsmann, ministerial director of the finance ministry; Martin Schiele, minister of food; Joseph Wirth, minister of the interior. In the center, Hermann Dietrich, vice chancellor and finance minister; next to him, Chancellor Heinrich Brüning and Hermann Pünder, state secretary of the chancellery. Opposite Dietrich (with back), Heinrich Hirtsiefer, welfare minister of Prussia.

BRÜNING STRUGGLES

THE PARTIES of the Weimar Coalition were breaking apart. The immediate reason was their inability to reach an agreement on a rate increase of the workers' unemployment insurance. The People's Party demanded a higher insurance rate and a cut in social services, while the Social Democrats opposed these as increased burdens on the working class.

Dr. Heinrich Brüning, leader of the Center party—the third party in the coalition—offered a compromise; when his suggestions were not taken, the Müller cabinet resigned.

President Hindenburg now asked Brüning to form a new cabinet and he accepted the appointment with the un-derstanding that he would be allowed to govern with emergency decrees without relying on parliamentary majority.

At the time Brüning became chancellor, three million men were out of work, and the government was facing a severe financial crisis. Brüning proposed new austerity measures, hoping to weather the economic storm.

1931:   *Photograph by Dr. Erich Salomon*
"HUNGER CHANCELLOR" BRÜNING INTRODUCES HIS AUSTERITY BUDGET IN THE REICHSTAG IN FEBRUARY 1931.

VOTING

THE EMERGING LEADER: Adolf Hitler, the idol of the National Socialist masses, welded his enthusiastic supporters into a homogeneous political force.

1930:
AT THE WEIMAR PARTY DAY, HITLER GETS SUPPORT FOR HIS POLICIES.

CHANCELLOR BRÜNING did not hide his intentions. On assuming office (on March 30, 1930), he told the Reichstag that if he was not given support he would govern through emergency decrees. He could do this by asking President Hindenburg to invoke Article 48 of the constitution.

Article 48 empowered the president, "in the event the public safety and order are *'gestört oder gefährdet'* [disturbed or jeopardized]," to temporarily annul the following articles of the constitution: Articles 114 (concerning the inviolability of the freedom of the individual), 115 (inviolability of the home), 117 (concerning privacy of mail and telephone), 118 (freedom of speech), 123 (freedom of assembly), 124 (freedom of association), and 153 (safeguard of personal property).

At first the Reichstag followed Brüning's proposals; the Social Democrats did so in a passive manner; they "tolerated" the government through a simple expedient: they refrained from voting on the issues and allowed them to pass without their approval. But when Brüning—in his effort to bring down the massive budget deficit—submitted stringent measures to deal with the worsening economic crisis, the Social Democrats balked. They resisted a further increase in unemployment insurance rates (from 3.5 per cent to 4.5 per cent) and they spoke out against additional taxes on income and on wages. When Brüning could not gain the Reichstag's support for his program, he submitted the presidential order invoking Article 48.

The Social Democrats promptly brought in a motion (which required only a simple majority) for an annulment of the order. Twenty-four hours later, when the vote was taken, a strange combination of political bedfellows—Social Democrats and Communists, joined by Nationalists and National Socialists—gave Brüning a resounding defeat. Shorn of his parliamentary support and blocked from

FOR THE FIFTH REICHSTAG

governing by emergency decrees, the chancellor now dissolved the Reichstag and set the date for the new election sixty days hence. In these two months Brüning hoped to convince the electorate of the soundness of his policies and expected that the early evacuation of the Rhineland by the occupation troops would sway the voters behind him and his party.

In the ensuing campaign the left and the right radical parties—the Communists and the Nazis—strove hard to win over the dissatisfied. The Nazis' main issue was *"Not und Elend"* (misery and hunger). They promised "bread and work for everyone," and an all-out fight against Bolshevism. Their campaigners, particularly Hitler, denounced the Social Democrats as traitors who helped the victors in the war keep Germany in bondage and assailed the Jews, the "nation's misfortune." Against such attacks and promises, the campaign of the moderate parties appeared listless.

The result of the election brought a stunning victory to Hitler and his supporters. The Nazis emerged as the second strongest party; their delegate strength rose from 12 to 107. The Communists gained as well. In the new Reichstag they would have 23 more delegates than in the fourth Reichstag.

(*continued next page*)

A NAZI RALLY in the Sportspalast with General Litzmann speaking. As wearing the brown shirt was forbidden by the government, the Nazis appeared in neat white shirts.

POSTERS OF THE RIVAL PARTIES. Left, a poster of the Social Democrats; center, a Nazi poster; and right, a poster of the Communists. The election brought victory to the Nazis—with 107 deputies, they grew into the second largest party in the country.

1930, October 12:

AFTER THE NAZI VICTORY. The newly elected Nazi members of the Reichstag—all one hundred and seven of them—assembled in the Hotel Kaiserhof to declare their fealty to their leader, Adolf Hitler.

At the head of the table Hitler is flanked by Gregor Strasser and Wilhelm Frick. Standing from right to left, General Franz von Epp (in civilian clothes) the Bavarian Nazi sympathizer, Alfred Rosenberg, Nazi racist philosopher and the editor of the *Völkischer Beobachter*, the party's newspaper, and Hans Frank, Hitler's jurist, who met his end in Nürnberg.

1930, December:
THE REICHSTAG WITH THE NAZIS. They obstructed the proceedings, turning

The great losers were the right-wing conservatives. The Nationalists lost 32 seats, the Peoples' Party 15. The losses of the Social Democrats were small, only 10 seats. Brüning's Center party gained, but barely; they were to have

1930, October 13:
THE NAZIS IN THE REICHSTAG
appeared in brown shirts.

their backs on the speakers. In the second aisle the man leaning on his hand is Joseph Goebbels, the party propagandist, probably composing a piece for his paper, *Der Angriff*.

6 more delegates.

At the opening of the new Reichstag, when the 107 brown-shirted Nazi deputies filed into the hall, the other delegates laughed with amusement. The uniformed Nazis presented a ridiculous picture. But their march into the hall, representing their Führer Adolf Hitler, to whom they had sworn personal fealty the night before, was a historic event; with it a new era in German political life began.

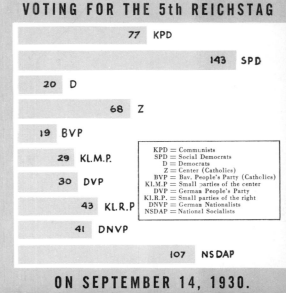

VOTING FOR THE 5th REICHSTAG

77	KPD	
	143	SPD
20	D	
	68	Z
19	BVP	
29	Kl.M.P.	
30	DVP	
	43	Kl.R.P
41	DNVP	
	107	NSDAP

KPD = Communists
SPD = Social Democrats
D = Democrats
Z = Center (Catholics)
BVP = Bav. People's Party (Catholics)
Kl.M.P = Small parties of the center
DVP = German People's Party
Kl.R.P. = Small parties of the right
DNVP = German Nationalists
NSDAP = National Socialists

ON SEPTEMBER 14, 1930.

1930, September 25:

HITLER WAS THE CHIEF WITNESS in the process against the three officers who were charged with conducting Nazi propaganda in the army. He told the court that his party would take power through parliamentary and not through revolutionary means. His testimony mollified the Reichswehr—the officers believed him. From then on his detractors nicknamed him "Adolf Légalité."

THE HIGH TREASON TRIAL against the officers Scheringer, Ludin, and Wendt before the Supreme Court. Hitler (fourth on the left in the first row) is marked with an x.

THE WITNESS

FIERCELY ATTACKING the regular army's nonpolitical position, Hitler argued that officers should be allowed to join the Nazi party.

When three lieutenants of the Ulm garrison were brought before the Supreme Court for spreading Nazi propaganda in the ranks, Hitler appeared as a witness in their behalf and gave the assurance that the storm troops would not be a threat to the army, and that the Nazis would not attempt to take over the state by force, but only by legal means.

190

HIS
MOVIE
STARS

1929:

LENI RIEFENSTAHL

was Hitler's particular favorite. For years she played in films made in the mountains. After he took power she created two memorable films: one of the Nazi Party Day, the other of the 1936 Olympic games in Berlin.

1930:   GRETA GARBO

Left Germany in 1925 for the United States, where she became a leading star. Hitler, who seldom missed a Garbo film and returned to see them again, was a connoisseur of her early ones: *The Torrent, The Temptress, Flesh and the Devil, Anna Karenina, The Divine Woman, The Mysterious Lady, The Green Hat, Wild Orchids, The Single Standard, The Kiss.* During the war the movies of Garbo were screened for the Führer.

1929:

OLGA TSCHECHOVA

was the niece of the actress Olga Knipper-Tschechova, the wife of the Russian writer Chekhov. Not a gifted actress but a charming person, she became the Führer's friend.

1936:   RENATE MÜLLER,

the actress, was rumored to be Hitler's paramour. Later she committed suicide. Here she is with Stefan Lorant and ski champion Hannes Schneider.

191

1931, July 20:   *Photographs by Dr. Erich Salomon*

CONFERENCES. The German and French delegations travel together in a special train to the seven power conference in London. From left to right: Philipp Berthelot, permanent undersecretary of the French foreign office; Chancellor Brüning; the foreign ministers Paul Hymans, Belgium; Julius Curtius, Germany; and Aristide Briand, France; Prime Minister Pierre Laval; and André François-Poncet, then the cabinet chief of Laval.

PARTICIPATORS IN THE LONDON CONFERENCE: Grandi of Italy; Curtius and Brüning of Germany; MacDonald of England; Briand, Laval, and Flandin of France.

HITLER GAINS

UNDER HITLER'S LEADERSHIP the Nazis grew at a phenomenal rate. When in 1919 Hitler first attended the meeting of the original party, 46 people were present; two years later the party had 6000 members. At the end of 1925 the membership reached 27,117; a year later it was 49,573, and in the 1930 Reichstag election 6,409,600 voted for the Nazis.

The main reason for the Nazis' success lay in the worsening economic crisis and also in the inability of the governing parties to agree on a constructive program. There were five million unemployed. Foreign countries withdrew their credits from Germany. In June 1931 President Hoover proposed a one-year moratorium on all reparations payments. A month later Chancellor Brüning journeyed to Paris, and from there to London, where the American president's proposals were accepted.

Campaigning against the Brüning government, Hitler used all the modern propaganda techniques. He reached the voters through specially made films

1931, July 20:
FINANCIAL CRISIS: The Darmstädter and Nationalbank became insolvent after the fall of the Österreichische Kreditanstalt.

BERLIN CONFERENCE
between Curtius, Brüning,
Laval, Briand, and Treviranus.

1931, October:

THE NUMBER OF NAZIS GREW BY LEAPS AND BOUNDS.
The economic crisis, unemployment, a divided government, violence in the streets, the threat and fear of Communism—all these issues made the people swell the Nazi ranks in the hope that Hitler had remedies for the problems. During the Braunschweig Party Day, enthusiasm for Hitler and S.S. chief Ernst Röhm ran high.

and phonograph records; he spoke to them over the radio and sent a constant stream of leaflets. His party grew like Topsy.

1931, August 20:
FINANCIAL CRISIS: Depositors in Berlin, fearing a collapse of the banking system, withdrew their savings from the banks.

HITLER'S FIRST VISIT TO THE PRESIDENT. In October 1931, not long after the suicide of his beloved niece Geli Raubal, Hitler had a conference with Hindenburg.

THE NATIONAL OPPOSITION

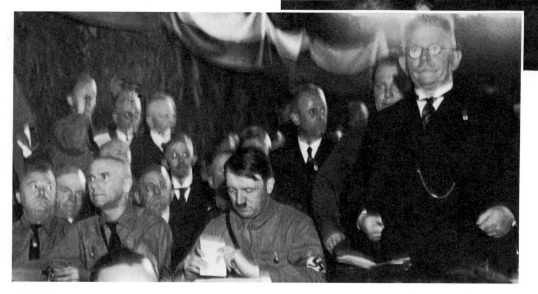

ALFRED HUGENBERG, the cement-headed leader of the German Nationalists, invited the rightist parties and organizations for a show of strength in a meeting at Bad Harzburg, the Thuringian resort town.

It was a well-organized and well-attended affair with a great number of leading figures of the nationalistic and reactionary forces in attendance. Two sons of the kaiser showed up: Prince

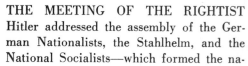

ALFRED HUGENBERG, NOW HITLER'S ALLY, SPEAKS TO THE ASSEMBLY.

THE MEETING OF THE RIGHTIST Hitler addressed the assembly of the German Nationalists, the Stahlhelm, and the National Socialists—which formed the na-

Eitel Friedrich, a member of the Stahlhelm, and Prince August Wilhelm, a high Nazi functionary. General Seeckt, the former head of the army, was present, as was Dr. Hjalmar Schacht, the former president of the Reichsbank. Industry and finance were well represented with Emil Strauss, director of

REVIEWING THE NAZI BRIGADES. Hitler, with Ernst Röhm and Hermann Göring, takes the salute. But before the troops of the Stahlhelm reached the stand, the Führer and his cohorts had departed, to the annoyance of the Stahlhelm leadership.

The meeting was held three weeks after Geli, his niece and beloved, had committed suicide, and only a day after he had his first interview with President Hindenburg—a parley which had not gone well. He felt uncomfortable among the conservative reactionaries, the bemedaled generals, titled aristocrats, and frock-coated industrialists. He knew what they were after —to harness the National Socialist movement for their political advantage. Hitler had come to Harzburg with his eyes open, ready to use the nationalist organizations to advance his own aspirations. He mocked and ridiculed his temporary allies. He left the reviewing stand before the arrival of the Stahlhelm marchers, antagonizing their leadership.

The Harzburg meeting—so highly praised in the Nationalist press—was not a success. Its chief purpose was unfulfilled: to bring about the fall of the national government of Heinrich Brüning and also the Prussian Social Democratic government of Otto Braun.

When the Reichstag met two days later, representatives of the parties at Harzburg brought a motion of no confidence against the Brüning cabinet. The motion was defeated 296 to 270. Chancellor Brüning reconstructed his cabinet, and it was not long thereafter that the "national opposition" of Hugenberg and Hitler—and its "unity"—was in shambles. Oil and water do not mix—neither did Hugenberg and Hitler.

NATIONAL OPPOSITION WAS HELD AT BAD HARZBURG ON OCTOBER 11, 1931.
tional front against the government. Next to Hitler are Hugenberg, leader of the German Nationalists; Reichstag Deputy Schmidt of Hannover; and Düsterberg, leader of the Stahlhelm. Dr. Schacht sits behind Hugenberg; on Hitler's right are Stöhr and Frick.

the Deutsche Bank, Wilhelm Poesgen, head of the Allied Steelworks, and other prominent industrialists.

In his opening remarks Hugenberg told the meeting: "A new world is coming. . . . we call out to the governing parties: we do not want you anymore." He spoke against "the creeping bolshevization of German culture," against "the deliberate exclusion of nationalist forces from the government." He asked for Chancellor Brüning's resignation, for the dissolution of the Reichstag, and for new elections.

Hitler, who had come to Harzburg with reluctance, was in a low mood.

REVIEWING THE STAHLHELM. Count von Goltz of the Pan German League with Stahlhelm chiefs Seldte, Düsterberg, Wagner.

THE ORGANIZER OF THE MEETING, Alfred Hugenberg, with Prince Eitel Friedrich, one of the sons of Kaiser Wilhelm II.

195

1932, March:

A STREET CORNER IN BERLIN WITH GIANT POSTERS FOR HINDENBURG AND HIS OPPONENT FOR THE PRESIDENCY.

1932, March:

A NAZI POSTER.   A NATIONALIST POSTER.   A COMMUNIST POSTER.   A SOCIAL DEMOCRATIC POSTER.

VOTING
FOR
PRESIDENT

1932, June 3:
HITLER BECOMES A GERMAN CITIZEN. His appointment as councilor of Brunswick made him a German, and eligible to run for the presidency.

The new German citizen leaves the Brunswick legation after his oath-taking with his adjutants Julius Schaub and Wilhelm Brückner and his deputy Rudolf Hess.

WHEN HINDENBURG's seven-year term expired in April 1932, Brüning attempted to keep the eighty-four-year-old general in office by extending his term through a constitutional amendment. But when he could not obtain the support of Hitler and Hugenberg, he was forced to call the election.

Three candidates opposed Hindenburg: Hitler for the National Socialists, Düsterberg for the Nationalists, and Thälmann for the Communists. To defeat Hitler, the parties of the middle were obliged to line up behind Hindenburg. When the vote for the general fell short of an absolute majority, a second election had to be held. In this Hindenburg won with 53 per cent of the votes to Hitler's 36 per cent and Thälmann's 10.2 per cent. Hitler's support was spectacular:11.5 million—one-third of the electorate—voted for him.

THE KAISER'S GRANDSON: Prince Hubertus chats with Nazi pollwatchers before the voting place in Potsdam.

1932, April:
A NAZI POSTER. AN ANTI-NAZI POSTER.

FINAL MEETING OF THE DISARMAMENT CONFERENCE IN LAUSANNE ON JULY 12, 1932, IN WHICH THE REPARATIONS

Count Schwerin-Krosigk, German finance minister (standing); at the table: Jules Renkin, Belgian prime minister; Dino Grandi, Italian foreign minister; Konstantin von Neurath, German foreign minister; Chancellor Franz von Papen; Édouard Herriot, French premier; Duncan Sandys of the British embassy; Georges Bonnet, French minister; Ramsay MacDonald, British prime minister;

ONCE MORE—REPARATIONS

In October 1922, after the German government asked for a moratorium on cash payments, a committee of international financial experts—among them John Maynard Keynes and Robert H. Brand from Britain, Gustav Cassel from Sweden—came to Berlin. They suggested a temporary moratorium and a stabilization of the currency.

In December the German government requested a time extension on their material deliveries. The French refused, and together with the Belgians, they moved into the Ruhr to seek "protective guarantees." The Germans called for passive resistance. This accelerated inflation; the mark's value sank to almost nothing.

After passive resistance ended and the currency had been stabilized, another group of international experts led by the American Charles Dawes met in Paris early in January 1924. Their suggestions were taken by the English, the French, and the Germans at the London Conference assuring Germany's entry into the League of Nations.

In 1929 another adjustment of payments was sought. In Paris a committee headed by the American Owen D. Young drafted a compromise plan which greatly reduced German indebtedness. This was accepted at The Hague Conference, but the world economic crisis which broke that autumn played havoc with the settlement.

After Brüning had been replaced as

1932, July:
DR. GOEBBELS stirs up his supporters against the Lausanne Conference decisions.

chancellor by Papen, another meeting was held at Lausanne on June 16, 1932. Papen, like Brüning before him, asked for the cancellation of all reparations. On July 9 the conferees reached agreement: the provisions of the Young Plan were discarded; Germany was to pay 3 billion gold marks into a general fund for European construction. Six months later when Hitler became chancellor, even this was forgotten. The reparation issue was "solved" —Nazi Germany paid nothing.

Photograph by Dr. Erich Salomon
PAYMENTS HAD BEEN REDUCED. Germain-Martin, French finance minister; Émile Francqui, Belgian finance minister. Standing right is Sir Maurice Hankey.

SINCE April 27, 1921, when the Reparation Commission made known that the Germans had to pay 132 billion gold marks for damages in the war, the argument over reparations went on.

NAZIS IN WHITE SHIRTS PROTESTING AGAINST THE LAUSANNE AGREEMENT.

1932, April 4:
HITLER ATTACKS THE GOVERNMENT. In rabble-rousing speeches throughout the year of 1932, Hitler inflamed the Germans against their government and incited his supporters against the Communists. Here he addresses a meeting attended by tens of thousands in Berlin's Lustgarten. At left: Count Helldorf and Hitler's adjutant Brückner; at the microphones, Dr. Goebbels.

THE NAZIS were not for peaceful times. What they needed was unrest, and the precariousness of people's existence. Violence in the streets brought them renewed support. Thus Goebbels, Göring, Röhm, Himmler kept the political pot boiling. Nazi troopers battled their enemies on street corners; they disrupted workers' meetings. The beating up of people whom they considered their enemies became every-day events. During 1932—the year of President Hindenburg's re-election and Chancellor Brüning's ouster—democratic institutions disintegrated rapidly. The very existence of the Republic was in jeopardy. Its paralyzed defenders hesitated to resort to illegalities, while the Nazis had no such qualms. Illegality, immorality, murder did not stop them as long as it furthered their aims.

Governments and chancellors changed. Papen followed Brüning and General Schleicher followed Papen—it made little difference. None of them had a parliamentary majority, none of them could restore order as long as Hitler kept passions aflame.

In the big industrial cities hardly a day passed without Nazis murdering Communists and Communists retaliating by killing Nazis. When a large segment of the population, under corrupt leadership, disregarded its laws, how long could the Republic last?

FIGHTING
IT
OUT

1932:
END OF A MEETING. It is the usual picture—repeated over and over again at many places. Nazi troopers enter a Communist meeting—such as this one in Berlin-Hasenheide —attack participants, break up furniture, then withdraw, leaving the hall a shambles.

1932:
DISORDER: POLICE BEAT UP WORKERS IN NEUKÖLLN.

1932:
ORDER: THE NAZIS SALUTE HITLER IN WEIMAR.

THE SQUIRE OF NEUDECK

THE PRESIDENT'S HOME AT Neudeck, the estate of his forebears, was presented to him on his eightieth birthday. Junker neighbors, Rhenish industrialists, and munitions makers helped toward its purchase.

1932, August 31:   *Photographs taken for the* Münchner Illustrierte Presse *by Helmuth Kurth*
THE GRAVEDIGGERS OF THE REPUBLIC, Franz von Papen, Oscar von Hindenburg, General Kurt von Schleicher, and Dr. Otto Meissner at Hindenburg's Neudeck home.

Wilhelm von Gayl, minister of the interior.

ON THE WAY TO NEUDECK:
Franz von Papen, the Reichs chancellor.

General von Schleicher, minister of war.

THE MEN WHO HAD THE PRESIDENT'S EAR. Hindenburg on his Neudeck terrace with his political intimates in late August, a few weeks after he appointed "Fränzchen" von Papen national commissioner for Prussia. The brash von Papen, helped by Schleicher and Gayl, removed Prussia's Socialist government from office, demolishing the power of the Social Democratic party in the state.

HINDENBURG WAS a figurehead in uniform—not a political leader. As age engulfed him, so did senility. Those around him—his son Oscar, Dr. Meissner, the secretary of state for his office, General Schleicher, "Fränzchen" Papen—wielded great power because they had the president's ear. Their determinations and intrigues could make and unmake governments.

The Junker landowners too, Hindenburg's East Elbian neighbors, had a profound influence on *"der alte Herr"*. It was the idea of his friend Oldenburg-Januschau to buy the lost Hindenburg family estate at Neudeck and present it to him on his eightieth birthday. The idea paid off well for the rich landowners and industrialists who contributed toward the purchase price. The grateful president upheld and defended their interests faithfully.

HINDENBURG, his daughter-in-law, and Dr. Meissner.

BISMARCK'S HEAD ADORNS the election posters of the German Nationalist party.

THE NAZIS GET THE MOST VOTES

IN THIS ELECTION the Nazis more than doubled their vote and became the largest party in the Reichstag. The newly elected delegates met in the Hotel Kaiserhof to swear loyalty to their leader, Adolf Hitler.

APPEAL OF THE IRON FRONT.

POSTERS OF COMPETING PARTIES.

A NATIONALIST POSTER.

"THE DAGGER THRUST with which Hindenburg felled Brüning on May 30, 1932, in an unexampled display of infidelity, murdered not only the German Republic, but also the peace of all Europe," wrote the liberal historian Erich Eyck. The old man would not allow Brüning to rule through emer-

gency decrees. "I have to move toward the Right," Hindenburg told his chancellor as he dismissed him, ". . . but you were always against it."

The chief instigator of Brüning's ouster was General Schleicher, an intriguant whose ambition was to wield the power behind the throne. Together

with Hindenburg's son Oscar and the president's state secretary, Dr. Meissner, Schleicher prevailed upon the president to replace Brüning with Franz von Papen, an empty-headed former cavalry officer. The general's idea was to bring the National Socialists into the government and give them

1932, August 29:

THE NIGHT BEFORE THE MEETING OF THE REICHSTAG the 230 new Nazi deputies were addressed by the Nazi leaders in the Hotel Kaiserhof. At the head table, left to right: Heinrich Himmler, Hermann Göring, Wilhelm Frick, Hitler, and Gregor Strasser.

responsibility, and at the same time to break the alliance between the Center and the Social Democrats.

Before Papen was appointed he met with Hitler, who made two demands: the lifting of the ban against the S.A., and the dissolution of the Reichstag so new elections could be held. Papen promised both.

The new cabinet represented the landed gentry and the industrial magnates; it was called a "cabinet of barons," or, in the words of the British ambassador, "a cabinet of mutual deception." A group of second-rate minds, many of them believers in monarchy, they spied on their political opponents, tapped their phones, shadowed their every move.

The new chancellor, unable to command a majority in the Reichstag, dissolved it and set a date for new elections. By then he had fulfilled his other promise to Hitler—the lifting of the ban on the S.A.

Once more the streets swarmed with brown-shirted rowdies. In a single month 99 men were killed and 1,125 wounded in street corner brawls. Two weeks before the election the Nazis paraded in Altona. The Communists looked upon it as a provocation, leading to a bloody battle with 17 dead.

In retaliation Papen declared a state of emergency for greater Berlin and the province of Brandenburg and in a coup d'état he ousted the Prussian prime minister, a Social Democrat; Prussia's minister of the interior, also a Social Democrat; arrested Berlin's Social Democratic police chief and his deputy; and made himself commissar of Prussia.

The election resulted in a stunning victory for the Nazis. They won 230 delegate seats, 123 more than they held before, and became the largest party in the Reichstag. In the new assembly Papen held only 44 votes.

VOTING FOR THE 6th REICHSTAG

89	KPD
133	SPD
4	D
75	Z
22	BVP
4	Kl.M.P.
7	DVP
7	Kl.R.P.
37	DNVP
230	NSDAP

KPD = Communists
SPD = Social Democrats
D = Democrats
Z = Center (Catholics)
BVP = Bav. People's Party (Catholics)
Kl.M.P = Small parties of the center
DVP = German People's Party
Kl.R.P. = Small parties of the right
DNVP = German Nationalists
NSDAP = National Socialists

ON JULY 31, 1932.

1932, September 12:

REICHSTAG CONFRONTATION. Chancellor Franz von Papen stands to be recognized, but the president of the assembly, Hermann Göring, looks the other way.

The leader of the Communists, Ernst Torgler, offered a resolution asking for the repeal of the president's emergency decree "for the revival of the economy," and a vote of no confidence in the government.

As the Nationalists remained silent, von Papen had to dissolve the Reichstag before the no confidence vote. However, when

THE REICHSTAG IS

THE DISSOLUTION ORDER OF THE PRESIDENT.

In the new Reichstag Chancellor Papen's "cabinet of barons" was supported by only 44 delegates. Hostile were the Nazis with 230 delegates, the Social Democrats with 133, the Communists with 89. But as long as Hindenburg backed him, Papen did not have to rely on a parliamentary majority, but he was able to govern by presidential fiat.

As soon as the opening session of the Reichstag got under way, the Communists brought in a motion to repeal the government's latest emergency decree "for the revival of the economy" and to express lack of confidence in the government. Their motion found Papen unprepared. Though he had persuaded the president to sign the dissolution order, he hadn't brought the document with him. Luckily the Nazis called a half-hour recess.

When the meeting resumed, the traditional red dispatch case, used by every chancellor since Bismarck, was on Papen's desk. He ceremoniously took out the order and prepared to read it. But Hermann Göring, who presided over the Reichstag—as his party was the largest in the house—would not recognize the chancellor. Looking ostentatiously away from Papen, he proceeded with the Communists' proposal—and the delegates began to vote on the no confidence motion. Papen, who as chancellor had the right to address the assembly at any time, was livid with anger; he waved the dissolution order under Göring's nose, but the Reichstag president remained unperturbed.

The result of the vote was a humiliation for the chancellor. Only 42 delegates supported him while 512 expressed no confidence.

After the session the dispute between chancellor and Reichstag president continued. Papen argued that Göring had had no right to proceed with the vote after the dissolution order was on the table, while Göring shot back that once the no confidence motion was before the assembly and the voting had begun, the house could not be dissolved.

Whatever the merits of the argument, the Reichstag was eventually dissolved and new elections were set for November 6, 1932. Thus the life of Papen's cabinet was prolonged by almost two months, during which he could stay in office, and he hoped that the situation would change to his benefit in that period. He had plans for a new constitutional reform which might give him the right to govern without the approval of the parties. In other words, he asked for dictatorial powers. How he expected his plans to succeed —after the resounding defeat he suffered in the Reichstag—remains a mystery. But Papen was not a bright man.

AFTER GÖRING REFUSED TO RECOGNIZE VON PAPEN, the government walked out—the seats of the cabinet were empty while the delegates proceeded with the voting.

he rose to announce the dissolution order, Göring would not recognize him but announced that the Reichstag would proceed with the vote. Only after the no confidence proposal won, with 512 to 42, did Göring take notice of the dissolution order.

DISSOLVED

VOTING FOR THE SEVENTH REICHSTAG

"NOTHING TO WEAR, but worried about the new hat fashion . . ." Karl Arnold's comment on the parties in *Simplicissimus*.

1932, November:

VOTING, VOTING, VOTING. The new voting for the Reichstag was set for November 6, 1932. Dr. Goebbels was ecstatic. He hoped to gain more supporters, particularly from the poorer classes. He wanted "voting, voting, and more voting." In these dilapidated houses in Berlin's Köpenickerstrasse, the families were on a rent strike. Both the Nazis and the Communists encouraged their discontent—election day was just around the corner.

IT WAS TO BE the fifth election in a single year: there had been two ballotings for the presidency, one for the Prussian diet, and one for the Reichstag. Even for Dr. Goebbels's propaganda machine—which called for "voting, voting, voting" and more voting—it was too much. The coffers of the party were empty, particularly since Papen had prevailed on his industrial and banking friends in the Rhineland and in East Prussia from giving more money to the Nazis.

Hitler, anxious about his political future, discussed three possibilities with Goebbels: to get Hindenburg's support for a presidential cabinet; to form a coalition with the Nationalists and the Centrum; or to go into opposition. None of these solutions seemed satisfactory.

A few days before the election the National Socialists joined the Communist transit workers in a strike against the municipally owned Berlin Transit Corporation, which had attempted to reduce wages. The Social Democratic trade unions opposed the strike; with millions of workers out of jobs, they considered it a futile attempt. But the Nazis were stirring up trouble. Goebbels wrote with elation: "Not a single streetcar or subway train is operating in Berlin. The general public is observing admirable solidarity with the workers. The Red press

Reichstagswahl
Wahlkreis Berlin

1	Nationalsozialistische Deutsche Arbeiter-Partei (Hitlerbewegung) Hitler — Dr. Frick — Göring — Dr. Goebbels	1	◯
2	Sozialdemokratische Partei Deutschlands Culsüpien — Aufhäufer — Frau Bohm-Schuch — Litte	2	◯
3	Kommunistische Partei Deutschlands Thälmann — Pieck — Torgler — Vogt	3	◯
4	Deutsche Zentrumspartei Dr. Brüning — Dr. Krone — Schmitt — Bernoth	4	◯
5	Kampffront Schwarz-Weiß-Rot Dr. Hugenberg — Laterrenz — Berndt — Wischnöski	5	◯
7	Deutsche Volkspartei Dr. Mahler — Dressler — Frau Haß — Müller	7	◯
8	Christlich-sozialer Volksdienst (Evangelische Bewegung) Hartwig — Frau Ulbrich — Lüthje — Krafeit	8	◯
9	Deutsche Staatspartei Dr. Schreiber — Dr. Claß — Frau Dr. Edelheim — Machuh	9	◯
10	Deutsche Bauernpartei Dr. Fehr	10	◯
12	Deutsch-hannoversche Partei Meyer — Pralle — Meier — Salter	12	◯
15	Sozialistische Kampfgemeinschaft Fahrenson — Schmitz — Schönborn — Reinhardt	15	◯

1932, November:

FLYING FROM PLACE TO PLACE. During the election campaign, Hitler was steadily on the go, addressing audiences and drumming up votes. He used a plane to be able to speak in different cities on the same day. He was a master of modern propaganda methods. Pilot Hans Bauer and "Putzi" Hanfstängl are with him.

THE VOTING BALLOT. The Nazis as the largest party are listed first, and they expected to keep that position. However, the result was disappointing; their number of deputies in the Reichstag declined from the previous 230 to 196. It appeared as if Nazism had reached its peak; the people of the country had had enough.

has been deprived of all its tools of propaganda against us."

When the returns of the election became known, they showed a Communist gain of 700,000 votes. After this, the Nazis promptly abandoned their support of the striking transit men in Berlin.

Another surprise was the substantial decrease in the Nazis' vote. Since the last election four months before, two million voters had abandoned them. Although with 196 deputies they still remained the largest party in the Reichstag, the loss of 34 seats in such a short time boded ill for the party's future.

The Catholic parties—the Center and the Bavarian People's Party—

also registered losses: the Center losing 300,000 votes and the Bavarian People's Party 100,000.

Interestingly, the votes of the two groups which supported the Papen government increased; the Nationalists gained 900,000, the People's Party well over 200,000 votes.

Yet all these gains were not enough to help Chancellor Papen to a majority. Of the 584 Reichstag delegates, he could only count on the support of 62 —a hopeless minority. Yet Papen, whom the French ambassador described as "a superficial, confused, and untrustworthy thinker and a vain, ambitious, and scheming intriguer," still expected to govern with emergency decrees—he still hoped that

President Hindenburg would sign them for him, he still thought that he could function with presidential approval. But the shadows of Schleicher and Hitler loomed large over his efforts.

VOTING FOR THE 7th REICHSTAG

100	KPD
121	SPD
2	D
70	Z
20	BVP
4	Kl.M.P.
11	DVP
8	Kl.R.P.
52	DNVP
196	NSDAP

KPD = Communists
SPD = Social Democrats
D = Democrats
Z = Center (Catholics)
BVP = Bav. People's Party (Catholics)
Kl.M.P = Small parties of the center
DVP = German People's Party
Kl.R.P. = Small parties of the right
DNVP = German Nationalists
NSDAP = National Socialists

ON NOVEMBER 6, 1932.

THE NEW CHANCELLOR

HE IS APPOINTED. On January 30, 1933, Hitler leaves the presidential palace after Hindenburg gave him the chancellorship. Until the last minute Hitler bargained with Hugenberg and his Nationalists, who were confident they could control him in the cabinet.

A DEMOCRATIC NEWSPAPER announces the formation of the new government of the Rightists, from which members of the Centrum, the Social Democrats, and the Communists were excluded.

RETURNING TO THE KAISERHOF, the freshly appointed chancellor receives the Nazi salute from his cheering supporters.

LEAVING THE KAISERHOF to drive to the Reichs chancellery in the Wilhelmstrasse for the first meeting of the new cabinet.

1933, January 30:
"LET'S POSE FOR A PHOTOGRAPH." Hitler asks the Nationalist members of his cabinet to join him for their first official picture. With him, his Nazi appointees: Prussian prime minister Hermann Göring and Wilhelm Frick, minister of the interior.

THE CURTAIN ROSE on the last act of parliamentary democracy. On stage were three men: Hindenburg, the old Reichs president; Papen, still his chancellor but without parliamentary support; and General Schleicher, the defense secretary with commanding influence over the army. All three tried to prevent Hitler and the National Socialists from taking power, yet all three bargained with him. Hitler was adamant: he demanded the chancellorship and would consider nothing less.

Papen was forced to resign when even his own cabinet refused to support him. General Schleicher, who followed him, was unable to build up the necessary parliamentary support and gave up after fifty-four days.

While Schleicher was chancellor, Papen met with Hitler in the home of banker Baron Kurt von Schröder in

THE CABINET: Seated: Göring, Hitler, and von Papen. Standing: Schwerin-Krosigk (finance), Frick (interior), Blomberg (defense), Hugenberg (commerce and agriculture).

211

THE NAZIS' GIGANTIC TORCHLIGHT PARADE ON JANUARY 30, 1933, AS RE-ENACTED FOR A PROPAGANDA FILM.

HIS FIRST RADIO ADDRESS TO THE NATION ON FEBRUARY 1, 1933.

Cologne, and the three reached an understanding. Schröder and the Rhenish industrialists were ready to accept Hitler as a chancellor.

Thus Hindenburg gave him the appointment on January 30, and named "reliable" men to the cabinet who would contain "the Bavarian corporal." General Blomberg became defense secretary and Papen vice chancellor; Neurath, minister of foreign affairs; Count Krosigk, finance minister; Eltz Rübenach, minister of transportation. Three Nationalists—Hugenberg, Seldte, and Gürtner—rounded out the cabinet. The remaining two posts were filled by the National Socialists Göring and Frick. The conservatives and the Nationalists thought that they had "framed in" Hitler—but the new chancellor did not seem worried over it.

1933, January 30:

THE POPULACE OF BERLIN CHEERS PRESIDENT HINDENBURG, WHO A FEW HOURS BEFORE GAVE HITLER THE POWER.

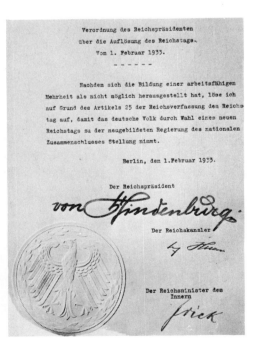

1933, February 1:

HINDENBURG'S ORDER dissolving the Reichstag so a new election could be held which gave Hitler the needed majority.

HITLER ACCEPTS THE CHEERS
from the window of the chancellery.

FLAMES BURST OUT OF THE BUILDING ON FEBRUARY 27, 1933.

THE
REICHSTAG BURNS

ON THE EVENING of February 27, 1933, soon after nine o'clock, flames burst out of the Reichstag. In less than an hour the inside of the building was gutted. As Chancellor Hitler rushed to the scene, he was heard hailing the fire as "a sign from heaven."

Ever since the Nazis assumed power on January 30, their propagandists had been searching for "something" that would swing more voters behind the Hitler regime. A new election for the Reichstag was scheduled for March 5, and the Nazis needed to increase their support to achieve a majority. The opposition was strong; the Social Democrats had 121 delegates and the Communists 100. Against them the Nationalist bloc amounted to 248—the National Socialists, 196 and the Nationalists, 52.

As the flames of the Reichstag painted the sky, Göring declared that the conflagration was the work of the Communists. Shortly thereafter the young Dutchman Marinus van der Lubbe was caught, admitting his Com-

THE CUPOLA OF THE REICHSTAG.

THE BURNED-OUT HALL.

THE HALL OF REPRESENTATIVES WAS DEVASTATED BY THE FIRE.

munist affiliation and confessing that he alone had set the fire.

With this the Nazis had the "something" they had so ardently sought. They made President Hindenburg sign an emergency decree against "Communist acts of violence endangering the state," which gave Chancellor Hitler the legal means to suspend civil liberties and the freedom of the press, to conduct searches without warrants, to confiscate property, to open people's mail, to listen in on their telephone conversations, to disregard all constitutional guarantees of the privacy of individuals. Opponents of the regime were arrested, and when the prisons were filled, they were thrown behind barbed-wire enclosures—the first concentration camps.

THE INVESTIGATORS CAME FAST. Shortly after the alarm was sounded, Hitler, Goebbels, Göring, and the kaiser's son "Auwi" (with black hat) arrived at the scene.

215

HITLER HAS THE POWER

THE REICHSTAG FIRE served its purpose. In the election held six days after the conflagration, the Nazis increased their delegate strength from 196 to 288. Yet the Social Democrats still retained 120 seats (losing only 1), and the Communists 81 (losing 19).

If the Communist delegates could be eliminated, the Nazis would have five more votes than a majority in the reduced Reichstag. Thus, disregarding legal niceties (and sanctioned by President Hindenburg's emergency decrees), they arrested the Communist deputies.

Hermann Göring, head of the Prussian ministry, and Wilhelm Frick, head of the ministry of the interior, used their powers with brutal effectiveness. They commanded the police forces of the state, and they saw to it that the police would serve the interest of the National Socialists. In a short time all Communist functionaries were put behind bars; the terror of the police engulfed the country. Dr. Goebbels's propaganda machine convinced the citizenry that the Nazis were only acting against the enemies of the state; the distorted reports in the press lulled the people into apathetic subservience. Even if the atrocities had been revealed—which, of course, they were not—the people would not have believed that a representative government, that a chancellor of the Reich, could act in such an illegal manner.

The Social Democrats, who had opposed the Communists since the beginning of the Republic, could do nothing against the gangster tactics of the Nazis. Their vacillating behavior during the previous decade reaped its reward—their party was destroyed by the Nazis. The Catholic Center party and the Bavarian People's Party—the third largest group in the parliament—fared no better. Their opportunism and the betrayal of their basic tenets led to their demise.

Hitler emerged as the triumphant victor. Through political cunning and finesse, he had reached the top of power. With the help of the emergency decrees, with the help of Goebbels's propaganda, of Göring's bayonets, of Röhm's rubber truncheons, he had all but annihilated his political adversaries. His enemies in prison and concentration camps, the opposing political parties wiped out, he was now the absolute ruler of Germany.

AN ELECTION POSTER linking Hitler, the corporal in the First World War to Hindenburg, the venerated field marshal: "They fight with us for peace and equality."

VOTING FOR THE 8th REICHSTAG

81	KPD	
120	SPD	
5	D	
74	Z	
18	BVP	
2	Kl.M.P.	
2	DVP	
5	Kl.R.P.	
52	DNVP	
288	NSDAP	

KPD = Communists
SPD = Social Democrats
D = Democrats
Z = Center (Catholics)
BVP = Bav. People's Party (Catholics)
Kl.M.P = Small parties of the center
DVP = German People's Party
Kl.R.P. = Small parties of the right
DNVP = German Nationalists
NSDAP = National Socialists

ON MARCH 5, 1933.

Title page of the Münchner Illustrierte Presse a few days after the imprisonment of Editor Lorant
THE FÜHRER LISTENS TO THE ELECTION RESULTS OF MARCH 5, 1933.

THE POWER IN THE LAND:
ADOLF HITLER

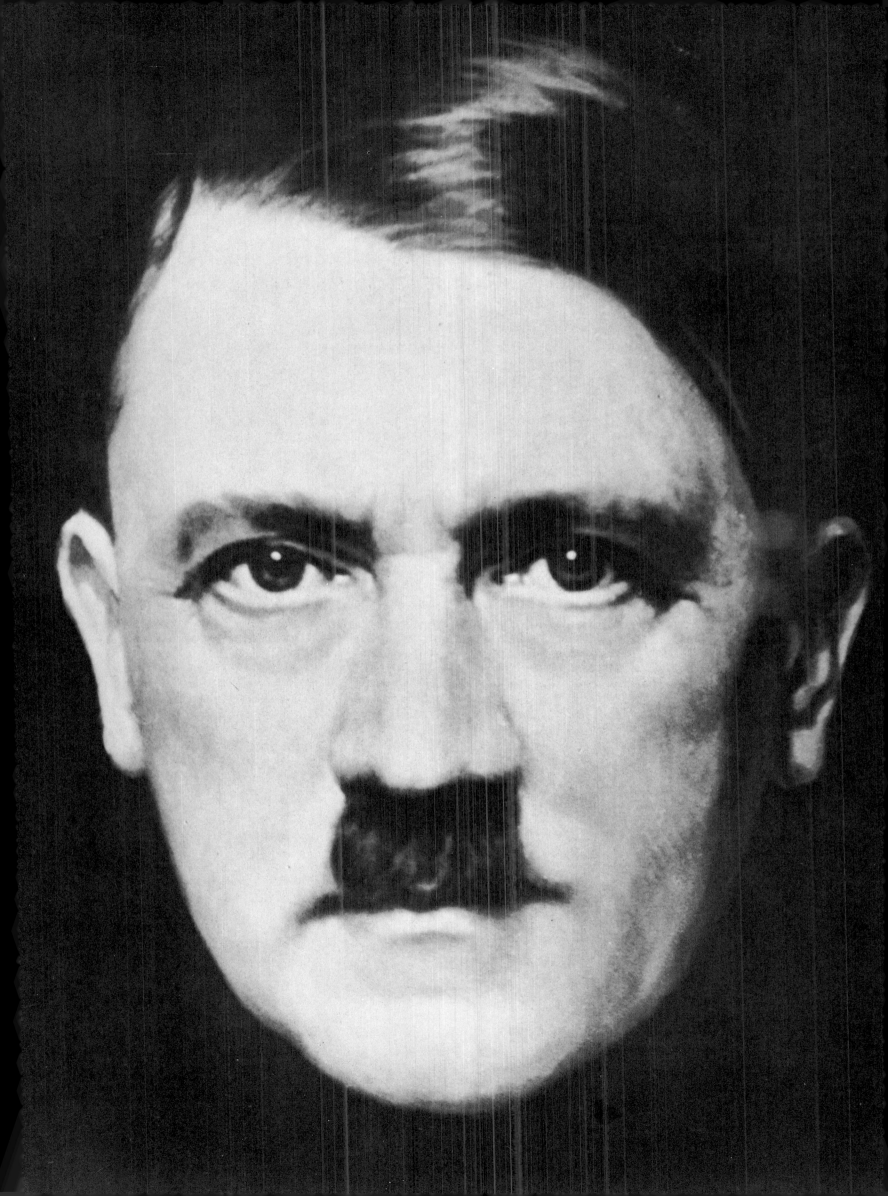

THE DAY
OF POTSDAM

THE TWO BOYS HAVE GROWN UP (see pages 42 and 43). Hitler and the former crown prince pose in front of Potsdam's garrison church while Göring (right) watches.

THE CABINET ON THE WAY TO THE CEREMONIES. Chancellor Hitler and Vice Chancellor von Papen as the leaders of the procession.

1933, March 21:
HITLER'S ADDRESS IN THE CHURCH. President Hindenburg, in general's uniform, sits opposite him; next to Hinden-

BISMARCK HAD OPENED the first Reichstag of the Second Reich on March 21, 1871. And Hitler—with an acute sense of tradition and theatrics—was to hold the opening of the Third Reich's first Reichstag on the anniversary of that day, on March 21, 1933, in the garri-

burg in cutaway is Hermann Göring, Reichstag president. Facing the camera is the cabinet: Seldte (labor), Hugenberg (agriculture), Schwerin-Krosigk (finance), Frick (interior), von Neurath (foreign affairs). Behind them: Admiral Raeder, Gereke, Dr. Goebbels (propaganda), Eltz Rübenach (transport), Blomberg (defense). In the pews: Prince August Wilhelm and Streicher.

son church of Potsdam where Frederick the Great lay buried.

President Hindenburg in his full field marshal's uniform walked down the aisle, saluting the empty place in the imperial gallery once occupied by the kaiser, and made a short speech.

Looking more like a maître d'hôtel in his cutaway than the head of the government, Hitler addressed the president:

"By a unique upheaval . . . our national honor has been restored, and thanks to your understanding . . . the union between the symbols of the old greatness and the new strength has been celebrated."

Bowing his head reverently, he grasped the hand of Hindenburg in a dramatic gesture; their handshake symbolized the unification of the old Germany with the new.

219

1933, March 23:

WHILE HITLER SPOKE, PLEADING FOR AN "ENABLING ACT," THE FACES OF HIS CABINET REMAINED SOLEMN.

In the first row: Frick, von Neurath, and Vice Chancellor von Papen; in the second row: Seldte and Hugenberg listen to Chancellor Hitler, who demands from the Reichstag exclusive legislative powers for the next four years.

As the proposals meant changing the constitution, Hitler needed a two-thirds majority. But how to increase his simple majority of only 16 seats to a decisive one? The Nazis found an easy solution. The 81 Communist delegates were arrested, as were a number of Social Democrats.

The Catholic Centrum, abandoning all decency, voted for the act; only the 89 Social Democrats opposed it. Thus parliamentary democracy in Germany ended. The Reichstag handed the power of its constitutional function to Hitler. The Weimar Republic was constitutionally dead, the way to the Nazi dictatorship open.

THE NATION ABANDONS ITS FREEDOM

FORTY-EIGHT HOURS after the Potsdam ceremonies, the Hitlerian Reichstag convened for its first business session. Before the house was the "law for removing the distress from the people and the Reich" (*Gesetz zur Behebung der Not von Volk und Reich*). It consisted of only five paragraphs.

The "Enabling Act," as the legislation became known, was to give the government for the next four years exclusive power to legislate (including control of the Reich budget), to make treaties, and the right to initiate constitutional amendments without the approval of the Reichstag.

In proposing the bill Hitler was reasonableness itself. He assured the assembly that "the existence of neither the Reichstag nor the Reichsrat was menaced"; he told the delegates that "the separate existence of the federal states will not be done away with," that "the position and rights of the president remain unaffected," and that "the rights of the churches will not be diminished."

When he had ended his peroration, the Social Democrat Otto Wels (the same Otto Wels who as military commandant of Berlin had been arrested by the rebellious sailors in 1918) rose to speak. It was the last time that the voice of a member of the opposition was heard in the Reichstag. With somber words Wels reiterated his party's philosophy—humanity, justice, freedom, and socialism—and declared the Social Democrats' opposition to the proposed legislation. Immediately Hitler was back on his feet. In a scathing and sarcastic rejoinder, he ripped into the Social Democrats, recounting their past sins. "I do not want your votes," he screamed. "You are no longer needed."

Of the 647 Reichstag members, Hitler had the support of the 288 from his own party and the 52 Nationalists—not enough for a two-thirds majority. But Göring and his police force saw to it that the chancellor was given what he asked for. The 81 Communist delegates were safely under lock and key when the session was called to order. About two dozen duly elected Social Democratic delegates shared the same fate. In this way the number of Reichstag delegates was reduced by over a hundred. And as the spineless leaders of the Catholic Center party were lured into voting for the Enabling Act, Hitler had his way. The delegates in the Reichstag, abandoning their prerogatives, handed the power to him on a silver platter.

The result of the vote: 444 for the legislation and 94 against it; all the opposing votes were cast by the Social Democrats.

As the meeting closed the Nazi deputies stood with raised hands and sang the Horst Wessel song—the scene marked the end of German parliamentary democracy. The days of the Weimar Republic—after fourteen tempestuous years—were over.

1933, MARCH 23: END OF THE WEIMAR REPUBLIC

Two days after the day of Potsdam, Hitler addressed the Reichstag, proposing a "law for removing the distress from the people and the Reich." The legislation, in five short paragraphs, was to give the government the power to make laws, to enter into treaties with foreign states, to initiate constitutional amendments—all without the Reichstag's approval. Laws which "might deviate from the constitution" might be drafted by the chancellor. In short, the elected deputies were to abandon their duties and place the governing power into the hands of a single man: Adolf Hitler. And they meekly did.

THE BURNING OF BOOKS

THOSE WHO FEAR ideas, fear books. The great majority of the National Socialists were scantily educated—they cared nothing for books.

The book burning in Berlin was a well-organized propaganda show. As the volumes were thrown into the flames, speakers chanted incantations such as: "Against class warfare and materialism, and in the name of national solidarity and high principles, I consign to the flames the works of Marx and Kautsky." Did the chanting students really believe that by burning them, the ideas in the volumes would be destroyed as well?

TORCHBEARING GERMAN STUDENTS drive through Berlin's streets to the ceremony of bookburning on the night of May 10, 1933.

DR. GOEBBELS AND HIS FRIENDS GLEEFULLY WATCH THE BURNING BOOKS.

STUDENTS THROW VOLUMES ON THE On the evening of May 10, 1933, one hundred days after Hitler became chancellor, Nazi propaganda minister Goebbels organized a scene which, in William Shirer's words, "had not been witnessed in the Western world since the late Middle Ages." Books which acted "subversively on our future or strike at the root of German

Photograph by Helmuth Kurth

PYRE AFTER GOEBBELS TOLD THEM TO BURN UN-GERMAN LITERATURE. thought, the German home and the driving forces of our people" were thrown into the flames. Copies of Remarque's *All Quiet on the Western Front,* Mann's *Magic Mountain,* Feuchtwanger's *Success,* Arnold Zweig's *Sergeant Grischa,* Brecht's *Baal,* and other books were burned. Works of Freud, Zola, Proust, H. G. Wells, Upton Sinclair, Hemingway, Gide were among the more than twenty thousand volumes consumed by the flames. Dr. Goebbels in a joyous mood told the students: "The soul of the German people can again express itself. These flames not only illuminate the final end of an old era; they also light up the new." These sentences introduced the barbaric age of Nazi culture.

A NAZI SALUTE TO THE FLAMES.

223

AGAINST THE JEWS

HITLER CHANGED his mind about many matters, but he never changed it about the Jews. Talking of them sent him into a frenzy, his mouth and hands trembling, his eyes popping, his voice screaming.

His violent anti-Semitism dates from his years in Vienna, where he devoured the racist anti-Semitic periodical *Ostara,* edited by "Jörg Lanz von Liebenfels," a crackpot and a swindler. *Ostara* extolled the virtues of the blond, blue-eyed Germans. Thirty-odd years later Hitler still remembered what he read and propagated the notion that "blond-blue" men should marry "blond-blue" women to produce a heroic and noble race.

Whether his anti-Semitism was sex-based is hard to prove. Rudolph Han-isch, who lived with him in the flop-house, told me in the thirties that Hitler's hatred stemmed from an incident in which a Jewish boy took a girl away from him. But Hanisch is not a reliable witness. Still, *Mein Kampf* contains salacious allusions to Jews who raped Christian girls and to the "nightmare vision of the seduction of hundreds of thousands of girls by re-

THE VULGARITY OF THE NAZIS' ANTI-SEMITISM REVEALS ITSELF IN THE POSTERS BELOW

A BAREFOOTED JEW who complained to the Munich police is led through the streets to the railroad station. The sign hanging around his neck reads: "I will never again complain to the police."

ARYAN JUSTICE. A middle-aged woman is forced to walk the streets wearing a sign accusing her of being a pig because she had sexual relations with a Jew "although I was married."

"DON'T BUY FROM JEWS!" read the posters which Nazi troops paste on the windows of Berlin's Jewish-owned department stores.

IN RESPONSE TO FOREIGN ATROCITY PROPAGANDA, the Nazis of Cologne exhort the people not to trade with the Jews.

THE SIGN CARRIED BY THE GIRL: "At this place I am the greatest swine: I take Jews and make them mine." The sign carried by the man: "As a Jewish boy I *always* take German girls up to my room!" And the Nazi troopers proudly pose with them.

pulsive, crook-legged Jew bastards."

From Vienna Hitler went to Munich, where apparently he met no Jews. Then came the war and four years at the front. Again he shunned Jews, although through a quirk of fate it was a Jewish officer—Hugo Gutmann—who recommended him for the Iron Cross First Class. Hitler never acknowledged the fact—if he knew about it—that during the First World War the proportion of Jews killed in battle was higher than the proportion of Gentiles. Out of Germany's 80,000 Jewish servicemen, 12,000 gave their lives for the Fatherland, while 35,000 were decorated for valor.

Was Hitler's violent anti-Semitism a reaction to stories that his father might have been sired by his grandmother's Jewish employer? Or was he bested in an argument with a Jew? No doubt he was influenced by the anti-Semitic policies of Schönerer and Lueger, but could they have made such an impression on him that every time he spoke of Jews he worked himself into a mad rage?

The basis of Nazi anti-Semitism was primarily greed and envy. Shopkeep-
ers wanted to wipe out Jewish businesses, lawyers and doctors desired to undermine their competitors' lucrative practices, people without means raged against wealthy Jewish bankers. In *Der Stürmer* the Franconian Nazi leader Streicher reveled in filthy and pornographic anti-Semitism.

The Nazis' official anti-Semitic attitude began with their twenty-five-point program in 1920 and ended with their "final solution"—the extermination of millions of Jews in the gas chambers of the concentration camps twenty-five years later.

225

REICHSTAG FIRE TRIAL

THE TRIAL was conducted with decorum before the State Supreme Court in Leipzig. The Nazi leadership was determined to prove to the world its innocence.

But German refugees in France and England flooded the foreign press with stories about the Nazis' guilt. Willy Münzenberg, the Communist propagandist, flatly charged the Nazi leaders as incendiaries. His "Brown Book," which appeared in ten languages, accused them of entering the Reichstag with torches and gasoline cans by way of the underground tunnel leading from Göring's palace.

The whole truth about the fire will never be known. Late research discloses that it was laid by a single man, Marinus van der Lubbe, a demented young Dutchman—the one found guilty by the court and executed. While the evidence of Fritz Tobias and Hans Mommsen is persuasive, it is still difficult to believe that the fire which consumed the huge building in minutes could have been started by a single person—and a foreigner to boot, who was not familiar with the surroundings. Whether Lubbe had any help from others, whether he was a dupe of Göring and Goebbels has never been ascertained, and probably never will be. When Göring was asked at the Nürnberg trial whether he had anything to do with the conflagration, he consistently denied it.

The defendants—Marinus van der Lubbe and his supposed accomplices, Ernst Torgler, chairman of the Communist faction in the Reichstag; Georgi Dimitroff, the Bulgarian Communist who later became prime minister of his country; and two other Bulgarians, Blagot Popoff, a student, and Wassil Taneff, a cobbler—were assigned leading lawyers. Lubbe was defended by Dr. Seuffert, Torgler by Dr. Alfons Sack, the Bulgarians by Dr. Paul Teichert. The indictment charged them with high treason, but the prosecution could not prove it—even after the Nazis raided the Communist headquarters in Berlin in search of incriminating material against the Communist participants. Lubbe insisted that he alone set the fire: "What did

1933, September 21–December 23:
THE TRIAL BEFORE THE PEOPLE'S COURT IN LEIPZIG. BEHIND THE JUDGES, DIAGRAMS OF THE REICHSTAG.

ADVERSARIES: Potsdam police chief Count Helldorf faces Lubbe in the courtroom. The interpreter translates his words into Dutch.

THE ACCUSED. Ernst Torgler, the Communist Reichstag deputy, Marinus van der Lubbe, who admitted setting the fire, and Bulgarian Communist Georgi Dimitroff. Before them, Torgler's counsel, Dr. A. Sack.

THE CHIEF DEFENDANT, the Dutchman Marinus van der Lubbe, was found guilty of the deed and sentenced to death.

1933, September:

AT THE CONFRONTATION with the Communist defendant, Minister Göring blew up when Dimitroff needled him with questions. He burst out, "In my opinion you are a scoundrel who should have been hanged long ago." After the Bulgarian was silenced by the president of the court for trying to elicit further answers (he wanted to know whether Göring was afraid to reply), Göring shot back: "You will be afraid when I catch you when you are out of this court, you scoundrel, you!"

it amount to, setting the Reichstag fire? It took ten minutes or at most a quarter of an hour. I did it all alone." And when experts testified that he could not have done it, he remained adamant. "I did it alone," he repeated over and over again.

The highlight of the trial was the confrontation between Göring and Dimitroff. Dimitroff argued that as only the Nazis gained from the fire, they alone must have done it—Lubbe must have been helped by the Nazis. "The poor Faust is here," said Dimitroff, "but Mephisto is missing." When he questioned Göring about his knowledge of Lubbe's party membership, Göring lost his composure, and the following dialogue ensued:

"The German people know how

DIMITROFF VS. GÖRING
Photomontage by John Heartfield

His brusque behavior disclosed the impudent arrogance and lawless attitude of the Nazi leadership.

DR. GOEBBELS BEFORE THE JUDGES. Seeing that Göring's blustering brashness failed to make an impression, Goebbels chose other tactics: to display reason and amiability, to be a "regular fellow."

THE BENCH OF THE ACCUSED DURING THE TRIAL.

ANNOUNCING THE JUDGMENT.

cheeky you are, that you came here to set fire to the Reichstag, and now you are impudent to the German people. I didn't come here to be accused by you."

"You are a witness."

"And in my eyes you are a scoundrel who should have been hanged long ago."

Before Dimitroff was silenced, he twitted Göring: "Are you afraid of my questions, Mr. Minister President?" And Göring, shaking with anger, shouted back: "You're the one who will be afraid when I catch you after you are out of this court, you scoundrel, you!"

The other Nazi leaders were more circumspect. Propaganda Minister Goebbels, Breslau police president Edmund Heines, and Potsdam police president Count Helldorf politely answered all questions put to them. They denied the accusations of the "Brown Book" and the foreign press.

The judgment was: death for Lubbe, acquittal for the four Communists. On January 10, 1934, three days before his twenty-fifth birthday, Lubbe was beheaded.

1934, January 1:
HITLER CONVEYS THE GOVERNMENT'S BEST NEW YEAR'S WISHES TO PRESIDENT HINDENBURG IN THE ESTAB-
Behind Hitler, the cabinet. From left to right: von Papen (vice chancellor); von Neurath (foreign minister); General Blomberg (defense); Göring (Prussian prime minister); Goebbels (propa- ganda); Schwerin-Krosigk (finance); and Gürtner (justice). It was all very civilized and proper—and the world was lulled into a false sense of security. Few would have believed that soon these

ON NEW YEAR'S DAY the political leaders of the country donned tails and, together with the heads of the army, navy and air force, and with members of the foreign diplomatic corps, offered their felicitations to President Hindenburg.

It all looked so very proper. The chancellor, neatly scrubbed, read his New Year's message to the old man; the smartly tailored cabinet ministers gathered around him, looking like figures from a fashion magazine. And the president replied in dignified manner, emphasizing the peaceful and friendly intentions of Germany toward all nations.

The picture—as they stood before President Hindenburg—was to show to the world that in Germany everything was in the best possible order, that Hitler and the National Socialist members of his cabinet were like any other politicians—well-mannered, civilized, peace-loving. And the neatly dressed men with their smoothly brushed hair and their restrained manners indeed presented the picture of civility. They did not look different from any other cabinet of democratic statesmen.

The photograph does not reveal what was really happening in the

THE PRESIDENTIAL PALACE

PAPAL NUNCIO ORSENIGO OFFERS HIS GREETINGS TO HINDENBURG.

Photographs by Helmuth Kurth

LISHED, TRADITIONAL CEREMONY. nattily dressed gentlemen would reveal themselves as cold-blooded murderers willing to exterminate anyone in their path.

country—that these were the same men who had sent thousands of their political opponents and tens of thousands of Catholics and Jews to concentration camps, where they suffered torture and death; that the hands of these men were stained with the blood of their victims. The photograph shows the surface of their behavior, what they themselves wanted the world to believe —not their barbarism.

THE PRESIDENT'S RESPONSE TO THE GOOD WISHES OF THE CABINET.

VISITING MUSSOLINI

1934, June 15:
SIGHTSEEING ON THE GRAND CANAL.

Photographs by Helmuth Kurth
THEIR FIRST MEETING IN VENICE.

FOR THE FIRST TIME they faced each other in person. Resplendent in his Fascist uniform, Mussolini greeted Hitler, who alighted from his plane in a rumpled raincoat.

Their meetings went badly. The Duce told the Führer that Austria must remain independent, that Britain and France as well as Italy were determined to see to that.

While Hitler profoundly admired Mussolini, he failed to impress the Duce, to whom he seemed to be "a barbarian with a modicum of ideas."

HITLER AND VON NEURATH AT ST. MARK'S SQUARE.

THE MASSES OF VENICE CHEER THE TWO DICTATORS.

THEY TALKED FOR TWO HOURS.

THE NIGHT OF THE LONG KNIVES

HINDENBURG'S DAYS were numbered. To insure his succession to the presidency, Hitler needed the good will and the support of the army.

The high command was willing to stand behind him, but only if he would restrain his storm troops who agitated for a "second revolution" and the merger of the S.A. with the Reichswehr.

Representatives of the generals met with Hitler, and they made a pact. The powers of the storm troopers would be severely curtailed.

Captain Röhm and the other S.A. leaders had no inkling of what was in store for them. They expected the Führer to come to their Tegernsee hotel to discuss the storm troops' future. The meeting was arranged for June 30, but when Hitler arrived, he came not to reason with Röhm, but to arrest him. Röhm was taken to Stadelheim prison and shot. Other S.A. officers suffered similar fates. And while the Nazi leadership was at it, all those who had opposed them, all those against whom they had personal gripes, were murdered as well. General Schleicher; Gregor Strasser; Gustav Kahr; two of Papen's closest associates, Herbert von Bose and Edgar Jung; and dozens of lesser figures were "promptly eliminated" in the purge. Hitler told the Reichstag afterward: "In this hour I alone was responsible for the fate of the German Nation; I alone was the Supreme Court." He was the law.

THE TWO GOOD FRIENDS—HITLER AND RÖHM IN EARLY JUNE 1934.

1934, June 28:
BEFORE THE BLOODLETTING. Hitler attended the wedding of his friend Josef Terboven on June 28, 1934. A day later Nazi troopers were on their way to kill the leaders of the S.A.—to pacify the army—and many thousands of others—from General Schleicher to Father Staempfle.

RÖHM IS KILLED
Photomontage for the Arbeiter Illustrierte Zeitung *by John Heartfield*

30. JUNI 1934

HEIL HITLER!

Fotomontage: John Heartfield

THE MURDER OF DOLLFUSS

THE AUSTRIAN CHANCELLOR, ENGELBERT DOLLFUSS, an enemy of Social Democracy, addresses a meeting in Vienna.

IN THE YEAR OF 1934 MANY AUSTRIANS WERE ARRESTED.

1934, April 30:
LAST SESSION OF THE AUSTRIAN

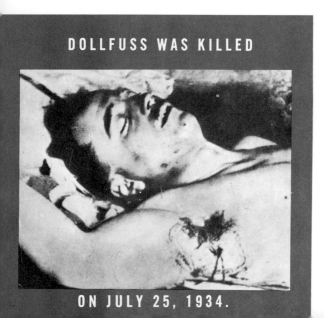

DOLLFUSS WAS KILLED

ON JULY 25, 1934.

1934, February:
THE GOVERNMENT GUNS ARE DIRECTED AGAINST THE HOMES OF WORKERS.

NATIONALRAT WITH CHANCELLOR DOLLFUSS PRESIDING. THIRD FROM RIGHT: KURT VON SCHUSCHNIGG.

AT NOON ON July 25, 1934, a large detachment of Austrian Nazis, dressed in army uniforms, stormed into the chancellor's office on the Ballplatz and shot Dollfuss. Another band moved into the radio station and broadcast the news that Dollfuss had resigned and had been replaced by Anton Rintelen, a National Socialist.

For many months the Austrian Nazis kept Vienna in a state of terror with their violent tactics, blowing up public buildings and power stations, mur-

dering their opponents. They believed that by killing Dollfuss they could take over the government—but loyal government forces moved against them, retook the occupied buildings, and arrested the murderers.

Over the border in Italy Mussolini placed four divisions at the Brenner Pass to be in readiness in case the German army marched into Austria.

The move of the Austrian Nazis turned out to be ill-timed; Germany was not yet ready for a showdown with

the big powers, whose wish was to keep Austria an independent nation. Hitler promptly disassociated himself from the adventure, labeling it an "Austrian affair." He recalled his minister from Vienna, dismissed his party inspector, and dispatched Franz von Papen—who had escaped the purge a month before—to that troubled country as minister extraordinary. Papen did what the Führer expected of him; in less than four years Austria ceased to be an independent state.

HINDENBURG DIES

1934, August 1:
THE LAST VISIT. Hitler was at Neudeck a day before the president's death. From left to right: Adjutant Julius Schaub, Hitler, Hindenburg's son, Adjutant Wilhelm Brückner, and State Secretary Dr. Otto Meissner.

WHEN 87-YEAR-OLD Hindenburg died, Hitler's affairs were in the best of order. He had already broken the power of the storm troops (S.A.) and had established a close alliance with the country's military leadership. The S.A. under its new chief, Viktor Lutze, who had replaced the murdered Ernst Röhm, was reduced to impotence. The power over the Nazi paramilitary organizations was wielded by Hermann Göring and Heinrich Himmler, commander of the Schutzstaffel (S.S.). This elite troop had broken away from the S.A. to become an independent unit. The high command of the army could not foresee that within a short span of time Himmler and his S.S. would become far more dangerous than Röhm and the S.A. had ever been. Having achieved control over local police and the Gestapo, Himmler kept a close watch on the generals— harassing, arresting, and—on occasion —executing them.

After Hindenburg's death the offices of president and chancellor were merged into one. The posts of president, chancellor, commander in chief of the armed forces were all held by one person: Adolf Hitler.

No longer was the oath of allegiance to be taken to the constitution and the Fatherland. Officers and men had to

PRESIDENT PAUL VON HINDENBURG DIED ON AUGUST 2, 1934.

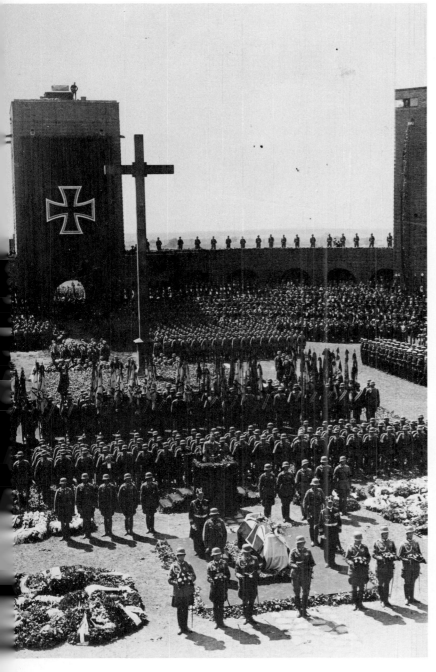

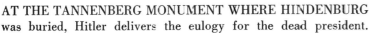

AT THE TANNENBERG MONUMENT WHERE HINDENBURG
was buried, Hitler delivers the eulogy for the dead president.

THE MEMORIAL SERVICE FOR PRESIDENT HINDENBURG
in Berlin was attended by masses of Nazi storm troopers.

pledge their oath to the new head of the country—the Führer and Reichskanzler, Adolf Hitler.

It was no secret that Hindenburg would have liked to see the monarchy restored. He had hoped that one of the Hohenzollern princes would follow him in office, and it was rumored that he had written a political testament to that effect. But soon after his death Propaganda Minister Goebbels made a hurried announcement that no will or testament had been found.

However, when the National Socialists decided to hold a plebiscite—asking the people's approval of Hitler's assumption to the presidency—Hindenburg's testament suddenly came to light, brought to Hitler by no less a man than Papen.

On the eve of the plebiscite—August 13—Goebbels arranged for Hindenburg's son to make a radio broadcast. And Oscar von Hindenburg announced: "My father himself saw in Adolf Hitler his own direct successor as head of the German State, and I am acting in accordance with my father's wishes when I call on all German men and women to vote in favor of handing my father's office over to the Führer and Reichs chancellor." By a curious coincidence Oscar von Hindenburg was promptly promoted to major general and not long thereafter was given hundreds of acres of land to add to his large estate in Pomerania.

The result of the plebiscite was as expected: 38,395,479 voted for Hitler. But it was unexpected that 4,300,429 Germans had the courage to say no, they did not want him as president, and another 873,787 protested by casting empty ballots.

239

FOLLOWING A DIPLOMATIC RECEPTION, CHANCELLOR HITLER INSPECTS THE HONOR GUARD IN THE COURTYARD

THE NEW HEAD OF STATE

LIFE IN GERMANY was calm. To a stranger looking at it from the outside, everything seemed peaceful. The government was stable; there was no more infighting between the political parties, because there were none—save the National Socialist party. All others had been dissolved. Economic conditions had improved; no more German money went for reparations. Unemployment was no longer a problem; there were plenty of jobs in armament industries, and the army needed men. The people had regained their self-esteem.

There were no pitched battles in the streets, no altercations between National Socialists and Communists. The

their former competitors, usually for a song.

Children joined the Hitler Youth—and loved it. For their parents there were holidays at home and abroad.

The revolutionary ferment in the S.A. had subsided; with the elimination of the old leadership, talk of a "second revolution" had ceased. The regular army was firmly in the saddle—rearmament of the country was proceeding with rapid strides.

In the seventeen months since Hitler had become chancellor, Germany had undergone a thorough change. And as people had jobs—even if the pay was less—and as there was order and stability, they appeared to be satisfied.

Freedom—or the lack of it—did not seem to concern them. They did not seem to care that their press was regulated. As long as there was food on the table, they did not mind whether they had freedom of speech.

If they were aware of the concentration camps, which were springing up all across the country, if they learned about the maltreatment of the Jews, they did what most people would do in the same circumstances: they put their heads in the sand, not wanting to hear about it. Yes, the persecution of the Jews and the opposition

was cruel, but as long as there was peace and work and food and they personally were not disturbed, they did not care.

A trained observer like William Shirer, who came to Germany around that time, "was somewhat surprised to see that the people of this country did not seem to feel that they were being cowed and held down by an unscrupulous and brutal dictatorship. On the contrary, they supported it with genuine enthusiasm. Somehow it imbued them with a new hope and a new confidence and an astonishing faith in the future of their country."

Hitler did reassure the Germans over and over again of how peace-loving he was, and how all "present-day problems should be solved in a reasonable and peaceful manner." He concluded a nonaggression pact with Poland, and he spoke honeyed words to France and England. "Trust me!" he cried out. "As long as I live I will never put my signature as a statesman to any contract which I could not sign with self-respect in private life."

He was reasonable and sensible, he was for justice for everyone. But secretly he pushed rearmament; factories worked day and night so that Germany would be ready for "the day."

OF THE PRESIDENTIAL PALACE.

Communists had vanished—many of them were in prison or in the ranks of their former enemies—the Nazis.

The actions against the Jews had boosted the fortunes of the Gentiles; they had taken over the businesses of

GREETING THE PEOPLE from the balcony of the presidential palace. Next to Hitler, his state secretary, Dr. Meissner; Foreign Minister Neurath; and photographer Hoffmann.

GÖRING THE PLAYBOY

1936:
THE TENNIS BUFF: A HAIRNET KEEPS HIS UNRULY LOCKS IN PLACE.

As a combat flier in the First World War, he earned the country's highest decoration, the Pour le Mérite. He was brave, fearless, without nerves. Drifting after the war, he settled in Munich, where he met Hitler and came under his spell. Following an unsuccessful operation for wounds suffered in the ill-fated putsch, he became addicted to the morphine given him to ease his pain.

Hitler learned to trust him and to take his advice. He said of Göring: "In time of crisis he is brutal and ice-cold. When it comes to the breaking point he is a man of iron without scruples." But behind this blustering, bombastic, larger-than-life façade there hid a child who played with electric trains, sailed a fleet of model boats, romped with lion cubs, a man who "could lie down like a tired child and weep away the life of care."

1916: *From Göring's private album*
A WORLD WAR I SNAPSHOT OF THE YOUNG GÖRING.

Photograph by Heinrich Hoffmann
MARRIAGE TO ACTRESS EMMY SONNEMANN IN 1935.

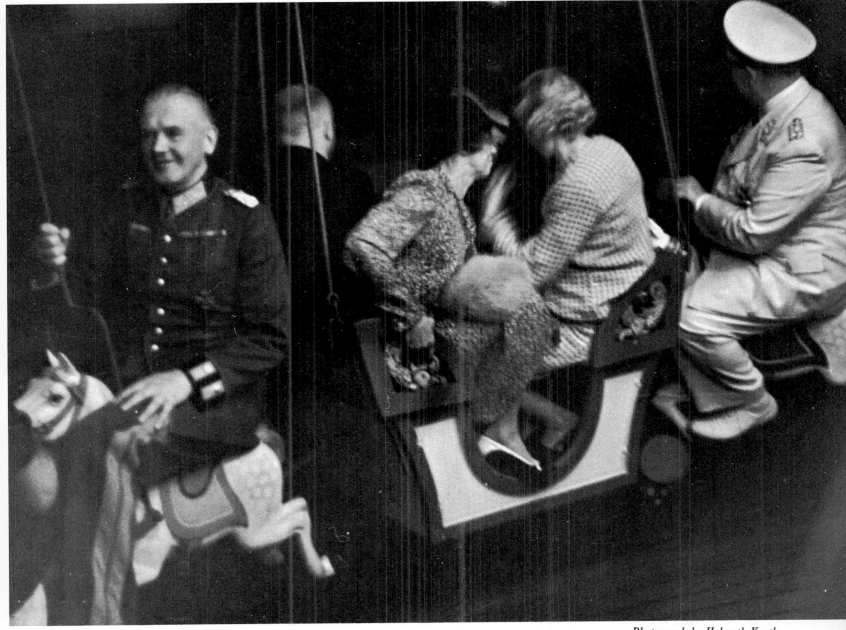

A VERBOTEN PICTURE—NOT TO BE PRINTED: ON THE MERRY-GO-ROUND WITH DEFENSE MINISTER BLOMBERG.

HE HAD THE PASSION OF A CHILD FOR MODEL BOATS.

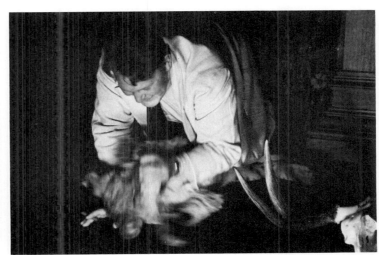

HE HAD A COUPLE OF LION CUBS TO PLAY WITH.

GOEBBELS THE PROPAGANDIST

1931, December 19:
GOEBBELS MARRIED Mrs. Magda Ritschel Quandt in Severin. She had been divorced from her first husband since 1929. Magda's ten-year-old son, Harold, is next to Goebbels in Hitler Youth uniform. Hitler (behind the couple), an admirer of the new Mrs. Goebbels, and General von Epp were witnesses.

GOEBBELS FORBADE PUBLICATION OF THIS PHOTOGRAPH

THE GOEBBELS FAMILY WITH UNCLE ADOLF, THE CHILDREN'S FAVORITE.

HE WAS A master of propaganda, a resourceful innovator.

Born in the Rhineland in 1897 the son of a worker, he was left with a short left leg after a childhood operation. People thought he had a club foot.

He studied at the universities of Bonn and Heidelberg and worked on his doctorate under Friedrich Gundolf, the Jewish literary historian. After his graduation he earned his living as a journalist, then became secre-

IN TWO OF HIS CHARACTERISTIC ROLES: AS AN ELOQUENT SPEAKER AND AS A TOP-HATTED POLITICIAN.

tary to Gregor Strasser, one of the leaders of the budding Nazi party.

In 1922 he heard Hitler speak and fell under his spell, noting in his diary: "At that moment I was reborn." Two years later when Hitler and Strasser split, he sided with Hitler. He was made Gauleiter of Berlin and as such he edited the party's newspaper, *Der Angriff* (The Attack).

In 1928 he was one of twelve Nazi members of the Reichstag; that same year he was put in charge of the party's propaganda. After Hitler's accession to power, Goebbels became the Third Reich's propaganda minister—an office of great importance. His maxim was to lie big and to repeat the lie often. Unscrupulous, without moral standards, he acted for the party's benefit. A fanatical Nazi, he was devoted to Hitler, a devotion bordering on mania.

Goebbels was an excellent speaker and a promiscuous lover. His marriage to Magda Quandt, a divorcée who was enamored of the Führer, did not keep him from having affairs with other women. His celebrated liaison with the movie actress Lyda Baarova ended only when Hitler interfered.

Until the last he stayed loyal to Hitler, remaining with him in the Berlin bunker. Before he and Magda committed suicide, they poisoned their six children: twelve-year-old Helga, eleven-year-old Hilde, nine-year-old Helmut, eight-year-old Holde, seven-year-old Hedda, and four-year-old Heide.

245

HIMMLER THE BLOODHOUND

HE WAS RESPONSIBLE for the torture and extermination of millions of human beings, yet if someone mentioned the sport of hunting at mealtime, he lost his appetite. Once on the eastern front he witnessed the execution of a hundred prisoners by a firing squad, and when two women did not die outright, he screamed and berated his men for their inefficiency.

Named for Prince Heinrich of Wittelsbach, he was born in Munich in 1900 to a conventional Catholic middle-class family. His father was a secondary schoolmaster who kept a tight rein on his three sons, and his mother was a model homemaker. Family life was pleasant and orderly. The hard work of the school year was rewarded with summer vacations in the country, where the boy Heinrich grew to love nature.

A model student, he consistently placed at the top of his class. He was the teacher's pet, collected stamps, played chess, studied piano, read adventure stories, and wrote poetry on martial themes.

He had always wanted to become an officer; toward the end of the war when he was seventeen, he joined the Eleventh Infantry Regiment, but the war ended before he had finished his training, and his unit was demobilized. Then he joined the Freikorps and dreamed of the restoration of German glory.

In his nineteenth year he began to study agriculture. He had an active social life, though his prudishness made contact with young women difficult. He was much more at ease with his fraternity brothers in the Bund Apollo, and despite initial qualms about whether dueling conflicted with the Catholic religion, he soon absorbed the ideals of male comradeship and honor typical of the German students who displayed their dueling scars as badges of valor.

His allegiance to the *völkisch* movement was strengthened by a summer spent on a farm where he began to read anti-Semitic publications.

His twenty-second year was a year of torment. Plagued by religious doubts, sexual conflicts, money worries, and uncertainties about his future, he took a job at a fertilizer factory at Schleissheim, researching manure, and he studied languages with the vague notion of emigrating as a farmer—to Russia, to Peru, to Turkey. The town was a center of right-wing activity, and before long Himmler had quit his job to join the Reichsflagge, one of the nationalist military groups. By August 1923 he was a card-carrying member of the National Socialist party, and took part in the putsch; and the following year, without telling his family where he was going, he went to Landshut to run the provincial office of Gregor Strasser's nationalistic splinter group. Later, after Strasser's group had become one with the National Socialists, Himmler was a local official of the enlarged organization.

His rise to power was swift. He grew to deputy leader of the Schutzstaffeln (S.S.) in the same year he married the daughter of a West Prussian landowner, and in 1929 while he was running a poultry farm in Waldtrudering, he advanced to Reichsführer of the S.S.

A skilled administrator with a fanatical devotion to the Fatherland, he added to his power as S.S. head the control of German police forces, and eventually the control of the interior ministry and the intelligence agency.

He envisioned a new morality for the German nation—the S.S. state was the institutional embodiment of his highest ideals: honor, loyalty, and the will to purity; and he molded his S.S. into an elite corps with elaborate ceremonial rituals expressing their loyalty and sense of duty to the Fatherland. He was a conventional petty bourgeois, always trying to do the right thing.

As "trustee for the consolidation of German nationhood," he administered a network of concentration camps which—in his opinion—enabled the Jews to atone for their "guilt" against Aryan civilization. He firmly believed that it was the duty of the good Germans to punish the "Jewish criminals" and exterminate them by "humane means." Inspecting a Polish camp, he consoled his men: "Most of you know what it means to see a hundred corpses lying together, or five hundred, or a thousand. To have gone through this, and yet . . . to have remained decent, this has made us hard. This is a glorious page in our history . . . ."

With ruthless devotion to duty, he hunted down and murdered millions of people. He ordered the razing of the Warsaw ghetto, carried out the idea of using human guinea pigs for hideous medical experiments, and expanded the Waffen S.S. and the secret police so that his personal power rivaled that of the Führer himself.

Hitler called him *"der treue Heinrich"*—but when the chips were down he betrayed his Führer. His wife looked upon him as a model husband, not knowing that he had steady affairs on the side. A weak man with thick glasses and a receding chin, he camouflaged his weakness in a martial black uniform. Stupid and opinionated, he was the most cold-blooded, dangerous, and feared Nazi leader.

HEINRICH HIMMLER,
the dreaded Gestapo chief.

BORMANN THE BUREAUCRAT

MARTIN BORMANN was born on June 17, 1900, in the small German town of Halberstadt. His father played the trumpet in the army band; retiring to civilian life, he worked in a post office. He died early, when his son was only four; his widow soon remarried a prosperous local banker.

In school Martin was no great light. He dropped out of high school to work on a farm. In the war he served as a gunner, and after the war he joined the Freikorps. Primitive and uneducated, he turned into a passionate Jew-hating nationalist. He became a member of the organization Rossbach—the group of Feme murderers. Among the Feme's victims were Matthias Erzberger, the Catholic deputy who signed the peace treaty for Germany, and Foreign Secretary Walther Rathenau, the liberal intellectual.

When a French court sentenced the German Albert Leo Schlageter to death during the Ruhr occupation for committing sabotage, the Rossbach group cried for revenge on those who denounced Schlageter. They accused a man—Walter Kadow—of the deed, dragged him into the forest near Parchim (close to Bormann's home), beat him to a pulp, cut his throat, and finally shot him. In the trial Bormann received a light sentence because he did not actually commit the murder.

After his release Bormann joined the paramilitary organization Frontbann, and when that group merged with the National Socialists (February 17, 1927), he became party member #60,508.

Two years later he married the daughter of Major Walter Buch, one of the prominent Nazis. It was a happy marriage. Gerda Buch, a fanatical Nazi and Jew hater herself, bore her husband in the years from 1930 to 1943 ten children (nine of them still living).

Bormann was a devoted family man. When he was away he communicated with his wife daily. He loved and trusted her, and she loved and trusted him. He also loved his mistress—an actress. He made no secret of his relationship and told his wife about it; she accepted it and suggested that if his illicit love should produce children, they might be brought up along with the legitimate ones.

Bormann, a hard-working bureaucrat, rose fast in the Nazi hierarchy. He began as Rudolf Hess's deputy, and after Hess made his flight to Scotland in 1940, he succeeded him as

"BORMANN WILL TRY TO COME TO YOU TODAY," Dr. Goebbels wired to Grand Admiral Doenitz from the Berlin bunker at 3:15 P.M., May 1.

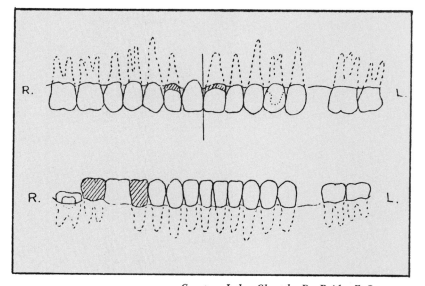

Courtesy Jada. Chart by Dr. Reidar F. Sognnaes

THE TEETH OF MARTIN BORMANN—a dental diagram by his dentist, Hugo Johannes Blaschke, submitted to American interrogators in 1945. A gold-backed porcelain tooth replaced the upper right central incisor. The lower right third molar had a cement filling; a gold bridge replaced the lower right front molar. Upper and lower first molars were missing. Simple comparison of this chart with the teeth of the men found in South America who resembled Bormann would have been incontrovertible evidence that none of them was the true Martin Bormann.

chief of the party chancellery, bearing the title "secretary to the Führer."

Hitler relied on him. Bormann, forever at hand, looked after his financial affairs and managed his estate in Berchtesgaden. He worshiped his master. So that Hitler's thoughts should be recorded for posterity, he assigned Dr. Henry Picker to make notes during the Führer's meals with his generals and to jot down his words. And he planned to buy all the buildings in which Hitler had lived during his lifetime so they would be preserved for posterity.

He kept other Nazi leaders jealously at bay, and they loathed him.

From early February 1945 Bormann was with Hitler in the chancellery bunker, working around the clock, sending out round-robin missives to the party chieftains. As the Russian tanks approached the Wilhelmstrasse, his hopes faded; but he believed that even if Hitler were to perish, Nazism would survive. On February 4 he wrote his wife: "Even after our death, the Reich must remain victorious for our children and the children's children"; and on February 24: "For us —there is only one possibility to remain alive; to be ready to die fighting and thus force victory."

Until the last he remained Hitler's devout slave and loyal servant—it was he who called a justice of the peace to the bunker to perform the marriage ceremony of the Führer; it was he who witnessed Hitler's political and private testaments; it was he who carried Eva's dead body to the courtyard to be put to the flames.

Shortly after midnight on May 1, Bormann wired Grand Admiral Doenitz, whom Hitler had named as his successor, that he would come to him as soon as he could. He said good-by to his secretary:

"Well, *auf Wiedersehen*! It makes no sense any longer. I will try it, but I don't believe I can get through to him."

Twenty-eight years after he left the bunker, a body found by street excavators was officially declared by the German government to be that of Bormann.

MARTIN BORMANN—who shadowed Hitler everywhere he went. Born in 1900, father of ten children, of whom nine are still living, he was officially declared dead by the authorities for the second time in 1972.

BORMANN'S LAST MESSAGE to Doenitz, sent at 10:53 A.M., May 1, 1945: "I will come to you as fast as I can."

PARTY DAY IN NÜRNBERG

THE NAZIS' PARTY DAY WAS a Roman circus. From their first modest celebrations in 1923, their gatherings grew into gigantic propaganda spectacles, with forests of uniformly clad marching men molded into an all-encompassing mass in obedience to one man—their leader, Adolf Hitler.

THE BIG SHOW—the phalanx of the Nazi battalions at the 1934 Nürnberg Party Day.

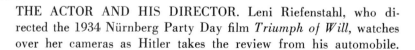

THE ACTOR AND HIS DIRECTOR. Leni Riefenstahl, who directed the 1934 Nürnberg Party Day film *Triumph of Will*, watches over her cameras as Hitler takes the review from his automobile.

LABOR BATTALIONS PARADE WITH THEIR SHOVELS.

250

THE SHACKLES OF VERSAILLES ARE BROKEN

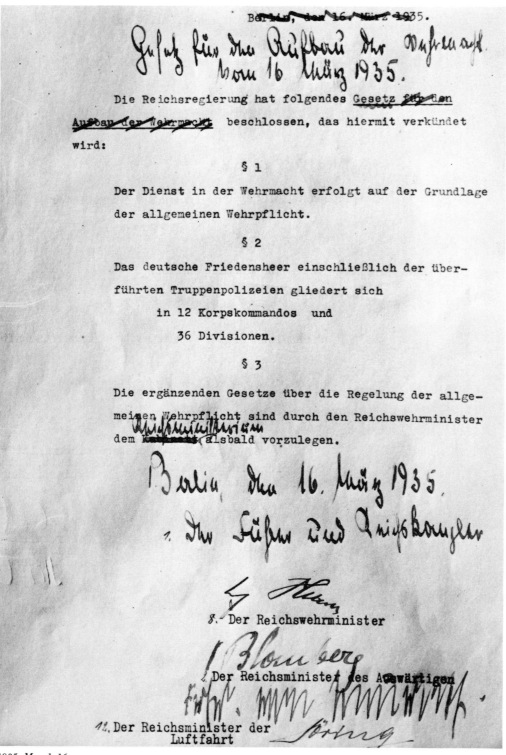

1935, March 16:
HITLER'S DECREE FOR REBUILDING THE ARMY. Disregarding the military restrictions of the Versailles treaty which allowed an army of 100,000, he decreed universal military service and a peacetime army of "12 Korpskommandos und 36 Divisionen."

WITH HITLER in power, Germany's rearmament accelerated at a fast rate. The armament industry worked around the clock. Ships, submarines, battle cruisers were built, some of them in foreign countries. An air force—expressly forbidden by the peace treaty —was formed; the League for Air Sports, supposedly a recreational organization, camouflaged the training of pilots. In less than two years the size of the army had trebled. In his conversations and addresses, Hitler hinted that Germany would soon be in a position to challenge its former enemies and that they would not have the strength to strike back.

On January 13, 1935—fifteen years after the signing of the Versailles treaty—a plebiscite was held in the Saar to determine the territory's future. Only 21,124 of the inhabitants voted to belong to France, while 477,119 opted to be with Germany. After the voting, Hitler gave his solemn promise that Germany had no further territorial demands on France, thus officially abandoning any claim to Alsace-Lorraine.

However, in Saarbrücken, at the celebration of the Saar's return to the Fatherland, he orated: "In the final analysis blood is stronger than all paper documents. The day will come when the writing of ink will be erased through blood. Woe betide him who does not learn this fact." And though the meaning of his words was clear, the nations of the world acted as if they had not heard it.

The timidity of Germany's adversaries encouraged Hitler to move forward boldly. On March 16 he decreed a law establishing universal military service and providing for an army of twelve corps and thirty-six divisions. With this he unilaterally annulled the military restrictions of the Versailles treaty and brought more than half a million new men into the army. The aim of the German military, for which the generals had fought ever since the inception of the treaty—a treaty which had limited their armed forces to 100,000 men—had come to pass.

Heroes' Memorial Day fell on the following day—Sunday, March 17, 1935. In the morning, the solemn ceremony held in the Berlin State Opera brought out the entire government and the military leadership.

The orchestra was filled by a forest of uniforms: high-ranking officers, generals, admirals, air force men. It seemed as if the clock had been put back to the time of the kaiser and Prussian militarism. The military came not only to honor the nation's dead, but to celebrate the end of the "obnoxious clauses" of the Versailles treaty.

After the ceremonies, Hitler took the salute of the honor guard at the square. Next to him walked the old field marshal Mackensen in his black death hussar uniform, a surviving military hero of the First World War; behind them the heads of the army, the navy, and the air force. Bugles sounded and music blared.

The "Bohemian corporal" had defied the world, had torn up the treaty which had caused so much real and imagined anguish and suffering to the Germans. They were now freed from their "enslavement," freed from their shackles, no longer restricted in their military expansion. Hitler had challenged France and England and—as he had predicted—they took the challenge and failed to respond to it.

1935, March 17:
ON HEROES' DAY Hitler walks before a line of military units with General Mackensen and with the heads of the army, the navy, and the air force. The world took the provocation of German rearmament with equanimity. England and France voiced a protest, but nothing else. Hitler gambled on the weakness of the Western democracies—and won.

THE LEADERS: Hitler, Field Marshal Mackensen, Defense Minister Blomberg (in front); Gen. Fritsch, Göring, and Admiral Raeder (rear).

DISCUSSING PEACE

THE BRITISH, troubled about Germany's illicit rearmament, were ready for an arms parity in exchange for the guaranteed security of Poland and Czechoslovakia. To their soundings the Führer gave a vague reply, but invited the British diplomats to Berlin to discuss the matter further. Before they arrived Hitler had declared compulsory military service. Still the blatant violation of the Versailles treaty did not bother the British; they came to Berlin as planned.

For some time in the past there had been conversations between England and Germany about the proportions of their navies. The peace treaty permitted Germany to build no more than four battleships of ten thousand tons' displacement, and six small cruisers. Hitler asked for more. Thus, when British foreign secretary Sir John Simon and Sir Anthony Eden met him in Berlin, he demanded their consent to a German fleet 35 per cent the size of the British. The British accepted the proposals without consulting their French allies or informing the League of Nations. When the naval agreement —allowing Germany to build five capital ships, two aircraft carriers, twenty-one cruisers, sixty-four destroyers, and submarines equivalent to 60 per cent of those of Britain— became a reality, Winston Churchill remarked wrily: "It is always dangerous for soldiers, sailors, or airmen to play at politics."

Hitler's diplomacy drove a wedge between Britain and France; the Versailles treaty provisions were smashed, the League of Nations was weakened.

The increase of the German navy kept her shipyards working at full capacity. When war came a few years later, Germany already had built fifty-seven U-boats and used them with effectiveness against British shipping.

1935, March 30:
DISCUSSING A NAVAL AGREEMENT. Left to right: Anthony Eden; Sir John Simon, British foreign secretary; Hitler; translator Paul Schmidt; German foreign minister von Neurath; Sir Eric Phipps, British ambassador in Berlin; Ribbentrop, German ambassador in London. Hitler proposed a German fleet whose total tonnage would be 35 per cent that of the British fleet—thus British superiority would be maintained. The English unilaterally grabbed at the proposal—a folly for which they paid dearly.

HITLER WITH THE ENGLISH DIPLOMATS Sir John Simon and Anthony Eden. They agreed that Germany be allowed to substantially increase the size of her navy. Though the deal looked advantageous to the British, the real winner was Germany. No longer hampered by the provisions of the Versailles treaty, Hitler could build the nucleus of a much desired naval force: five battleships; twenty-one cruisers, sixty-four destroyers, and up to 60 per cent as many submarines as owned by Great Britain.

"I WANT PEACE"

ONCE AGAIN HITLER's prediction was right. The French and the English, weary of the continuous quarrels and arguments against the Versailles treaty and against reparations, tired of an agreement which did not work, did nothing when Hitler renounced it. In the decade and a half since its signing, it had become obvious that the treaty was a failure—that instead of creating a peaceful and unarmed Germany, it had helped the rise of that country's militarism and spawned the war-mongering Nazi party.

In response to Hitler's action, Allied statesmen made speeches—but little else. The British and French met with Mussolini at the Stresa conference, where they issued a high-sounding statement about the independence of Austria.

A few weeks later—on May 21, 1935—the Reichstag was convened to hear the Führer. He used the assembly as a film director uses extras—the delegates were to cheer him and make approving noises.

The tenor of his speech was an appeal for peace. He asserted that Germany had no desire to conquer other nations. "No! National Socialist Germany wants peace because of its fundamental convictions. . . . Germany needs peace and desires peace." His words sounded reasonable and they seemed conciliatory. He reiterated that Germany had "renounced all claims to Alsace-Lorraine [and] concluded a nonaggression pact with Poland" and that she had no wish to "interfere in the internal affairs of Austria, to annex Austria, or to conclude an *Anschluss.*" As always, he evaded the real issues, raising a smoke screen around his intentions.

He started out with the promise that he would speak "with absolute sincerity and honesty" and would hold nothing back. He told the Reichstag that he was the best democrat Germany ever had, because he was elected as the nation's only representative, and because "the German people gave their 38 million votes for a single deputy." Their confidence and overwhelming support made him their true representative. It meant "that I am as responsible to the people as any parliament in any other country." He reiterated that his word alone was as good as the signatures under the collective pacts. "When I, as leader and representative of the German nation, assure the world that now that the Saar issue has been solved, I will make no other territorial request of France, that is a contribution to peace far greater than any signature under any pact."

As usual, he recited the accomplishment of Germany's disarmament, listing the figures of the war materiel destroyed: 59,000 guns, 130,000 machine guns, 38,750,000 rifles, 15,714 aircraft, 26 battleships, 315 U-boats, and so on, and on. He loved to cite figures; he was fascinated by numbers. He quoted at some length what foreign statesmen had said on disarmament and gave details of the rearmament of other countries, their new weapons, their new planes and ships. For a full hour his speech touched on nothing else.

He dwelled on the danger of Russia (this for English consumption) and stressed that Lithuania's march into Memel twelve years before in 1923 was against all treaties and agreements. (With such irrelevancies he was preparing the ground for his already planned invasion of the Rhineland.) He asserted that the newly signed Franco-Russian agreement was a "military alliance" (which it was not), and in contradiction of the statutes of the League of Nations and probably of the Locarno treaty (to presage any agreements he might make with other nations).

In conclusion—following the example of President Wilson's Fourteen Points—he offered a thirteen-point proposal for the solution of the problems. His Point 1 argued that the "Diktat of Versailles" had been invalidated not by the unilateral action of the German government, but by those powers who would not disarm. His Point 2 said that the German government would never enter into an agreement which could not be kept. Point 6 declared his willingness to enter into nonaggression agreements with Germany's neighbors. Point 8 reiterated that the Anglo-German naval agreement was binding and final (which he later in his April 28, 1939, speech unilaterally terminated). In the concluding points he reiterated over and over again his desire for peace. And finally he cried out: "Whoever raises the torch of war in Europe will only bring about chaos."

The main purpose of the address was to woo the peace-loving, Communist-hating British establishment and to win it over to his "moderate and modest" ideas. In this he was eminently successful.

Following the address, the *Times* of London editorialized that the Führer's proposals "may fairly constitute the basis of a complete settlement with Germany—a free, equal and strong Germany instead of the prostrate Germany upon whom peace was imposed sixteen years ago." Apparently the editorial writer had forgotten that the "prostrate Germany upon whom peace was imposed" had been soundly beaten on the battlefield, and that she had lost the war. Had she won, the kaiser and his generals would have forced a peace on her enemies not unlike the peace forced by them on the Russians at Brest-Litovsk. Such a peace would have been far more severe than anything contained in the "Versailles *Diktat.*"

ON OCTOBER 3, 1935, MUSSOLINI'S CARABINIERI INVADED ETHIOPIA.

THE AXIS AGREEMENT between Italy and Germany—a secret protocol outlining the foreign policies of the two countries—was signed by Italy's foreign minister Count Galeazzo Ciano (left) in Berlin on October 21, 1936.

THE DICTATORS tested world opinion to see how far they could go with their aggressive actions. When Mussolini saw that Britain would not oppose him, he invaded Abyssinia. And when Hitler was convinced that neither England nor France would intervene if he moved into the Rhineland, he ordered the army to march. He gambled—and won. Years later he admitted that if the Western powers had fought him in the Rhineland, he would have committed suicide, as at that time Germany was not yet ready for war.

He kept the Western democracies and Italy in the dark about his ulti-

ON MARCH 7, 1936, GERMAN TROOPS

That morning Neurath, the German foreign minister, called in the ambassadors of France, Britain, and Italy to his Berlin office, handed them a note denouncing the Locarno treaty and making new proposals for peace. It was a typical Hitler maneuver

PEACE?

Photograph by Robert Capa

IN 1936 NAZIS ASSISTED FRANCO AS CIVIL WAR FLARED IN SPAIN.

THE ANTI-COMINTERN PACT with Japan, which was directed against Russia, was signed on November 25, 1936. A reception in Berlin's Japanese embassy was held on the first anniversary of the signing of the agreement.

MARCHED INTO THE RHINELAND.
to send a military force into an adversary's territory and at the same time to declare: "I bring you proposals for peace!" But the disunited and defeatist French—abandoned by their English allies—took Hitler's challenge without responding to it with arms.

mate goal. He used the Spanish Civil War as a testing ground for German arms, sending Franco tanks, antiaircraft guns, airplanes. The constant tension in the Mediterranean forced Mussolini to enter into a secret agreement with the Germans. For the Duce the agreement constituted an "axis" around

which the European powers "may work together." And German diplomacy persuaded Japan to enter into an anti-Comintern pact with Germany.

Hitler, the consummate politician, played friends and enemies off against each other, always keeping the initiative, pushing, demanding, threatening.

GÖRING'S OPERA BALL

GÖRING LIVED more ostentatiously than any of the Nazi leaders. Most of the others came from poor backgrounds, most of them had scant education; but Göring had never known poverty, he had never been short of money. He married a rich woman; they had a comfortable home and were surrounded by the luxuries of life.

As he rose up the political ladder—Reichstag president, Prussian prime minister, chief of the Luftwaffe, economic dictator—his way of living rose as well. In Berlin he took over a small palace, and outside the capital he built an opulent hunting lodge in which to hang masterpieces taken from museums and from requisitioned art treasures. He gave hunting parties and soirees, imitating the style of a Roman emperor. He dressed flamboyantly in colorful uniforms; on his chest he displayed rows of medals which tinkled like bells.

Any occasion was an excuse for a party, for a celebration. If an artist friend—like Richard Strauss, the composer—had a birthday he threw a dinner to which he invited luminaries from stage and film. Foreign diplomats were taken hunting, and on their return servants awaited them with champagne and caviar. When his first wife's remains were reinterred in Carinhall, he turned the event into a dramatic pageant with Hitler and his military leaders taking part in the tableau. And when he married actress Emmy Sonnemann in 1935, the whole city of Berlin became part of the celebration.

His prominence growing, his parties grew as well. They became bigger and bigger. Finally they were given at the opera house—with a full symphony or-

1936, January 12:
THE OPERA BALL GIVEN BY THE GÖRIN

chestra and a whole corps de ballet furnishing the entertainment. To be invited was a privilege and a duty. All foreign ambassadors attended, as did the heads of industry and commerce, with Göring the center of attention. He loved to autograph programs, he loved to be flattered, he loved to be loved.

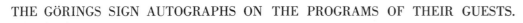

THE GÖRINGS SIGN AUTOGRAPHS ON THE PROGRAMS OF THEIR GUESTS.

Photographs by Helmuth Kurth

—THE HIGHLIGHT OF THE SOCIAL SEASON—WAS ATTENDED BY LUMINARIES OF GOVERNMENT, ART, AND INDUSTRY

THE RIBBENTROPS WITH KING BORIS OF BULGARIA.   RUDOLF HESS'S WIFE (left) WATCHES THE BALLET.

1937, August 8:
MEMBERS OF THE SAN FRANCISCO SINGING CHOIR VIE FOR THE PRIVILEGE OF SHAKING THE FÜHRER'S HAND.

THEY ALL CAME TO SEE HIM

THE WHOLE WORLD came to his door. In the six years before the war, great and small knocked and asked admittance. They did not come and demand explanations for the murders of thousands of innocent victims, they did not take him to task for flouting treaties or for invading countries without provocation; they came to flatter, to cajole, and to court. Ex-President Hoover came, and ex-Prime Minister Lloyd George, Charles Lindbergh, and the Duke of Windsor. Journalists came—formerly their papers paid Hitler fat fees for interviews—now he talked to them without fees, expecting them to write friendly pieces. Occasionally a critic slipped in, like Dorothy Thompson, who wrote disparagingly and made false and fatuous prophecies about his future. Foreign industrialists begged admittance and made propositions for alluring business deals.

The economic circles in the United States and England welcomed Hitlerism. The Du Ponts were for it, as was Sir Montagu Norman of the Bank of England. For Lady Astor the Nazis constituted "a bulwark against communism," and Charles Lindbergh in a speech to the America Firsters declared that the Nazis were "the wave of the future."

Hitler received his visitors in a royal manner. Guests were taken by his charm and his polished manners. He impressed them with his reasonableness. To them he stressed how moderate his policies were, that he wanted nothing but peace, that he had no territorial ambitions, no desire for the lands of other nations, but that he would fight Communism to the bitter end. And those who sat at his feet believed him—perhaps because they desperately wanted to believe him. They fed his egomania and thus they gave him encouragement—until he brought the world of those who had come to shake his blood-stained hands to the brink of disaster.

1938, September 8:
THE FRIENDLY LLOYD GEORGE is warmly received by the German Führer.

1937, October 23:
THE HUMBLE HITLER greets the Duke and Duchess of Windsor at Berchtesgaden.

1937, July 28:
THE JOYOUS GÖRING entertains Charles Lindbergh and his wife (right) during their tour of Nazi Germany.

1938, March 2:
AFTER HERBERT HOOVER CONFERRED WITH HITLER, LITTLE WAS SAID ABOUT THE VISIT OR WHAT WAS DISCUSSED.
At right: Hitler's translator Paul Schmidt and Hugh Wilson, the American ambassador in Germany. *Photograph by Heinrich Hoffmann*

1938, March 13:
SALZBURGERS ARE JUBILANT AS GERMAN TROOPS ENTER THEIR CITY.

ON HIS WAY TO VIENNA HITLER

AUSTRIA IS TAKEN

IN 1935 HITLER announced that he had no desire "to annex Austria or to conclude an *Anschluss*." In 1936 he signed an agreement recognizing the sovereignty of that country and pledging noninterference in her internal affairs. But his promises were—as usual —written in the sand. On November 5, 1937, he told his generals that "the aim of German policy is to secure, preserve, and enlarge the racial community." And he hinted that the *Lebens-*

THE TRIUMPHANT ENTRY INTO VIENNA: HITLER AT THE BURG THEATER.

HITLER AND HIS ENTOURAGE IN THE

REACHES THE FAMOUS MELK ABBEY.

AT KUFSTEIN THE "HERO'S ORGAN" PLAYS THE HORST WESSEL SONG.

raum (living space) which Germany so badly needed could be secured in the "immediate proximity" of the Reich.

To "soften up" Austria, the Austrian Nazis—directed from Germany—created civil disturbances and clashed with the police. Hitler summoned Chancellor Schuschnigg to Berchtesgaden and told him: "I am determined to make an end to all this." He demanded that the Austrian Nazis should be represented in the govern-

ment and that the two countries' economic systems be merged. He shoved an agreement under Schuschnigg's nose. "You will either sign it as it is and fulfill my demands within three days, or I will order the march into Austria," Hitler screamed.

But even after Schuschnigg signed, agitation by the Austrian Nazis continued. They bombed public buildings, they tore down the Austrian flag and replaced it with the swastika. In des-

peration Schuschnigg planned a plebiscite to ask the country to vote for a "free, independent, social, Christian, and united Austria." He set the date for Sunday, March 13. In response, the enraged Hitler ordered the invasion of Austria for March 12—the day before.

From his ministry in Berlin Göring directed the Austrian operations. In phone call after phone call—twenty-seven on March 11 alone—he demanded the cancellation of the pleb-

CITY TAKE A REVIEW ON MARCH 16.   HITLER WITH THE NEW NAZI GOVERNOR OF AUSTRIA, DR. SEYSS-INQUART.

Photograph by Hanns Hubmann

THE ENTHUSIASTIC VIENNESE—EXPECTING A ROSY FUTURE FROM THEIR NEW LEADERS—CHEER AND CHEER.

THE FÜHRER ADDRESSES THE MASSES OF VIENNA ON MARCH 15, 1938.

iscite and the appointment of the pro-Nazi Seyss-Inquart as chancellor.

In the evening of March 12, the German troops swarmed across the Austrian border. Neither Britain nor France interfered; Italy and Czechoslovakia watched from the sidelines.

Göring forced Austrian president Miklas to appoint Seyss-Inquart chancellor—and when this was done the new chancellor was told he must ask the German government to "send German troops as soon as possible" to Austria to restore order. This gave Germany the legitimate excuse for the invasion. Within a few short hours the whole of Austria was occupied.

Jubilantly cheered by the population, Hitler drove into the land of his birth and proclaimed it a province of the German Reich. Independent Austria—abandoned by the free world—ceased to exist.

Sieg Heil
The Viennese cheer thei
annexation by Germany

1937, April 20:
HE IS 48. Hitler with General Sepp Dietrich, publisher Max Amann, and S.S. chief Heinrich Himmler listens to the band.

THE FÜHRER'S BIRTHDAY

1933, April 20:

HE IS 44. Hitler's birthdays were celebrated with great pomp and festivities. Propaganda minister Goebbels arranged monster reviews and parades. Presents by the thousands filled the Reichs chancellery, where tables were decorated with swastika birthday candles.

THE BAND SERENADES THE FÜHRER, who listens to the music from his residence.

1938, April 20:

HE IS 49—and the favorite birthday gift was the model of the Volkswagen, designed by Ferdinand Porsche (left), who explains the car's intricacies to him.

HITLER'S BIRTHDAYS were celebrated with Byzantine pomp. The day began with the playing of military bands and ended with the mile-long parades of torchlit troops. At noon the cabinet, the heads of the army, the air force, and the navy clicked their heels before the Führer, offering their good wishes.

The birthdays were propaganda shows aiming to bring the people of Germany closer to their leader—the celebrations and parades were to take their minds off the grind of their drab, everyday existence.

HE IS 50.
A torchlight parade in celebration of his birthday.

THE CZE

WITH AUSTRIA incorporated into the Reich, Hitler turned his attention toward Czechoslovakia. His ambassadors abroad spread the word that if the Czech government did not heed the demands of the Sudeten Germans, the German army would move into Czechoslovakia and "liberate" them.

ON THE WAY TO GERMANY.

A COFFEE BREAK in the negotiations. Around the table: Foreign Minister Ribben-

1938, September 14, morning:
FULL OF CONFIDENCE.
A cocky Neville Chamberlain leaves 10 Downing Street.

CH CRISIS

Early in May 1938 the British and French governments pleaded with the Czechs to make concessions to the German dictator.

After a tense summer of diplomatic maneuvering, the London *Times* suggested on September 7 "making Czechoslovakia a more homogeneous state

ARRIVING AT BERCHTESGADEN.

trop; Chamberlain; Hitler; Dr. Schmidt; and the British ambassador Henderson.

1938, September 16, afternoon:
STILL FULL OF CONFIDENCE.
Returning to London from Germany with his political adviser Sir Horace Wilson.

BEFORE FLYING TO GERMANY AGAIN, THE CHAMBERLAINS TAKE A WALK.

1938, September 22:
ARRIVING IN GODESBERG . . .

. . . AND WELCOMED BY HITLER.

by the secession of that fringe of alien populations who are contiguous to the nation to which they are united by race." The editorial omitted to say that by ceding the Sudetenland to Hitler, the Czechs would relinquish both their natural mountain defenses and their military fortifications against Germany.

Two days later, during the Nürnberg Party Rally, Hitler, in an all-night conference with his generals, ordered them to prepare for an all-out attack.

In his speech at Nürnberg—on September 12—the Führer hedged, sounding as if he would be willing to negotiate the issue rather than go to war. He reiterated over and over again that he wanted only "justice" for the Sudeten Germans.

The confused politicians of France begged Chamberlain to approach Hitler.

Hitler now saw that neither the French nor the British would send military aid to the Czechs—thus he pressed his demands more boldly.

Chamberlain let the Führer know that he was ready "to come over at once to see you with a view to trying to find a peaceful solution. I propose to come across by air and am ready to start tomorrow." After reading Chamberlain's note, Hitler burst out: *"Ich bin von Himmel gefallen"* (I've tumbled from Heaven)—a phrase expressing delighted surprise.

On September 15 the sixty-nine-year-old Chamberlain, who had never been in an airplane before, flew to Germany. From the outset Hitler subjected him to an avalanche of words. The peak of his violent outburst was that "the three million Germans in Czechoslovakia must return to the Reich." If Chamberlain had had an elementary knowledge of German history, he could have responded that the Sudeten Germans had never in the past belonged to Germany, but to Austria, though it is doubtful whether such a fine point of truth would have impressed the Führer. Hitler reiterated that he "would not tolerate a small second-rate country treating the mighty thousand-year-old Reich as something inferior," and declared that he "would

THE COCKINESS OF CHAMBERLAIN IS GONE NOW. It seems as if the British prime minister and his ambassador Neville Henderson did not get what they hoped for. Even the face of the German interpreter Paul Schmidt (background) looks gloomy.

face any war, even a world war, for this."

The Führer's diplomatic cunning bore fruit. By continuing his threat to invade Czechoslovakia, he kept increasing his demands. Originally, he asked only "justice" for the Sudeten Germans; then he proposed "secession of the land" they inhabited on the basis of self-determination; and finally the "incorporation of the Sudetenland into Germany."

CHAMBERLAIN'S HEADQUARTERS were at the Hotel Petersberg in Königswinter am Rhein, which flew a solitary Union Jack.

HITLER'S HEADQUARTERS were at the Hotel Dreesen in Godesberg am Rhein, decorated profusely with swastika emblems.

1938, September 29:

AT THE MUNICH CONFERENCE. Chamberlain flew to Germany for the third time within a fortnight, this time to Munich, where on September 30, 1938, an agreement was reached among the four powers—England, France, Italy, and Germany. Foreign Minister von Neurath; French premier Daladier; Chamberlain; and Ambassador François-Poncet at the reception which followed the meeting.

Photographs by Helmuth Kurth

ALL SMILES. The Italian dictator Benito Mussolini jovially shakes hands with the English prime minister. Behind them are Göring, Hitler, Count Ciano, and Daladier.

Hitler impressed Chamberlain, who did not see in the Führer the unscrupulous liar whose political tactics were based on bluffs and misrepresentations.

Following the prime minister's return to London, the English and the French cabinets presented the following proposals to the Czechs:

All Czechoslovakian territories in which more than half of the inhabitants were Sudeten Germans should be turned over to Germany. After this was done Britain and France would join in "an international guarantee of the new boundaries"—a guarantee to supersede the former mutual assistance treaties.

The Czechs rejected the proposals as they felt they would bring them "under the complete domination of Germany sooner or later."

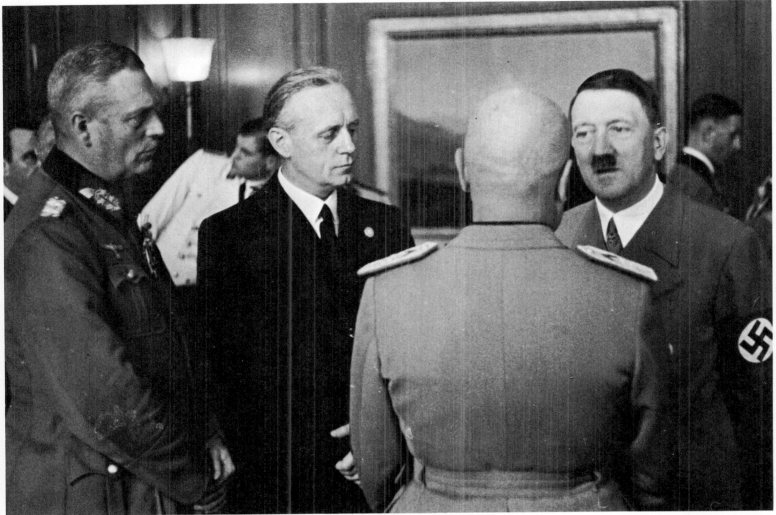

THE END OF THE MEETING. Hitler has an animated conversation with his Fascist partner Mussolini while Field Marshal Keitel and Foreign Minister Ribbentrop listen.

Photographs by Helmuth Kurth

These pictures, never published before, were taken by Göring's personal photographer, Helmuth Kurth, for Göring's own use—to be pasted in one of his many leather-bound volumes.

Meanwhile Hitler proceeded with his invasion plans. A Sudeten Freikorps within Czechoslovakia provoked "disturbances and clashes." The Hungarians moved their troops to the Czech frontier, threatening to recapture the territory they had lost through the peace treaty. The Poles, mobilizing their units, demanded a plebiscite in the Teschen district, which was inhabited by a large Polish-speaking minority.

The Czech government, surrounded by her enemies and "basely betrayed" by her allies, was forced to accept the Anglo-French proposals.

Next day Chamberlain returned to Germany to meet with Hitler in the Rhenish city of Godesberg and give him the news. Hitler wanted to know: "Do I understand that the British, French, and Czech governments have

AT THE BUFFET. Göring, hungry as always, was first. Hitler approached and involved him in conversation; they stopped talking as the French ambassador approached.

275

WHAT DO YOU THINK? Mussolini is all smiles about how things are going.

WHAT DO YOU THINK? Mussolini puts on a dictatorial mien for Chamberlain.

agreed to the transfer of the Sudetenland from Czechoslovakia to Germany?" And when Chamberlain replied that that was indeed the case, Hitler told him that "after the events of the last few days, this plan is no longer of any use." The flabbergasted Chamberlain was enraged. To soothe his feelings Hitler told him that "the Czech problem was the last territorial demand" which he would make in Europe.

Yet back in London Chamberlain urged his cabinet to accept Hitler's demands—but some of the ministers hesitated to sell out Czechoslovakia and to submit to the Führer. On September 26 Hitler was to deliver a speech at the Berlin Sports Palace. Three hours before the meeting, Chamberlain's emissary Sir Horace Wilson reached Berlin, bringing with him a personal message from Chamberlain in which he implored Hitler not to resort to war, but to settle the issue through negotiation.

Three days later, at another meeting, Wilson told the Führer that in case of war England would join with France, to which Hitler replied that if that was so, "by next Monday, we shall be at war."

However, the Führer had second thoughts about his belligerency—he realized he had gone too far. He dictated a letter to Chamberlain promising to negotiate the details directly with the Czechs and "to give a formal guarantee for the remainder of Czechoslovakia."

When the message reached London, the British navy was already on alert, and school children of London had been evacuated to the countryside. Chamberlain, in a final effort to save the peace, sent a message to the Führer: "I am ready to come to Berlin myself at once to discuss arrangements for transfer with you and representatives of the Czech government, together with representatives of France and Italy, if you so desire. I feel convinced we can reach agreement in a week."

Hitler was willing to confer with Britain, France, and Italy, but not with

1938, September 29:   *Photographs by Helmuth Kurth*

WITH BISMARCK'S PORTRAIT LOOKING DOWN ON THEM, THE NEGOTIATORS FINALLY REACH AN AGREEMENT.

We, the German Führer and Chancellor and the British Prime Minister, have had a further meeting today and are agreed in recognising that the question of Anglo-German relations is of the first importance for the two countries and for Europe.

We regard the agreement signed last night and the Anglo-German Naval Agreement as symbolic of the desire of our two peoples never to go to war with one another again.

We are resolved that the method of consultation shall be the method adopted to deal with any other questions that may concern our two countries, and we are determined to continue our efforts to remove possible sources of difference and thus to contribute to assure the peace of Europe.

September 30, 1938.

CHAMBERLAIN SIGNS THE AGREEMENT AIDED BY ADJUTANT SCHAUB.

THE AGREEMENT OF MUNICH between Great Britain and Germany signed by Adolf Hitler and Neville Chamberlain.

277

"PEACE FOR OUR TIME," EXCLAIMS CHAMBERLAIN AT HESTON AIRPORT ON HIS RETURN FROM MUNICH,

the Czechs, and wanted representatives of the three great powers to meet with him in Munich the following day.

They came promptly and all issues were settled in quick order, and on Hitler's terms. At 10 P.M. on September 29, Sir Horace Wilson informed the Czech representatives waiting outside that the four powers had reached an agreement, and handed them a map of the Sudeten areas which had to be evacuated right away. "If you do not accept," the Czechs were told, "you will have to settle your affairs with the Germans alone."

The pact of Munich was signed an hour after midnight on September 30. A few hours later German forces marched into the Sudetenland.

Returning to London, Chamberlain waved a document which Hitler signed

AFTER MUNICH

WAVING THE SIGNED AGREEMENT.

the day before and exulted: "I believe it is peace for our time."

Not everyone thought so. Winston Churchill warned: "We have sustained a total, unmitigated defeat. . . . We are in the midst of disaster of the first magnitude."

PICTURE POST

Vol. I. No. 3   October 15, 1938

THE HAPPY ELEPHANTS.
The elephants are happy. They are flying about in the sky. The elephants are happy because they have got peace. For how long have the elephants got peace? Ah, that alas! no one can say.

Photomontage by John Heartfield in Picture Post, *1938*

A MINORITY COMMENT ON CHAMBERLAIN'S OPTIMISM. The caption beneath this front-page photomontage in Britain's leading weekly reads: "THE HAPPY ELEPHANTS—The elephants are happy. They are flying about in the sky. The elephants are happy because they have got peace. For how long have the elephants got peace? Ah, that alas! no one can say." This comment turned out to be more pertinent than the optimistic utterances of the politicians. Then hardly a year later Britain was at war with Germany.

WOMAN CHARMER

HITLER WITH SONJA HENIE.

FOR A MAN who considered women of little importance, the list of his conquests is impressive.

He first fell in love when he was a sixteen-year-old schoolboy. Though he hardly knew the girl he glimpsed on the promenade at Linz, he was determined to marry her. But alas, when he left Linz for Vienna, the buxom Stephanie was soon forgotten.

It was said that in the seven years he lived in Vienna—until he was twenty-four—he indulged in love affairs, but there is no evidence of this. Nor is there a hint of any involvement with women during his Munich years, or in the four war years at or near the front.

The blossoming of his sex life coincided with the beginning of his political career—after he was thirty. And he was almost forty before he had his first great love affair—with Geli Raubal, the daughter of his half-sister. The twenty-year-old Geli lived with him in his Munich apartment, and their idyll ended when she committed suicide in 1931, leaving her lover disconsolate. Why she killed herself has never been satisfactorily explained.

Before Geli entered his life, he had a number of flirtations, but he felt more at ease with older women than with girls of his own age—Frau Bechstein, Frau Bruckmann, Frau Hanfstängl—who admired their young "Wolf."

As chancellor he was surrounded by the wives of his associates—Magda Goebbels, Inge Ley, Jenny Haug (his driver's sister), and by movie stars like Leni Riefenstahl, Renate Müller, Lil Dagover, Jenny Jugo. He had with them flirtations—but no sex. A more serious relationship was that with Winifred Wagner, the English-born daughter-in-law of the composer; he even toyed with the idea of marrying her.

A year or two after Geli's death he met Eva Braun. A secretary in Hoffmann's photographic studio, she fell in love with the famous man. And Hitler felt comfortable with her. He held on to the simple and unsophisticated girl as long as he lived.

WITH WINIFRED WAGNER.

WITH HIS BRITISH FRIEND UNITY MITFORD AT THE ENGLISH GARDEN.

WITH EVA BRAUN.

THE NIGHT OF THE BROKEN GLASS

HE UNLEASHED THE STORM. On November 7 in Paris, the 17-year-old Jew Herschel Feibel Grynszpan shot Ernst vom Rath, third secretary of the German embassy. His act led to Jewish prosecutions.

THE VICTIM. Vom Rath's bier in Paris. Though Rath was not a Nazi nor an anti-Semite, he became a hero of Nazi Germany.

WHEN THE SEVENTEEN-year-old Jewish refugee Herschel Grynszpan killed Ernst vom Rath, the third secretary of the German embassy in Paris, Dr. Goebbels in Berlin ordered the Nazis to respond to the deed with "spontaneous" demonstrations.

Storm troop leader Reinhard Heydrich instructed the police force and the security service to ally with the S.S., join in the demonstrations, burn down synagogues, destroy Jewish businesses, and arrest their owners. The night of November 9—forty-eight hours after Grynszpan shot vom Rath—became a night of terror for Germany's Jews. Their homes, their belongings were put to the torch. Within hours, so Heydrich reported to his superiors, 815 Jewish shops and 171 dwellings were destroyed, 119 synagogues burned, and twenty thousand Jews arrested.

Store windows of Jewish shops were smashed in every city. Insurance companies wailed that they would face bankruptcy if they had to make restitution for the damage. The claims for broken glass alone came to five million marks.

Göring, fuming in anger, berated Heydrich: "I wish you had killed two hundred Jews instead of destroying so many valuables." When asked at the Nürnberg trial whether he had really made that remark, he admitted he had, but only "in a moment of bad temper and excitement."

The civilized world was enraged. All over the globe a cry went up against the barbarism of the Nazis. Hitler was perplexed at this concern for "the fate of Germans within the frontiers of the Reich." To him it seemed added proof of the international Jewish conspiracy.

Three days after the *Kristalnacht*—"the night of broken glass"—as the Nazis' reaction to vom Rath's murder became named—Göring held a conference in his office to discuss the future of the German Jews. The field marshal, who liked to pretend that he was not swept up by the Nazis' vulgar anti-Semitism, declared: "German Jewry shall, as punishment for their abominable crimes, . . . make a contribution of one billion marks. . . . The swine won't commit another murder."

The Jews were to be eliminated from Germany's economic life; their businesses and property were to be taken away, and they themselves were to be "kicked out" of the country.

DRAWINGS FROM *DER STÜRMER* WERE EXHIBITED IN EVERY VILLAGE.

1938, November 10:

"ALL JEWISH SHOPS MUST BE DESTROYED . . ." read an order of the S.A. on the day vom Rath died. The night of November 9–10 became a night of horror for German Jews. In his report to Goebbels, Gestapo chief Reinhard Heydrich listed "815 shops destroyed, 171 dwelling houses set on fire . . ." Also 119 synagogues burned, another 76 destroyed, and 20,000 Jews were arrested.

Göring's declaration became the country's official policy. The clock was set back hundreds of years; Germany moved beyond the bounds of humanity.

If at this point the civilized world had united against the Nazis' barbarism, the future might have been different. But the anti-Semitic propaganda was reaping its dividends. The Jews were the first victims; after them came the Catholics, the Czechs, the Poles, the Russians, and finally everyone who did not belong to "the master race."

It was some time before the world realized the eternal truth of John Donne's words: "No man is an Island, intire of itselfe; every man is a peece of the Continent, a part of the maine . . . any man's death diminishes me, because I am involved in Mankinde."

ILLUSTRATION FROM A CHILDREN'S BOOK ISSUED BY *DER STÜRMER.*

283

HITLER RECEIVES THE HEAD OF CZECHOSLOVAKIA, Dr.
Emil Hácha, after midnight in the Reichs chancellery in Berlin.
Standing in the back, Lammers and Dr. Meissner.

Hácha was informed that the invasion was under way and that
Czechoslovakia was to be incorporated into the Reich. Hácha, after a fainting spell, was compelled to sign the official communiqué.

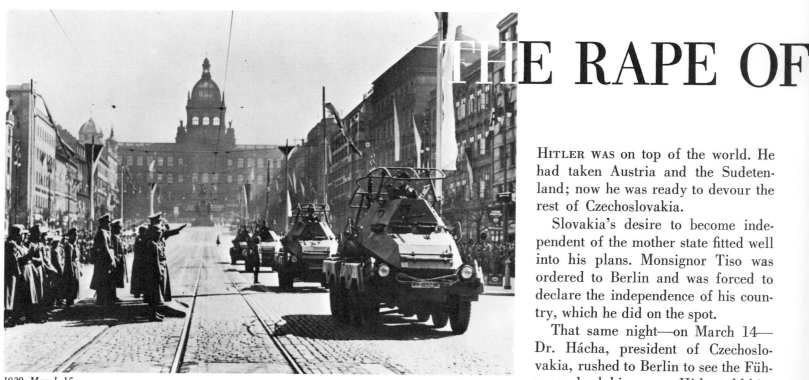

1939, March 15:
GERMAN ARMORED VEHICLES MOVE INTO THE HEART OF PRAGUE.

THE RAPE OF

HITLER WAS on top of the world. He
had taken Austria and the Sudetenland; now he was ready to devour the
rest of Czechoslovakia.

Slovakia's desire to become independent of the mother state fitted well
into his plans. Monsignor Tiso was
ordered to Berlin and was forced to
declare the independence of his country, which he did on the spot.

That same night—on March 14—
Dr. Hácha, president of Czechoslovakia, rushed to Berlin to see the Führer and ask his mercy. Hitler told him
that he had decided to occupy Czecho-

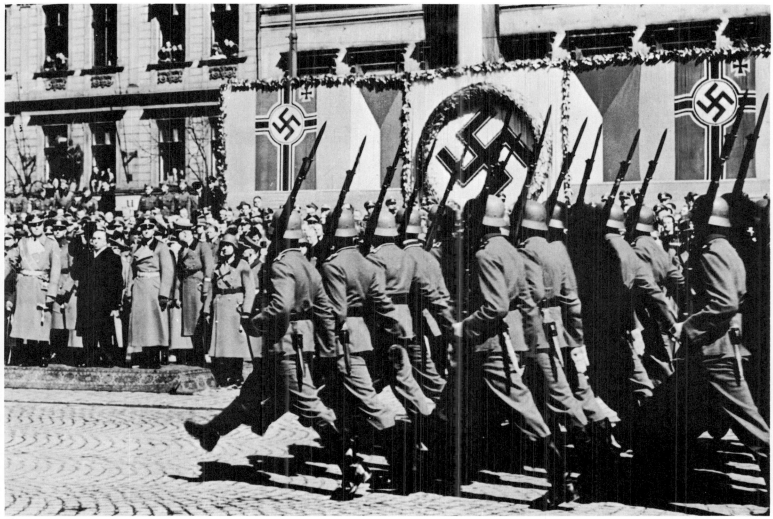

1939, March 15:
GERMAN TROOPS IN PRAGUE. The day before Hitler declared the end of the Czechoslovak state and proclaimed a Protectorate of Bohemia and Moravia. Neurath, the former foreign minister, was appointed as protector. Hácha, the president of the country, had to stand on the reviewing stand alongside the "Protector" and General List to take the review of the invading German troops.

CZECHOSLOVAKIA

slovakia—beginning at six o'clock the next morning. To avoid bloodshed, Dr. Hácha signed the surrender terms. Czechoslovakia ceased to exist. Neville Chamberlain, who had agreed in Munich to guarantee that country's borders, declared glibly that the independence proclamation had "put an end to the State whose frontier we had proposed to guarantee." The shameless betrayal by the English gave Hitler a free hand. Occupying Bohemia and Moravia, he cried out: "This is the greatest day of my life! I shall go down in history as the greatest German."

1939, March 23:
JOSEF TISO, THE NAZI PUPPET PRESIDENT OF SLOVAKIA, VISITING HITLER.

1939, July:
HITLER VISITED THE SARCOPHAGUS OF BISMARCK IN FRIEDRICHSRUH WHEN HE WENT TO HAMBURG TO LAUNCH

FOR BISMARCK — AGAINST

THE BATTLESHIP *BISMARCK*.

F.D.R.

THE WORLD HAD the jitters. Hitler's preparations for war, his repeated threats against Poland forced the other European nations into alliances. On April 6 Poland signed a mutual assistance pact with Great Britain; on April 13 Britain and France guaranteed the independence of Greece and Rumania. (By then Mussolini's army had already invaded Albania.)

In mid-April, shaken by Hitler's speech in Wilhelmshaven hinting at the incorporation of European countries into the Reich, President Roosevelt sent an urgent message to Hitler and Mussolini. He asked the two dictators for assurances that their "armed forces will not attack or invade the territory of the following independent nations"—Finland, Latvia, Lithuania, Estonia, Norway, Sweden, Denmark, the Netherlands, Belgium, Great Britain, Ireland, France, Portugal, Spain, Switzerland, Lichtenstein, Luxemburg, Poland, Hungary, Rumania, Yugoslavia, Russia, Bulgaria, Turkey, Iraq, Arabia, Syria, Palestine, Egypt, and Iran.

Hitler convened the Reichstag on April 28 to answer Roosevelt. He spoke for almost four hours, giving one of his characteristic addresses—full of venom, laced with sarcasm and irony. It was a set piece of demagogic oratory. After the ritual recitation of the party's history, of figures about Germany's disarmament, of his "moderate and modest policies" toward Austria and Czechoslovakia, he gave his replies to Roosevelt—twenty-one of them, each introduced with the word *Antwort* (answer) delivered in a mocking tone. The delegates rolled with laughter, savoring the Führer's performance.

Hitler assured Roosevelt that the thirty countries had nothing to fear from Germany—that she had no intention to attack them nor to invade North America. While his cheap polemic—treating the president as if he were a local German politician—impressed the Germans, the world was not hoodwinked. It had its fill of Hitler's promising peace while his armies were making ready for war.

HITLER'S PORTRAIT OF CHURCHILL. On May 4, 1940, Hitler ranted against Churchill:

"He is the most bloodthirsty and amateurish strategist in history. . . . As a soldier he is a bad politician and as a politician an equally bad soldier. . . . His abnormal state of mind can only be explained as symptomatic either of a paralytic disease or of a drunkard's ravings."

Prime Minister Winston Churchill with Stefan Lorant at Chartwell in 1940, about the time of Hitler's speech.

1939, August 23:
MOLOTOV SIGNS FOR RUSSIA. Next to Stalin, German legation counselor Gustav Hilger and German ambassador Schulenberg.

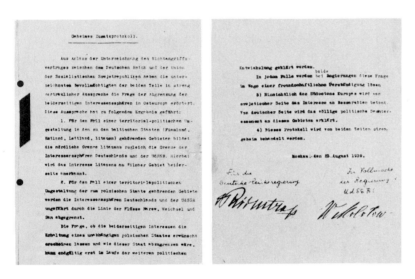

THE FIRST AND LAST PAGES OF THE PACT.

RIBBENTROP SIGNS FOR GERMANY. Left: Friedrich Gauss of the German foreign office; Hilger and Schulenberg watch.

THE NAZI-SOVIET PACT

THE NAZI timetable called for a move on Poland by the first day of September, but before that attack could be launched, Russia had to be neutralized.

Hitler's foreign minister Ribbentrop tried to convince the Russian government that "there exist[s] no real conflict of interest between Germany and Russia," and that the two countries should not be divided over the Polish-German controversy. He offered to go to Moscow himself and settle any outstanding issues on the spot. Ribbentrop slyly hinted at the possibility of dividing Poland between Russia and Germany.

After Molotov, the Russian foreign minister, read Ribbentrop's message he inquired whether Germany would be interested in a nonaggression pact. Hitler replied with an instant "Yes!"

Seeing the Nazis' haste for a treaty, the Russians upped their demands: they now also asked for a trade and credit agreement. The German answer again came fast: "Yes!" Hitler hoped for "quick results." In less than five days the negotiations for the trade treaty were concluded and signed in Berlin. "German foreign policy today has reached a historic turning point," crowed Ribbentrop on August 18, and Hitler wired Stalin "not to lose any time" but to receive the German foreign minister, who had "the fullest powers to draw up and sign the nonaggression pact and the protocol."

On August 23 Ribbentrop arrived in Moscow, and on the very evening signed the nonaggression pact. Russia and Germany pledged not to make war on each other, and in case one was at-

1939, August 23:   *Russian press photograph*

THE NEGOTIATORS ARE IN COMPLETE AGREEMENT: BOTH STALIN AND RIBBENTROP BEAM WITH HAPPINESS

tacked by a third power, the other promised not to assist that power. In a secret protocol the two signatories set down "their sphere of interest"—the partition of Poland.

A day later Ribbentrop was on his way home with the pact. His whirlwind diplomacy opened the way for a German invasion of Poland.

Photograph by Eva Braun

IN BERCHTESGADEN Hitler waits for the telephone to ring with the news from Moscow. With him, as usual, Martin Bormann.

Russian press photograph

STALIN TOASTS Heinrich Hoffmann, the photographer and intimate friend of Hitler from their earliest days in the movement.

289

1939, September 1:

ANNOUNCING THE WAR. On the morning of September 1, 1939, a few hours after the Germans invaded Poland, a distraught and fidgety Hitler told the Reichstag that Germany was at war. For the more than one hundred deputies already in service who could not be present, Reichstag president Göring substituted Nazi party functionaries, empowering them to vote. They did—approving the incorporation of Danzig into Germany. The vote of the Reichstag indirectly gave approval to Hitler's war policy.

MOVING INTO POLAND

HITLER NEEDED an excuse for ordering the army into Poland. So S.S. men in Polish uniforms attacked the radio station at Gleiwitz inside German territory. The Führer told the world: "A series of violations of the frontier, intolerable to a great power, proved that Poland is no longer willing to respect the frontier of the Reich. In order to put an end to this lunacy, I have no other choice than to meet force with force from now on."

And while he spoke the German army began its march into Poland, wreaking havoc and destruction.

The Führer thought that England would react to the German assault, as so often in the past, with words of protest only. But he miscalculated.

At nine o'clock in the morning on September 3—a Sunday—the British ambassador in Berlin appeared in the foreign office and read his country's ultimatum to Ribbentrop. When the document was translated to Hitler, the Führer turned to his foreign minister: "What now?" and all Ribbentrop could say was: "I assume that the French will hand us a similar ultimatum within the hour." Göring, who was with them, moaned, "If we lose this war, then God have mercy on us!"

With the rejection of the ultimatum, the Second World War broke out.

THIS IS HOW WORLD WAR II BEGAN: At daybreak on the first of September the German army poured across the Polish frontier, converging on Warsaw. The excuse for the invasion was the Polish attack on the German radio station at Gleiwitz. The world learned later that the attack was a fake one perpetrated by Nazi storm troopers in Polish uniforms. In "retaliation" German soldiers, German airmen, German guns, and German bombs showered destruction on Poland—soon to be subdued by the "master race."

WITH EVA BRAUN AT SUNDAY DINNER IN BERCHTESGADEN.

A MEAL IN THE TEAHOUSE

"IT IS WISER to have a mistress than to be married," said Hitler, and he reasoned, "then there is no burden to carry and everything is simply a beautiful gift. This, of course, only holds true in the case of an exceptional man." And to Adolf Hitler no man on earth was more exceptional than himself. Thus his relationship with Eva Braun.

She came into his life after his *Sturm und Drang* years, and after the suicide of Geli, his niece and his great love. He was then forty-three and Eva was twenty; he at the pinnacle of power, she an ordinary working girl.

They met at Heinrich Hoffmann's photographic studio in Munich, where Hitler's propaganda pictures were taken and where Eva was a secretary. It was in Hitler's nature to impress any girl he met; before long he began taking her out, to the Carlton Tearoom, to the Osteria Bavaria, to theaters, and to the movies. Eva, an unsophisticated girl, fell in love with the famous man.

Their affair had its ups and downs. Her diary leaves from 1935 which survived give a picture of their relationship. On her twenty-third birthday Eva noted: "If only I had a puppy I wouldn't be so lonely. But that is asking too much." Hitler did not present her with the little dachshund she desired. "He didn't even ask me if I wanted anything for my birthday."

Two weeks later she noted: "I am enormously happy that he loves me so, and pray that it will always be like this." But hardly a fortnight went by when she wrote (on March 4, 1935): "I am once more abysmally unhappy. Since I am not allowed to write to him, this book must hear all my laments." Jealous, she spied on him, keeping an eye on his house, waiting for three hours outside the Carlton Tearoom, "and had to watch while he bought flowers for the other and invited her for dinner." The "other" was a movie actress, Hitler's flame for the present.

Another entry reveals her dark mood: "I have just sent a letter to him which is decisive for me. . . . If I don't get an answer by ten tonight I'll take

LIKE ANY OTHER HUSBAND AFTER A SUMPTUOUS SUNDAY MEAL, HITLER TAKES A NAP IN HIS COMFY CHAIR.

my twenty-five pills and slumber into the other world in peace."

But gradually they grew together. He bought her a house in Munich—in the Wasserburger Strasse—and she accepted her role as backstairs wife. Still, most of the time she stayed with him in Berchtesgaden; when guests came or important personages, she had to disappear. He insisted that she call him "My Führer"; he called her "Tschapperl." When Goebbels said in a speech that Hitler was totally devoted

to the nation and had no private life, Eva remarked bitterly: *"Ich bin Fräulein Kein Privatleben"* (I am Miss No-Private-Life).

Yet with the passing of the years their relationship settled down. She became as comfortable to him as an old shoe.

On Sundays they used to take their meals in the teahouse, a small building on the Mosslahnerkopf with a view of Salzburg and the mountains. They seemed like an old married couple.

But in time of danger their emotions surfaced. After the attempt on his life, Eva, frantic with fear, wrote him: "I am beside myself. Desperate, miserable, unhappy. I am half dead now that I know you are in danger. Come back as soon as possible, I feel slightly crazy. . . . I've always said that I shan't go on living if anything happens to you. From the time of our first meeting I promised myself to follow you everywhere, even in death. You know that my whole life is loving you."

293

HITLER'S BLITZKRIEG

ALL WAS quiet on the western front. Hitler had lulled the world into false security. "A phony war," headlined the English newspapers. Everybody joked about the situation, so sure they were that Hitler and the German army could not possibly wage a serious, proper war against them.

In France most of the people felt equally secure. The French army, believing itself to be safely entrenched behind its "impregnable" Maginot Line—the ultimate defense system on which hundreds of millions of francs had been spent—was idle.

In London, Neville Chamberlain, oozing self-confidence, told the House of Commons that by failing to make war in the west, Hitler had "missed the bus." But even while the prime minister was uttering those fatuous words, the German army was on the march, striking against Denmark, Norway, and France.

On April 9, Hitler's ambassadors presented ultimatums to the Danish and Norwegian governments, demanding that they accept the "protection of the Reich" so they would not be occupied by the British and the French. It was a typical Hitler ploy, using euphemisms and lies to justify aggression. The Führer had tried it with Austria, he had tried it with Czechoslovakia; now he was using it with Denmark and Norway. Small Denmark, too weak to defend herself, yielded to the demands, but Norway would "not submit voluntarily."

The German fleet—in a daring move—steamed into Norwegian waters, "completely outwitting" the British admirals, as Churchill later wrote. German destroyers pierced the shield of the British navy guarding the Norwegian coast and, assisted by Nazi sympathizer Vidkun Quisling (whose name later became a synonym for traitor), occupied Narvik, the shipping port for Swedish iron ore. The other great cities—Oslo, Trondheim, Bergen, Stavanger, Kristiansand—fell soon in the well-nigh bloodless conquest.

But King Haakon VII of Norway would not surrender, and he refused to obey the German demand to name Quisling as prime minister. He fled to the north, from where he called on his

1940, April:

DENMARK was invaded on April 9, 1940, but King Christian stayed in Copenhagen during the period of occupation, riding through the streets of the city in silent protest.

NORWAY was taken by the Germans in the second week of April. Vidkun Quisling, the Nazi collaborator whose name became synonymous with "traitor," was named premier.

AGAINST EUROPE

subjects to resist. When the invading German troops neared his headquarters, he and his government moved to London where they remained in exile until Norway was liberated.

By the time the English navy—at last waking from its torpor—landed British troops on the Norwegian coast, it was too late. German armored columns had already secured their hold on the country; Norway was safely under German control.

The successful occupation of Norway was a stunning victory for Hitler and a humiliating defeat for England. The Führer had achieved his objective: he secured Germany's iron ore supply and prevented Norway from being occupied by the English. With Norwegian ports in Nazi hands, German submarines could move from safe harbors into the North Atlantic and prey on English shipping.

Once Norway was secured, one of Hitler's first acts was to appoint his trusted gauleiter, Josef Terboven—the same Terboven whose marriage he had witnessed on the eve of the "Night of the Long Knives" six years before —as Reichscommissar of the occupied nation.

The fury of the British over the defeat swept the Chamberlain government out of office and made Winston Churchill prime minister. The very day Churchill took over—on May 10— the Germans were on the move again. On that day their forces—eighty-nine divisions—stormed across the borders of Holland, Belgium, and tiny Luxemburg. They overran the Dutch and Belgian defense systems; their parachutists captured vital bridges before they could be destroyed by the retreating defenders. Within two days their armies were at the French border. The Dutch and the Belgians, helped by the French and the British, put up a heroic fight; but in six short weeks they were subdued. German arms, German strategy won. Hitler's armored columns—

over a hundred miles long—were rolling into France. Bypassing the Maginot Line, they advanced swiftly, paralyzing the French forces.

In the House of Commons Churchill rose and spoke the immortal words: "I have nothing to offer but blood, toil, tears, and sweat."

1940, May:

BELGIUM fell prey to the Germans in May 1940. Though the Belgians fought valiantly, King Leopold III surrendered on May 28, after much of his country had been devastated.

HOLLAND succumbed only five days after the German army invaded the country. The city of Rotterdam surrendered on May 14, 1940; Queen Wilhelmina fled to England.

295

HE LOVED THE CHILDREN HE KNEW

CHILDREN LIKED him. They were constantly about his home. The Bormann children (there were ten), the Speer children (there were five), the Goebbels children (there were six), and those of lesser National Socialist officials who lived in the neighborhood were welcome to play in the Berghof.

CHILDREN'S PARTY. "Uncle Adolf" and Eva Braun entertain the children of the Martin Bormanns and the Albert Speers.

Photograph by Eva Braun

WITH HIS FAVORITE, "Uschi," the daughter of Eva Braun's friend Herta Ostermeyr, who was married to Erwin Schneider.

He entertained them and brought them presents. And Eva, who longed to have children of her own, arranged special chocolate parties, celebrated their birthdays with them, took them on outings, showered them with love and affection.

Hitler loved the children he knew, but had no feeling or compassion for children who were not personally known to him. Jewish children by the thousands found death in the gas chambers of the extermination camps. Yugoslav babies by the hundreds were taken from their parents and shipped to Germany, where they were farmed out to Nazi families to be raised as good Nazis and future soldiers of the Reich.

He had no remorse for his deeds, no respect for human life; and until the end, he did not comprehend the enormity of the crimes he had committed.

PHOTOGRAPHER EVA BRAUN took this snapshot of her man together with Speer's children on the terrace of the Berghof.

Photograph by Eva Braun

THERE WERE ALWAYS CHILDREN AROUND. His Berchtesgaden retreat was the playground for the many children of his high-ranking Nazi officials.

297

MIRACLE AT DUNKIRK

THE RETREATING British and French were trapped in a pocket with their backs to the English Channel; they faced annihilation. They were saved by Hitler himself, who ordered General Guderian to stop his tanks and not pursue the enemy. Why did the Führer make the strategic blunder?

Three explanations are given for his order: one, because he did not want to humiliate the British, with whom he hoped to make peace; two, because he was trying to avoid fighting the war's decisive battle—as he thought—on Flemish soil; and three, to avoid large losses to his precious tank force.

The halting of the panzer division gave the British Expeditionary Force time to strengthen its defenses and to cover their army's escape to safety.

In the evening of May 26 the evacuation of the troops began. Large and small craft, motorboats, sailboats raced across the channel to bring them safely to the shores of England. The Luftwaffe was out of commission because of bad weather, and the German generals were confident that a mass rescue by "miserable pleasure boats" could not succeed.

But nine days later when the evacuation was completed, 338,226 British and French soldiers had been taken over the channel and saved. On that day—June 4, 1940—Winston Churchill spoke: "We shall go on to the end, we shall fight in France, we shall fight in the seas, and oceans . . . we shall defend our island . . . we shall fight in the fields and in the streets, we shall fight in the hills, we shall never surrender. . . ."

THE EVACUATION OF THE TRAPPED ENGLISH ARMY. Hundreds of boats converged on Dunkirk to save the remnants of the encircled British army. On May 27, 1940, and in the following days, well over 300,000 troops were taken safely across the channel.

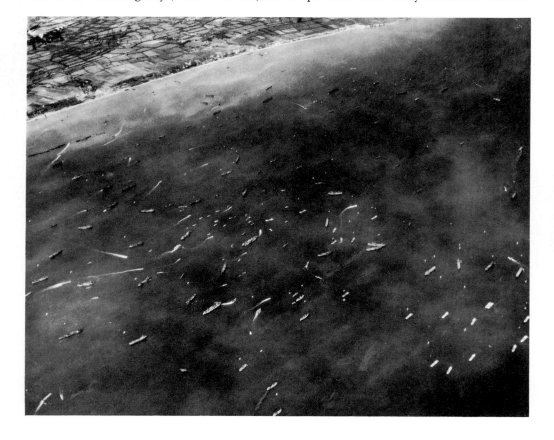

1940, May:

THE BEACH AT DUNKIRK after the evacuation. Wrote R. L. Duffus in an editorial for the *New York Times:*

"So long as the English tongue survives, the word Dunkerque will be spoken with reverence. For in that harbor, in such a hell as never blazed on earth before, at the end of a lost battle, the rags and blemishes that

have hidden the soul of democracy fell away. There, beaten but unconquered, in shining splendor, she faced the enemy.

"They sent away the wounded first. Men died so that others could escape. It was not so simple a thing as courage, which the Nazis had in plenty. It was not so simple a thing as discipline, which can be hammered into men by a drill sergeant. It was not the result of careful planning, for there could have been little. It was the common man of the free countries, rising in his glory out of mill, office, factory, mine, farm and ship, applying to war the lessons he learned when he went down the shaft to bring out trapped comrades, when he hurled the lifeboat through the surf, when he endured poverty and hard work for his children's sake.

"This shining thing in the souls of free men Hitler cannot command, or attain, or conquer. He has crushed it, where he could, from German hearts. It is the great tradition of democracy. It is the future. It is victory."

THE FRENCH SURRENDER

AFTER THE GERMANS moved into Paris on June 14, 1940, Marshal Pétain, who replaced Reynaud as premier, asked for an armistice.

On Hitler's orders the negotiations were conducted in the woods of Com-

piègne—at the same spot and in the same railroad car where the French had given their *dictée* to the Germans at the end of the First World War.

In the afternoon of June 21 Hitler arrived at the spot. With a contemptu-

AMERICAN NETWORK REPORTERS William Kerker, NBC correspondent, and William L. Shirer of CBS, outside the Compiègne communications center.

1940, June 21:
IN THE COMPIÈGNE RAILROAD CAR

NEGOTIATIONS INSIDE THE RAILROAD CAR. Members of the French delegation, headed by General Charles Huntziger, listen gloomily as the harsh armistice terms are presented to them. The Germans, led by Field Marshal Keitel, are sitting on the right.

ous expression he read the inscription on the granite block at the site: "Here on the eleventh of November 1918 succumbed the criminal pride of the German Empire—vanquished by the free peoples which it tried to enslave." He then entered the old *wagon-lit*, letting himself down on the chair on which Marshal Foch had sat in 1918.

For two days the negotiations dragged on until General Keitel's patience snapped. He told the French that either they would accept the German proposals within an hour or the fighting would continue. Twenty minutes later—at 6:50 in the afternoon of June 22—the French signed.

WHERE GERMANS SIGNED THEIR SURRENDER AFTER WORLD WAR I, HITLER FORCES THE FRENCH TO CAPITULATE.

NEGOTIATORS ENTER THE RAILROAD CAR in which General Foch handed the Germans his demands on November 11, 1918.

OUTSIDE THE RAILROAD CAR Hitler dances a happy jig while the French are forced to accept the terms of surrender.

HITLER IN PARIS

A PHOTOGRAPH HE SENT TO EVA FROM PARIS. On June 25, 1940, three days after the signing of the armistice, Hitler made a quick sightseeing tour of Paris, landing at Le Bourget at 6 A.M. and leaving the airport at 9 A.M. He told Speer that it was his life's dream to see Paris: "I am overjoyed that my dream today became a reality."

THE OCCUPYING GERMANS RIDE THROUGH THE STREETS OF PARIS.

As GERMAN TROOPS moved into Paris, Hitler remained at his headquarters in the village of Brûly-de-Pesche, not far from Sedan, where the decisive battle against the French was fought in 1871. He invited Albert Speer—who was to rebuild the German capital—to fly with him to the city which had fascinated him all his life. It was not to be an official visit, but an art tour.

The Führer and his entourage landed at Le Bourget airport at dawn on June 28. Three big Mercedes were waiting to speed them to the Opéra, which Hitler wanted to see more than anything else. It was seven in the morning when they arrived at the building—all the lights were on and the white-gloved attendants were on duty to show them around. But Hitler needed no guide—he knew what he wanted to see. He showed off his architectural knowledge. He held forth on the intricacies of Garnier's design, he waxed enthusiastic over the monumental staircase, he examined the boxes, walked through the orchestra, tried out the seats. He may have been thinking of incorporating the details into the opera houses of Berlin or Linz.

At the proscenium box he asked the whereabouts of a small salon which he remembered from the plans. And when he was told that indeed there had been such a salon, but that it had been eliminated during alterations, he told Speer proudly: "You see how well I know my way about."

From the Opéra the party drove along the Champs Elysées to the Arc de Triomphe, stopping at the grave of the unknown soldier. Then on to the Trocadéro, the Eiffel Tower, and from there to the Dôme des Invalides, where the Führer stood silently on the balcony for some time, looking down on the sarcophagus of Napoleon.

302

1940, June 25:
SIGHTSEEING INSIDE NOTRE DAME CATHEDRAL. LOOKING DOWN AT THE TOMB OF NAPOLEON.

They moved on—to the Pantheon, to Notre Dame, and finally to the Sacré Coeur, the church of Montmartre well-known from picture postcards and from the paintings of Utrillo.

Though they passed the Louvre, Hitler was not inclined to step inside and see the Mona Lisa or the Winged Victory. During the drive he discussed a celebration in Paris, but discarded the idea because of the danger of English air raids. "In any case, I am not in the mood for a victory parade. We aren't at the end yet."

The Führer felt he had seen enough, and they drove back to the airport. At nine o'clock—three hours after he had set foot in the French capital—he left it. "It was the dream of my life to see Paris," he said to Speer with satisfaction. "I am overjoyed that my dream today became a reality."

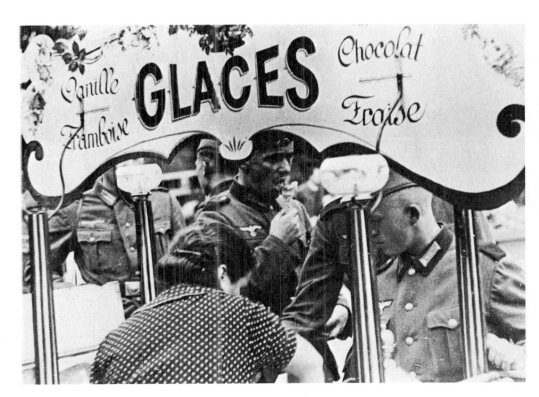

GERMAN SOLDIERS DISCOVER THE DELICIOUS ICE CREAM OF PARIS.

THE BATTLE
OF BRITAIN

By SUMMER 1940 Hitler was the master of Europe. He was convinced that he had won the war—and that only England remained to be dealt with.

He could not comprehend why the British treated him "so shabbily" and rejected his peace overtures. "I can see no reason why this war must go

THE HAVOC OF GERMAN BOMBING IN LONDON'S WEST END.

1940, December 31:
AFTER AN AIR RAID IN LONDON, THE INJURED ARE CARRIED AWAY.

1940, December 31:
THE CATHEDRAL OF ST. PAUL,

on," he said in his peace-offering speech on July 19.

He thought that air attacks would cause London to be "seized by hysteria" and the "population to flee." And Göring boasted that his Luftwaffe would destroy the Royal Air Force in two to four weeks. Thus September 20 was set as the date for the German invasion of England.

In the middle of August the Battle of Britain began. German bombers and fighters raided English cities and

304

CHRISTOPHER WREN'S MASTERPIECE, ON THE LAST DAY OF THE YEAR 1940 AS GERMAN BOMBS FELL ON LONDON.

installations. In the fortnight between August 24 and September 6, a thousand German planes attacked the island daily to soften it up for the invasion. But the RAF fought the Luftwaffe with bravery and determination. It also inflicted such heavy damage on the invasion fleet waiting across the channel that when invasion day arrived, a great number of German boats were out of commission.

On September 7 the Luftwaffe staged its greatest assault against London. Within a few minutes the city was in flames. Yet the spirit of the English remained undaunted. A week later outside of London a decisive battle was fought between the two air forces, in which the Germans suffered such heavy losses that Hitler had to call off his invasion plans.

The Luftwaffe was crippled. And Churchill's thanks to the RAF pilots echoed across the free world: "Never in the field of human conflict was so much owed by so many to so few."

WESTMINSTER ABBEY is inspected by its dean in the wake of a Nazi bombing attack.

305

HITLER AT HEADQUARTERS READING DISPATCHES WITH FIELD MARSHAL KEITEL AND GRAND ADMIRAL DOENITZ.

Photographs by Heinrich Hoffmann

DICTATING AT RASTENBURG. Behind Hitler: Walter Hewel of the foreign ministry; Field Marshal Keitel; press chief Dietrich; General Jodl, chief of operations; Julius Schaub, Hitler's adjutant; and Karl Heinrich Bodenschatz, general of the air force.

THE SUPREME WARLORD

HE BELIEVED in his own destiny. He was convinced he could do anything. When President Hindenburg died in 1934 he succeeded him—as "Führer" —retaining the chancellorship and becoming also supreme commander of the armed forces. And in 1941, with General Brauchitsch's fall from grace, he assumed the duties of commander in chief of all forces in the field. The ultimate political and military power was in his hands.

HITLER WITH RIBBENTROP AND MARTIN BORMANN AT HEADQUARTERS

THE WAR IN RUSSIA

THE ATTACK...

WORLD WAR II: NIGHTTIME PATROL DEEP INSIDE THE RUSSIAN HEARTLAND.

THE INVASION of Russia to secure more *Lebensraum* for Germany was an old dream of Hitler's. The vast land between the Vistula and the Urals—with its food and industrial resources—lured him. Convinced that Britain had already lost the war—and that the final blow could be dealt from the air, he felt the time opportune to move toward Russia and conquer her.

The prelude to his unprovoked aggression was a document, handed to the Russian government on June 21, 1941, containing feeble excuses for an invasion. Russia was accused of breaking her pact with Germany, of conspiring with Rumania and Bulgaria against the Reich, of adopting a "more and more anti-German policy." Therefore, the German armed forces were ordered to oppose the threat "with all the means at their disposal."

A day later—on the first anniversary of the French armistice at Compiègne—the German forces marched into Russia. Hitler was so confident of a quick victory that he made no preparations for a winter campaign. He told General Jodl that all that had to be done was to kick the door "and the whole rotten structure will come crashing down."

The campaign was carefully designed—a war of "destruction and annihilation." Communism was to perish so Nazism could live. It was a struggle of ideologies and racial differences—therefore it "will have to be conducted with unprecedented, unmerciful, and unrelenting harshness." Hitler ordered that all commissars should be liqui-

TO SLOW DOWN THE ENEMY, THE RUSSIANS SCORCHED THEIR LAND.

308

...AND THE RESULT

THE SNOW-COVERED LANDSCAPE IS LITTERED WITH DEAD SOLDIERS.

quate clothing. Hitler was still convinced of Russia's imminent collapse. He saw himself as the ruler of the greatest empire in the history of the world and envisioned roads to the Caucasus and to the Crimea "studded along their whole length with German towns and around these towns new colonists will settle." He vowed to Germanize Russia "by the immigration of Germans and to look upon the natives as Redskins"—to keep them as slaves.

On the second day of December, General Kluge's Fourth Army tried to breach the Russian defenses and capture Moscow—but was repulsed. Four days later the Russians launched their counteroffensive, relieving the pressure on the city. And a day after that—on December 7—the Japanese bombed Pearl Harbor. The war had spread into the Pacific—with the United States as an active participant.

Hitler relieved General Brauchitsch and became supreme commander of all German armies in the field (O.K.H.). The two-front war—the nightmare of the First World War which Hitler had tried to avoid—became a reality.

dated and the Russian people starved.

German armored divisions thrust across the border with lightning speed. Within three weeks they were 200 miles from Moscow, while another German army marched toward Leningrad, which Hitler had ordered "wiped off the face of the earth." The encirclement of the Russian army in the south succeeded; more than half a million Russian prisoners were taken. Early in October, with the offensive against Moscow in full swing, Hitler declared "that the enemy in the east has been struck down and will never rise again."

But his optimistic prediction turned out to be premature. Though the Russian forces retreated, they remained intact, and Germany was lured deeper and deeper into Russian territory. Winter came with snowfalls and frost —and neither Leningrad nor Moscow had fallen. German soldiers had to fight in subzero weather without ade-

LIKE NAPOLEON'S MEN, GERMANS SUFFERED UNDER THE RUSSIAN WINTER.

309

HESS FLIES TO ENGLAND

IN THE EARLY HOURS of the morning on May 10, 1940, Rudolf Hess, the deputy of the Führer, took off in a Messerschmitt-110 fighter plane from Augsburg. His destination was Scotland, where he was to see the Duke of Hamilton, whose acquaintance he made at the Olympic games in Berlin. That such a high-ranking Nazi as Hess should fly to the enemy in time of war was incredible.

He bailed out on target—only ten miles from the duke's home at Dungavel. The following morning when he was led to the duke, Hess told him that he had come on a "mission of humanity and that the Führer did not want to defeat England and wished to stop the fighting." After that he had three long talks with Ivone Kirkpatrick of the British Foreign Office, and Churchill informed President Roosevelt of these interviews.

Hess, so Churchill's cable read, was certain of German victory "due to development in combination of submarine and air weapons, steadiness of German morale, and complete unity of German people behind Hitler." And he told his English interviewer "that the Führer had never entertained any designs against the British Empire, which would be left intact save for the return of former German colonies, in an exchange for a free hand for him in Europe. But the condition was attached that Hitler would not negotiate with the present Government in England."

Later on Hess revealed to the English physicians who examined him that he came to Scotland "as an emissary of peace" because his teacher—Professor Haushofer—dreamed about him "on three occasions ... piloting an aeroplane he knew not where."

Whether Hess knew of Germany's impending attack on Russia has never been ascertained. Stalin was convinced that he had taken the flight to make a deal with the British so Germany would not have to fight on two fronts. When Churchill was in Moscow Stalin asked him for the "true story" behind the flight; Churchill told him what he knew, but Stalin made a doubting face. Churchill grew angry: "When I make a statement of facts within my knowledge I expect it to be accepted." Stalin glossed it over with a smile: "There are lots of things that happen even here in Russia which our secret service does not necessarily tell me about."

1941, May 11:
RUDOLF HESS'S SPECTACULAR FLIGHT as reported in an English newspaper. Hess, the deputy leader of the Nazi party, on his own accord flew to Scotland in a Messerschmitt-110 fighter plane to inform the Duke of Hamilton that he was on "a mission of humanity and that the Führer did not want to defeat England and wished to stop the fighting." Churchill thought at first that the flight was too incredible to believe.

310

1942, June 22:

ROMMEL WAS MADE A FIELD MARSHAL a day after he took Tobruk, the key to British defenses in Africa. Aiming to drive into Egypt and into the rich Middle Eastern oil fields, the "desert fox" massed his troops at El Alamein, facing the British army under General Montgomery. In a battle that marked the turning point of the African war, Rommel suffered a disastrous defeat and soon was routed out of Africa. Two years later, after the plot in July 1944 against Hitler, he was forced to commit suicide.

CAMPAIGN IN AFRICA

To BAIL OUT the Italians in North Africa, Hitler dispatched an armored division under General Erwin Rommel. In a dashing move Rommel, now commander in chief of the Italo-German forces, recaptured the provinces which the Italians had previously lost, took Tobruk, and moved within a few miles of Egypt and the Suez Canal. The British predicament was grave; with Greece occupied, their hold on the eastern shores of the Mediterranean was in jeopardy.

THE DESERT FOX. Field Marshal Erwin Rommel with his panzer division moved forward in the African desert with lightning speed, threatening Egypt and the Suez Canal. With Britain in a desperate position, Churchill implored Roosevelt to enter the war.

311

PAULUS' DEFEATED

THE COMMANDER OF THE GERMAN ARMY, Field Marshal Friedrich Paulus (left), surrendered with his army to the Russians. Hitler ordered him to stand firm and not to retreat. But by the end of January 1943, with the enemy encircling his army, resistance had become hopeless—there were only two alternatives: to surrender or to die.

GENERAL FRIEDRICH PAULUS, the commander of the Sixth Army, told the Führer he would capture Stalingrad by November 10. But the date came and Stalingrad still held out.

On November 19 the Russians began their big offensive; their aim was to cut off the city. Paulus had to withdraw his forces or face the chance of being encircled. Yet Hitler would not allow him to retreat; he ordered him to hold firm.

Four days after the Russians began their move, their two armies from the north and the south linked up at the bend of the Don. Twenty German and two Rumanian divisions were caught inside the net. Hitler promised Paulus to supply his army from the air. But it was sheer fantasy to promise 750 tons of supplies daily to the encircled troops. Where were the planes to come from?

To bring relief to Paulus's army General Mannstein launched an attack from the southwest on December 12. His troops came within thirty miles of Stalingrad. Hitler was begged by the general staff to let Paulus break out of the ring and to join up with the "liberating" forces; again the Führer would not allow it.

DISASTER AT STALINGRAD. Ninety-one thousand starving and half-frozen soldiers, including twenty-four generals, gave up their arms to their Russian foe.

OFF TO SIBERIA. Captured German soldiers in Stalingrad head for imprisonment

ARMY
IN RUSSIA

THE ATTACKERS OF STALINGRAD—now prisoners of the Russians. The defeat of the city marked the turning point of the war. From then on the Germans no longer held the initiative; they were forced on the defensive. At home Hitler proclaimed five days of national mourning to mark the greatest defeat that a German army had ever suffered.

Worse was to come—as the Russians farther up the Don opened a gap through the Italian Eighth Army, the left flank of Mannstein became imperiled. The troops had to be drawn back, leaving Paulus to his fate. Two hundred thousand Germans, surrounded by Russians, faced annihilation. On January 8, 1943, the Red commander offered Paulus terms for honorable surrender. He was given twenty-four hours to reply—once more Hitler ordered Paulus to hold out.

A day after the expiration of the ultimatum, a thousand Russian guns began their bombardment. Soon the pocket of Germans had been reduced by half and split in two as the Russians pulled the net tighter. On January 24 there was a renewed Russian

offer. Hitler radioed Paulus: "Surrender is forbidden. Sixth Army will hold their position to the last man . . . [for] the salvation of the Western world."

On January 30—the tenth anniversary of Hitler's taking power in Germany—Paulus sent this message: "Final collapse cannot be delayed more than twenty-four hours." He surrendered with the remnants of his army shortly thereafter.

in far-off Siberia. Only one man in twenty survived the grueling, Russian ordeal.

THE REMNANTS OF THE SIXTH ARMY GIVE UP. Of the 285,000 soldiers less than one-third remained alive. Their Führer wanted them to hold out and never surrender.

1943, April:
FORCED OUT of their bunkers by the Germans, Jews await their fate among the rubble.

THE DESTRUCTION OF THE GHETTO BY THE GERMANS.

CAPTURED JEWS AGAINST THE WALL, their possessions on the ground. Some were executed, others sent to the gas chamber.

IN THE FALL of 1940 the Germans built a high stone wall around the old ghetto in Warsaw and kept 400,000 Jews within its confines. Food was scarce in the enclosure, living conditions miserable. Thousands of orphaned children roamed the streets in rags. In three years the ghetto's population was reduced to 60,000; the rest

BEFORE THE "FINAL SOLUTION": ARRESTED JEWS IN THE GHETTO ARE LINED UP BY THEIR CAPTORS.

THE END
OF THE WARSAW GHETTO

were taken to extermination camps.

In 1943 the Germans decided to level the ghetto; the Jews were causing them too much trouble. But the "trash and subhumanity" fought; knowing their fate, they resisted their oppressors with heroic bravery. Then the exasperated Nazis destroyed "the entire Jewish area by setting every block

on fire." Still the Jews would not give up. They preferred to die, "insane from the heat, the smoke, and the explosions." Yet as the battle came to a close on April 25, the S.S. could report the capture of 27,464 Jews, whom they sent to Treblinka—the greatly dreaded extermination camp. After all was over General Stroop, who led the

operation, blew up the synagogue and reported to Heinrich Himmler:

"Of the total of 56,065 Jews caught about 7,000 were destroyed in the former ghetto. . . . 6,929 Jews were destroyed by transporting them to Treblinka. . . . Five to six thousand Jews were destroyed by being blown up or by perishing in the flames."

315

D-DAY

The year 1944 opened badly for the Germans. In January the Russians broke the lock in Leningrad, in February they were at the old Polish frontier. The war came near to the German homeland. On June 5, a day before the Allies landed on French soil, Field Marshal Rundstedt, commander in chief in the west, reassured Hitler that the expected invasion was still far off.

And General Rommel was so convinced that there would be no immediate invasion that he left the front to see his family, and afterward to visit Hitler. That same evening the Germans intercepted coded messages from London to the French resistance, announcing that the day for which they had been waiting had arrived.

An hour before midnight one Brit-ish and two American airborne divisions began landing on French shores in what the German command regarded as a minor operation. But when dawn came and more and more Allied troops waded ashore, there could be no further doubt—this was the showdown.

At first Hitler took the news calmly, confident that the Allies could be

Photograph by Heinrich Hoffmann

HITLER ON JUNE 6, 1944: In this unusual photograph, Hitler wears glasses. The place: Castle Kleissheim in Salzburg. From left to right: Günther Korten, air force chief of staff; Marshal Her-mann Göring, air force supreme commander; Alfred Jodl, chief of staff; General Walter Warlimont, General Wilhelm Keitel's deputy; General Keitel, chief of the army's supreme command.

Photograph by Robert Capa

D-DAY—JUNE 6, 1944—AMERICAN TROOPS UNDER EISENHOWER LAND ON THE NORMANDY BEACHES IN FRANCE.

thrown back into the sea. And even as further messages poured in and the commanders in the field implored him to send panzer divisions to relieve the pressure, he played for time. He retired in the belief that the invading troops of the Allies could do no great harm. By the time he awoke that afternoon, the invaders had established three beachheads and were moving inland at considerable speed. Still not comprehending the massiveness of the Allied attack, Hitler issued a fatuous message ordering the Seventh Army to clean up the beachheads "by no later than tonight."

Two tank divisions were sent to help the defending German troops; however their investment came too late. By then the Allies had driven the German navy from the sea and their air force from the skies; they were undisputed masters of the battlefield.

Eleven days later—on June 17—in a conference with his generals at Margival near Soissons, Hitler gave his two field marshals—Rundstedt and Rommel—a tongue-lashing for not halting the invasion and followed it with a pep talk about the new "V" weapons and the jet planes which would bring England to her knees.

Rommel attempted to argue, pointing out that the great Allied superiority in the air, at sea, and on land made the "struggle hopeless," and suggested that the time had come for negotiating a peace. Hitler cut him short: "Don't you worry about the course of the war. Look to your own invasion front."

Four days later the Russians, who had waited for the spring thaw before resuming operations, were on the move again. Marching through Poland, they were approaching East Prussia, heading straight for the German heartland.

In the meanwhile the invading Americans and English had established a solid front in France. "The mistake of the First World War," which Hitler had tried to avoid, had happened. Once more Germany had to fight in the east and west—once more it was a two-front war.

317

MEN OF THE AMERICAN 9TH ARMY TOGETHER WITH THE BRITISH OCCUPY GEILENKIRCHEN IN NOVEMBER 1944.

AMERICANS IN GERMANY

MOVING INTO THE CITY OF AACHEN IN THE MIDDLE OF OCTOBER 1944.

In August 1944 General Patton's new Third Army was on the move. In the second week of September American units reached the German border before Aachen. The Germans halted Patton on the Moselle, Hodges's First Army outside of Aachen, and inflicted heavy casualties on Montgomery's British units at Arnhem.

Paris had been liberated on August 25, after which the German forces were in full retreat from French soil. In the Balkans, Bulgaria threw in the sponge on August 26, forcing the Germans to leave that country. In the first week of September Finland gave up, Belgium and Holland were freed. Field Marshal Rundstedt, who had been reinstated as commander in chief in the west, admitted later that for him "the war was ended in September."

The big push of the Allies commenced again in October, when supplies caught up with the armies. After a hard-fought battle Aachen surrendered to the First Army on October 24 —it was the first great German city to fall to the Americans and the British. All along the front fighting raged with violent intensity.

Hitler ordered his generals to mount a massive offensive for the middle of December. He still believed he could reverse the outcome: split the American armies, take Antwerp, and close Eisenhower's main supply port, defeat the British-Canadians guarding the entrance to Belgium and Holland, and win the war. His generals, who listened to his exhortations at that crucial conference, were shocked at his appearance. He looked like a shadow of his former self—his arms twitched, his leg dragged as he walked, "a stooped figure with a pale and puffy face ... his hands trembling." Yet, he remained undaunted about the offensive, and the generals obeyed.

The 101st American Airborne Division raced to Bastogne to stop the German advance toward the Meuse. They succeeded and held on to the city. When the commander of the German Armored Corps asked for surrender two days before Christmas, General McAuliffe, leader of the 101st Airborne, shot back: "Nuts!"

1944, May 24:
ALLIED BOMBING OF BERLIN. The French church near the State Theater is hit. The air attacks by the Allies brought home to the German populace the high price of war.

AN AMERICAN CAMP for German war prisoners toward the end of 1944 bulges at the seams as more and more Germans are captured.

AN ATTEMPT ON HITLER'S LIFE

1944, July 20:
Photograph by Heinrich Hoffmann
A FEW HOURS AFTER THE EXPLOSION at his Wolfsschanze headquarters, a badly shaken Hitler tells Göring and the visiting Mussolini about the attempt on his life.

THE DESTRUCTION ON JULY 20, 1944:

THERE WERE GERMANS who recognized the immorality and inhumanity of the Nazi regime and who felt that if Hitler was not stopped Germany would be destroyed. In the year of 1943 alone, six attempts were made on the Führer's life, but all attempts were unsuccessful.

In March 1943 two officers—Tresckow and Schlabrendorff—put a time bomb on a plane in which Hitler was to fly, but the bomb—hidden between bottles of brandy—failed to explode.

Count von Stauffenberg, thirty-seven years old, a former cavalry officer, believed that the only way to save Germany was to kill Hitler—and he had

access to the Führer. On July 1, 1944, with a time bomb in his briefcase he attended a military conference in Berchtesgaden. But as neither Himmler nor Göring was present, he decided to put off his attempt. Four days later Stauffenberg was at the Führer's headquarters in East Prussia with his bomb; however, when he was ready to activate it, the Führer had already left the meeting.

On July 20 Stauffenberg once more flew from Berlin to headquarters; again he had the bomb in his briefcase, set to explode ten minutes after the activation of the timing device. At the conference he took his place near

the Führer and placed his briefcase under the large table, then made an excuse to leave the room. A few minutes later—at 12:45 P.M.—the bomb exploded. Though those near the point of explosion were killed, Hitler—his hair scorched and singed, his eardrums shattered, his pants partially blown off—walked out of the room alive. The heavy oak table upon which he had been leaning saved him.

Stauffenberg, believing that the explosion had taken the life of the Führer, flew to Berlin to assist with the take-over of the government. Within hours he and his co-conspirators were arrested and executed.

320

Photograph: Luce, Roma

MUSSOLINI, WHO REACHED HITLER'S HEADQUARTERS SOON AFTER THE BOMB EXPLODED, VIEWS THE SCENE.

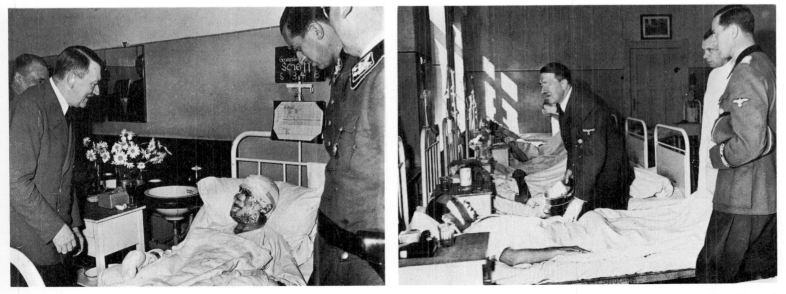

HITLER VISITS THE SEVERELY WOUNDED MEN; THEY WERE CONFERRING WITH HIM WHEN THE BOMB WENT OFF.

ULRICH VON HASSELL, the former German ambassador in Rome, on the stand before the People's Court. He was sentenced to death and executed. (At right, Hassell with Hitler in Rome.)

THE TRIAL OF

COUNT ULRICH WILHELM SCHWERIN VON SCHWANEN-FELD testifies in the ornate and swastika-decorated courtroom.

ROLAND FREISLER, the coarse and vindictive Nazi jurist, was the president of the court. He was later killed in an air attack.

COUNT WERNER VON SCHULENBERG, the former ambassador in Moscow, answers the judge's questions. He was found guilty and executed. (At left, in former days with Stalin.)

THE PLOTTERS

FIELD MARSHAL ERWIN VON WITZLEBEN, who was to become commander in chief of the army after Hitler was killed.

CARL GOERDELER, the former mayor of Leipzig, was slated to lead the new government after the success of the murder plot.

323

THE CLOCK RUNS OUT

HITLER ASKED THE GERMANS IN 1933: "Give me ten years and you will not recognize Germany." And he kept this promise. In 1945 Germany was not recognizable.

[Sign in image reads: "Gebt mir 10 Jahre Zeit und ihr kennt Deutschland nicht wieder — Adolf Hitler"]

HITLER COULD NEVER form a clear picture of his adversaries. Never having visited a foreign country, not speaking any other language but German, he never grasped the mentality of the English, the French, the Americans, the Russians. He constantly misjudged and underestimated them.

He was bewildered when in the spring of 1939 the British prime minister made a sudden about-face, offering Poland a pact against aggression, after in 1937 Chamberlain, through Lord Halifax, had indicated to him that England would not put any obstacles in the way of German expansion in the east. He misunderstood the diplomatic, urbane appeals of President Roosevelt, mistaking his restrained tone for weakness and fear of becoming involved in the European conflict. And he vastly underrated Stalin's hold on Russia, and the strength of the Red Army.

Roosevelt was for him a pitiful cripple, Churchill a hopeless drunkard, Stalin a murderer and a brigand. He was convinced that the German army could subdue Russia in a single

"THE GREAT CARTHAGE WAGED THREE WARS. IT REMAINED POWERFUL AFTER THE FIRST, IT WAS STILL

BAMBERG

HAMBURG

ON HITLER'S GERMANY

push, and that the Russian people would rush to throw off the Communist yoke. He fancied that the German air force was strong enough to bomb England into submission, and that the English could not halt a German invasion. He never doubted that France was an easy prey to German might, or that America would stay away from a European war.

At first — after he took power — everything went swimmingly. The democracies had not stopped him when he marched into the Rhineland, when he grabbed Czechoslovakia, when he annexed Austria. He scored his victories through bloodless conquests. And when war came and he took Norway, Denmark, Holland, and Belgium and overran France within a few short weeks, his star was shining bright.

But then the fortunes of war turned. Russia counterattacked, the Allies sent their invasion force to Europe. By 1944 Hitler had no hope of taking England or defeating Russia. His armies in the East were in retreat; his armies in France battled against superior American forces. Vastly outnumbered in men and material, the Nazis would soon be brought to their knees. Had the Allies not demanded "unconditional surrender," Hitler would have been deposed by his generals who wanted to end the war before Germany suffered unmitigated defeat. But the Allies demand solidified the people's support for their Führer.

Hitler still hoped that the democracies — particularly England — fearing and hating Communism, would turn against Russia and side with him in a holy crusade against the Bolsheviks. When this hope faded he had no more rabbits to pull from his hat. He had no rational proposal for survival; all he offered was to step up the war, to fight to the last man, to ask for more sacrifices.

He identified his personal fate with that of Germany. Like General Ludendorff in the First World War, who, when asked what would happen if the army lost its final offensive, answered: "Then Germany must perish," Hitler held that if the troops could not be

NÜRNBERG

BONN

HABITABLE AFTER THE SECOND — IT DISAPPEARED AFTER THE THIRD."
Bertolt Brecht.

HANNOVER

MANNHEIM

WÜRZBURG

MUNICH

BERLIN

victorious Germany had no right to exist. A romantic like the kaiser, he gambled with the destiny of his nation. Until the last he hoped for a miracle; he hoped to escape from final disaster. In adversity his true character surfaced — a man of limited intelligence, with a vulgar and cruel mind, an egotistical megalomaniac and a raving paranoid who charged the high command with inefficiency and who accused those around him of disloyalty.

The Allied air forces brought the dreadfulness of war to the German mainland. Germans now suffered a fate to which they had earlier subjected the English, the French, the Dutch. During the night the Royal Air Force kept on its saturation bombings, while during daylight hours American pilots pursued their pin-point bombing inside the Reich.

At the beginning of the war Göring had boasted that if a single bomb were to fall on Berlin people could call him "Meyer." As the Germans huddled in their cellars and their shelters they whispered, "Where is Meyer? Where is the Luftwaffe?"

In the months of February and March 1944, the battle between the Allied and German air forces reached its climax. During this period the British and Americans shot down well over 800 German planes; German production could not keep pace with such losses. Thus, by the time of D-Day, the Luftwaffe ceased to be an effective weapon.

The bombing wrought devastation to German cities. The houses of Hamburg were left without roofs, the industrial cities and harbors were demolished one after the other. Essen, Frankfurt, Kiel, Bremen — not one of them was spared. Bombs rained on Leipzig, Augsburg, Stuttgart, and other cities. In Cologne the majestic cathedral stood alone above the pulverized buildings. Before the Allied invasion in June all major German oil plants had been hit by bombing strikes. The lack of oil forced German planes to be grounded, German tanks to sit idle. By October the Krupp works at Essen ceased production; Aachen and other places on the Ruhr and Rhine were in ruins. The clock was running out on Hitler's Germany.

Before the year was out, Hitler, in a last desperate move, lashed out against the Allied invaders in the forest of Ardennes. The Germans penetrated the American lines, driving a "bulge" through them. Both sides suffered tremendous losses, but the superior resources of the Americans prevailed. The "Battle of the Bulge" ended in an Allied victory.

Meanwhile Russia was preparing for her great offensive. Since the summer of 1943 the Russians had recaptured territories wrested from them; they were now back in the Ukraine, in the Crimea, in eastern Poland and invaded Rumania, Bulgaria, and Hungary. The Germans were squeezed between the Allied and Russian forces.

Hitler returned to Berlin to direct the last battle for the capital. Cut off

NÜRNBERG

STUTTGART

HITLER LOOKS GLUMLY AT THE DAMAGED REICHS CHANCELLERY. THE END OF THE 1000-YEAR REICH IS NEAR.

from the world which was smolder-ing around him, isolated from the pop-ulace, seeing no one save members of his staff and the military leaders, he still believed his destiny; he clung to the myth promulgated by the party that he was a genius among men, that

God had invested him with the leader-ship of the "master race."

To the end he deluded himself that the tide would turn. He could still have saved untold thousands of lives, he could still have prevented the total destruction of Berlin, but he would

not step aside. He held on to his office with desperate tenacity. If he was to perish, so must Germany.

A new year was approaching—the year of 1945. With it the curtain was rising on the final act of the German tragedy.

1945, March 20:
ONE OF THE FÜHRER'S LAST PHOTOGRAPHS in the chancellery garden. Gone is the bravado—he is now a beaten man.

THE BLOWN-UP BUNKER under which Hitler spent his final days.

THE LAST BIRTHDAY GREETINGS. On April 20, 1945, Hitler's fifty-sixth birthday, banners with inscriptions like this ("We greet the first worker of Germany: Adolf Hitler") were hung around Berlin. Few people saw the irony of it.

WHAT
NAZISM WROUGHT

IN THE EARLY DAYS of the regime Jews were shot one at a time either in police prison or in Gestapo headquarters, but as time went on extermination methods were developed and refined. With the elaborate installations in concentra-tion camps, the killing was done at a fast rate.

In the dread Auschwitz camp alone —according to the boast of camp com-mander Rudolf Hoess at his trial—no less than three million Jews fell victim to the "final solution."

The bodies of the dead were dis-posed of mechanically, with nothing wasted in the process. Bones were con-verted into fertilizer for agricultural purposes. The gold fillings from their teeth, their gold wedding bands and jewelry were melted into ingots, sold on the regular market, and the finan-cial yield was deposited in the Reichs-bank to the account of the S.S.

"History does not record a crime ever perpetrated against so many vic-tims or one ever carried out with such calculated cruelty," said Justice Jack-son during the Nürnberg trials. And Adolph Eichmann, chief of the Ges-tapo's Jewish section, confessed to a friend that if he were ever forced to

A SIGN IN BERLIN after the war, list-ing the names of the dreaded concen-tration camps—the "Places of Horror."

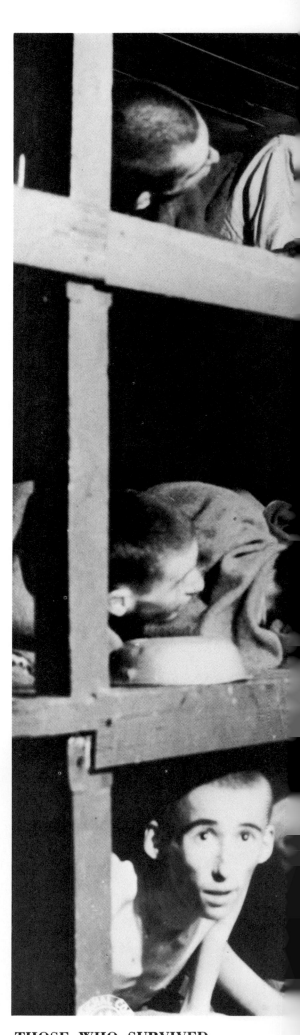

THOSE WHO SURVIVED . . .

. . . AND THOSE WHO DID NOT.
Grave pit at Belsen concentration camp.

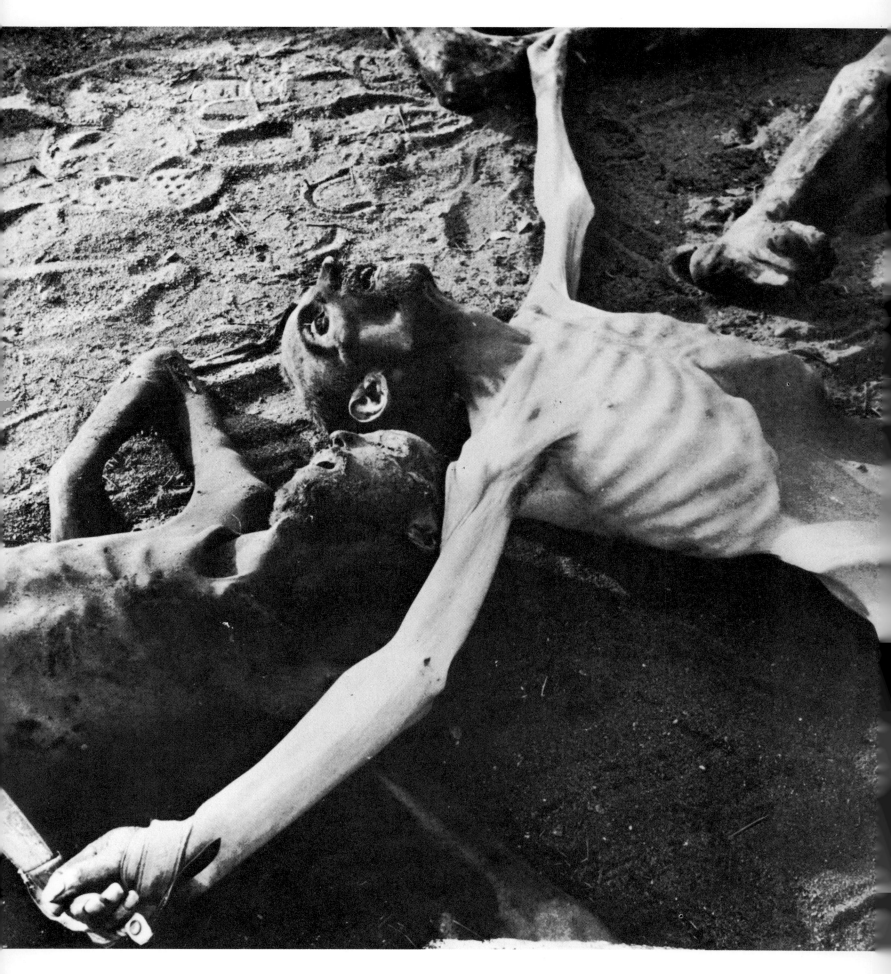

ECCE HOMO! CONCENTRATION CAMP VICTIMS OF THE NAZIS AS PHOTOGRAPHED BY THE AMERICAN LIBERATORS.

commit suicide, he "would leap laughing into his grave because the feeling that he had five million people on his conscience would be for him a source of extraordinary satisfaction."

Nazi bestiality did not restrict itself to the elimination of Jews, but to all "misfits" and people who opposed the regime. These "enemies" were harassed by the police, thrown into concentration camps, tortured, and killed. Unwarranted accusation, personal grudges, bureaucratic errors could lead to executions. The names of the artists, writers, scientists who chose exile is endless. Hitler's "master race" had no place for them.

The war which Hitler waged against the world resulted in staggering losses in human lives and material resources. The total casualties are estimated at 22 million dead and 34 million wounded. But the millions killed, the millions of refugees uprooted from their homes and homelands, the cities and houses destroyed, the lives shattered, were not the only legacy of Nazi tyranny. Hitler's arrogance of power, his brutal suppression of personal liberties, his monumental propaganda distortions and deceptions, his wanton disregard of laws have been emulated by others. His blatant lies, his spying on opponents, his pocketing money from industrialists, his harassment of critics, his immoral appeal to the basest instincts of mankind have been taken either whole or piecemeal by heads of state even in democratic societies.

The doctrine that the end justifies the means, the subversion of humanistic moral and ethical values led to a crisis of the human spirit—to collective guilt and individual despair. Nazi Germany revealed man the political animal as a ravening beast. It will be a long time before the nightmare can be erased from memory.

THE FINAL SOLUTION. The ovens of the concentration camp in which the remains of countless murdered victims were disposed.

THE GOLDEN WEDDING RINGS, torn from the fingers of the exterminated victims, were later changed into money by the S.S.

AFTER NAZI TROOPS ENTERED A POLISH VILLAGE, they executed everyone whom they suspected of being against them.

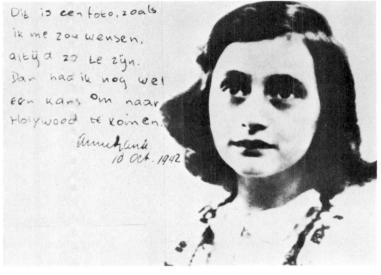

THE YOUNG JEWISH GIRL Anne Frank, whose diary of her life in hiding in an Amsterdam house laid bare Nazi brutality.

333

Photograph by

GONE ARE THE DAYS OF MAGNIFICENCE: MUSSOLINI'S OFFICE IN THE PALAZZO VENETIA, WITH THE FASCIST

MUSSOLINI AND HIS mistress had been taken by partisans to a hillside cottage near the town of Guilano di Mezzegere on the shores of Lake Como. The partisan Valerio, leader of the little group, was determined to bring to justice "those responsible for the catastrophe into which Italy had been led." When the Duce realized that he was not going to be freed, he begged for his life, offering his captors "an empire." But to no avail. He and his mistress were shot, their bodies taken to Milan and dumped in the Piazzale Loreto, where the year before fifteen Italian patriots

THE END OF A DICTATOR

THE FURY OF THE BETRAYED. After Mussolini was killed, his body was hung at the Piazzale Loreto in Milan in front of a filling station, with the body of his mistress.

Felix H. Man for the Münchner Illustrierte Presse
EMBLEM OVER THE FIREPLACE.

had been executed by the Fascists. For hours they lay on the pavement, then were hung heads down from the girders of a nearby garage. In a savage display people kicked and spat on them. Emptying a pistol into Mussolini's corpse, one woman shouted, "Five shots for my five murdered sons!" Soon the body of the former dictator was reduced to shapeless pulp.

MUSSOLINI WAS KILLED

ON APRIL 29, 1945.

GÖTTERDÄMMERUNG

1945, February: Photographs by Margaret Bourke-White

AS THE AMERICANS MARCHED INTO GERMANY, they came upon the bodies of Nazis who sought death through suicide rather than be captured by the Allied soldiers.

GÖTTERDÄMMERUNG (The Twilight of the Gods) was Hitler's favorite opera. He boasted that he had seen it over a hundred times. What entranced him about Wagner's music drama? Did he see himself in Siegfried, the hero who wrested the ring of the Nibelung from the giant? Or did he identify himself with Brünnehilde, the Valkyrie, who took upon herself the sins of the gods and "by her expiation freed the world from the curse of lust for wealth and power"?

Götterdämmerung closes with Valhalla, the home of the gods, in flames, and with a hope for a new era—that of human love. Hitler once said: "We may be destroyed, but if we are, we shall drag the world with us—a world in flames." He was prepared for his own Götterdämmerung.

And when the end came—when German cities were reduced to rubble, when the streets were littered with thousands of bodies, when resistance no longer made sense—he insisted that the nation must perish with him. In those last weeks in 1945, reality and fantasy, sanity and madness, life and death became indistinguishable.

Many of the Führer's followers preferred to die rather than live in a world without Nazi mythology. As the American and English liberation forces advanced, they came upon men and women who had snuffed out their own lives. Hitler in his Berlin bunker soon followed them.

He left the world of the living with the woman whom he had married in the last hours of his life—with a flourishing operatic gesture. As the guns and mortars of the Russians lit up the sky, as Berlin—Valhalla—was burning, Siegfried dead and Brünnehilde riding into the flames—Hitler killed the woman he had married a few hours earlier and then put an end to his own life.

A NAZI SUPPORTER in Schweinfurt who killed her two children and committed suicide.

TO LIVE OR DIE UNDER HITLER. A Leipzig lawyer and his family committed suicide, preferring death to living in a free world.

GENERAL KASTNER WAS DEAD IN BERCHTESGADEN.

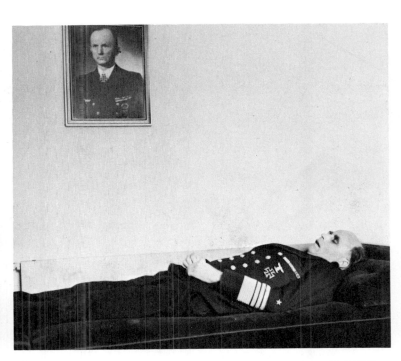

ADMIRAL GENERAL VON FRIEDEBURG IN FLENSBURG.

JOSEPH GOEBBELS'S CHARRED REMAINS IN THE BERLIN CHANCELLERY.

Goebbels:
"Germany today, and tomorrow the world!"

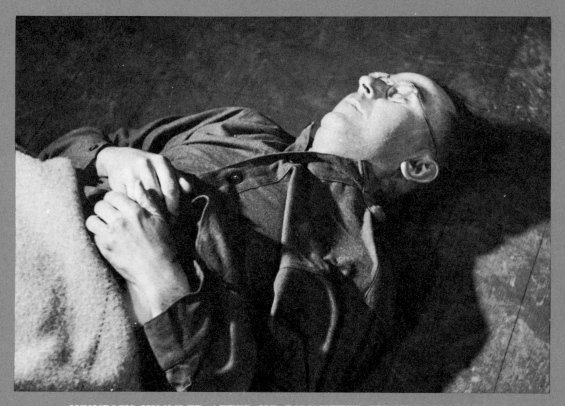

HEINRICH HIMMLER AFTER HE COMMITTED SUICIDE IN LUNEBURG.

Himmler:
"We are grateful for the wisdom of our great Führer."

THIS WAS THE END

THE YEAR 1945 came—it heralded the downfall of Nazi Germany. Hitler, a broken, sick, and dissipated man, had now established his headquarters in his Berlin chancellery; from there he tried to stem the tide of disaster. But the ring around him tightened; the end was near. The Russian bombard-ment of the chancellery forced him and his entourage into the shelter fifty feet below ground.

The chronology of events reveals the onrushing catastrophe:

January 1: German divisions under the command of Gestapo chief Hein-rich Himmler charge against the Al-

Hitler:
"I ask for your trust and confi-
dence—you will not repent it."

ADOLF HITLER'S ASHES IN THE YARD OF THE CHANCELLERY BUNKER.

Göring:
"Iron makes a nation strong—
butter makes the people fat."

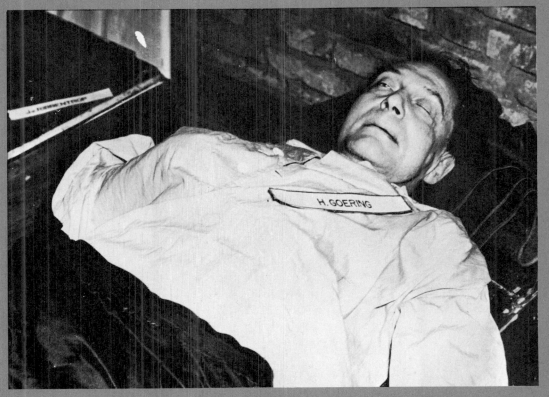

HERMANN GÖRING'S LAST PHOTOGRAPH, TAKEN IN NÜRNBERG.

lies in the Saar, but are stopped.

January 3: A German all-out assault against the American defenders of Bastogne ends in failure.

January 12: The Russians begin their great offensive; in five days they take Warsaw, the Polish capital.

January 27: East and West Prussia are cut off from the Reich. General Zhukov crosses the Oder and is one hundred miles from Berlin. The Russians take Silesia, occupying its rich coal mines.

January 30: The twelfth anniversary of the Nazis' "taking power." Hitler in the bunker is isolated from reality, he indulges in fantasies; he still hopes for peace with England and dreams of a German-British alliance against the "common enemy," the Russian Communists.

February 8: General Eisenhower's armies close in on the Rhine, reaching it before the month is out. In fierce

1945, June:

"I AM LEADING YOU TO MARVELOUS TIMES" proclaimed the Kaiser, and Adolf Hitler repeated the promise in the nineteen-thirties. Yet after twelve years of Nazi dictatorship this was the portrait of the Reichstag. By the end of the war, Berlin, which

battles against the Allies, the Germans lose 350,000 men—killed, wounded, captured.

March 7: The U.S. Ninth Armored Division reaches the Remagen bridge on the Rhine and establishes a bridge-head to the east bank.

March 19: Hitler issues a general order to destroy all military, indus-trial, transportation, and communica-tions installations. His minister of ar-mament—Albert Speer—remonstrates that "we have no right . . . to carry out demolitions which might affect the life of the people. . . . We have the duty to leave to the nation every possibility of insuring its reconstruction in the fu-ture." To this Hitler responds: "If the war is lost, the nation will also perish. . . . Only the inferior will remain after the battle, for the good have already been killed." Luckily, the rapid Al-lied advance and the reluctance of high-ranking German officers to carry out Hitler's "Nero order" saves the land from total destruction.

March 22: Patton's army crosses the Rhine at Oppenheim. Next day General Montgomery's Allied army moves over the river heading for the

340

Hitler planned to make into the grandest city in the world was reduced to rubble.

Ruhr.

April 12: The Russians are at the Elbe only sixty miles from Berlin. In the bunker the weird, fantastic, insane life goes on. Horoscopes, astrological predictions are consulted. Everyone hopes for a miracle. And when on this day the news of Franklin D. Roosevelt's death reaches the bunker, Goebbels is elated. Now that Roosevelt, "the

greatest war criminal of all times," has been taken away, Hitler (remembering the story of the Seven Years' War, when the czarina died at the critical moment) predicts that "the war will take a decisive turn."

April 16: Americans march into Nürnberg.

April 18: Field Marshal Model's army in the Ruhr capitulates; his 325,000 soldiers are taken prisoner.

April 20: Hitler's fifty-sixth birthday is celebrated in the bunker with the chief Nazi military leaders—Göring, Goebbels, Himmler, Ribbentrop, Bormann—in attendance. The Führer sets up two separate commands "in case" the Americans and Russians join forces and cut Germany in two. Admiral Doenitz is to be the commander in the north and General Kesselring is to lead the armies in the south. Hitler makes the decision not to go south, but to stay in the bunker. If Berlin falls, he will perish with it.

April 21: The Russians reach the outskirts of the city; Hitler orders a

counterattack. But S.S. general Steiner does not have the troops to launch it.

April 23: General Koller, chief of staff of the Luftwaffe, flies to Berchtesgaden to see Göring, his chief, with the news that the Führer has broken down and no longer knows what he is doing; he implores Göring to assume power. Göring sends Hitler a telegram, asking whether he can "take over at once total leadership of the Reich, with full freedom of action at home and abroad as your deputy; in accordance with your decree of June 29, 1941." (Speer, who was in the bunker, recorded Hitler's rage at Göring's "betrayal.") The Führer dictates a reply, charges Göring with high treason, and orders him to resign all his offices. Bormann, on his own, orders Göring's arrest.

April 25: The Russian and Allied armies join; north and south Germany are severed. Eisenhower's strategy is triumphant.

April 26: General Greim arrives in the bunker, flown in by Hanna Reitsch.

1951, September:

THE BRANDENBURG GATE IN 1951. Shorn of its glory, the Quadriga carted away by the Russians, its columns pockmarked by bullets, it gives a pitiful picture. No longer do the returning troops march under its columns as they did in 1871 (see page 22), or in 1918 (see page 73), nor do Nazi battalions celebrate their victory as they did in 1933 (see page 212).

The Führer tells him that Göring has "betrayed and deserted both me and his Fatherland," and that "he has established contact with the enemy." Hitler appoints Greim to succeed Göring as the new commander in chief of the Luftwaffe. He wails: "Everyone has deceived me! No one has told me the truth!" Even in the hour of reckoning he blames everyone for the disaster but himself.

April 28: While the Russian shelling of the chancellery increases, a foreign broadcast reports Himmler's secret negotiations with Swedish count Bernadotte in Lübeck, offering to surrender the German army on the western front, but to keep on fighting against the Communists in the east. Hitler is beside himself. "His color rose to a heated red and his face was virtually unrecognizable," recalled Hanna Reitsch. He fumes that Himmler's dealings are "the worst act[s] of treachery" he has ever known.

April 29: It is now Sunday; the Russians are less than a mile from the bunker. Greim and Hanna Reitsch have left. In the early morning hours Hitler marries Eva Braun. In legitimizing his affair with the woman with whom he has lived for more than a decade, the little bourgeois does what the bourgeois moral code taught him. After the ceremony champagne and delicacies are served. Then he dictates his last will and political testament. In the last hour of his life he rants about the Jews and blames the war on "international statesmen who either were of Jewish origin or worked for Jewish interests." He shields himself in lies and deceptions.

In the political testament Göring and Himmler are read out of the party, because they "brought irreparable shame on the whole nation by secretly negotiating with the enemy without my knowledge and against my will." As his successor Hitler appoints Admiral Doenitz for the presidency of the Reich and supreme commander of the armed forces. Goebbels is to be chancellor, Bormann the party minister (a new office), and Seyss-Inquart foreign minister. And he concludes: "Above all, I charge the leaders of the nation and the people with scrupulous observance of the racial laws and with merciless opposition to the universal poisoner of all peoples, international Jewry."

It is now four o'clock in the morning—April 30, 1945. The testament is signed and witnessed by Goebbels and Bormann for the party, and by Burgdorf and Krebs for the military. Copies are dispatched by special messengers to Admiral Doenitz.

Hitler prepares for the end. He destroys his papers and orders the shooting of Blondi, his Alsatian dog, he says farewell to his secretaries and all those in the bunker.

At noon he holds his last conference, sits down for a meal with his new wife, takes farewell of the Goebbels family—then walks into his room for the final act. Around 3:30 shots are heard—the lives of Hitler and Eva are over. Their bodies are taken to the chancellery garden; the 180 gallons of gasoline collected by chauffeur Erich Kempka are poured over them and ignited.

Goebbels and Bormann are still working in their cubicles, signing papers, sending out messages. Early in the evening Goebbels and his wife poison their six children and then commit suicide.

The Russians are only yards away. Bormann with Dr. Stumpfegger and others break out to go to Doenitz and hand him the Führer's last orders. Near the Bahnhof Friedrichstrasse Bormann is seen entering a tank; but before the vehicle can move it is hit by a Russian mortar and bursts into flames.

The noise of the guns is deadening. Each time a shell is exploded the skies light up — then darkness again. Along the walls of the crumbling buildings the men of Hitler's élite guard are searching for their lost comrades. The dying whine of a wounded soldier pierces through the night. He no longer shouts "Sieg Heil!"

A week after Hitler's death all German armies surrendered. The Third Reich came to an end. It lasted twelve years, four months, and eight days—and not a thousand years as Hitler had predicted.

NO MORE CHEERS..

...AND NO MORE Sieg Heil **AT THE STATUE**

(Turn back and see pages 23, 53, and 267)

THE END OF THE THOUSAND-YEAR REICH.
It lasted twelve years, four months, and eight days.
Photo: Hannes Rosenberg

Contents and Bibliography

There is a voluminous mass of literature on the Weimar Republic, National Socialism, and the Nazi leaders. The Wiener Library Catalogue, *From Weimar to Hitler Germany, 1918–1933* (2nd enlarged ed., London, 1964) lists 2990 titles. The *Vierteljahrshefte*

für Zeitgeschichte, Munich, prints a bibliography on contemporary Germany since 1953.

I gave preference to the publications in English, and to those works which are available in paperback.   S.L.

Pages 8–9 THE KING IS IN TROUBLE

On the general history of Germany, I suggest four books: Koppel S. Pinson's excellent *Modern Germany* (2nd ed., New York, 1970) ; Golo Mann's *The History of Germany since 1789*, a brilliant work by the son of Thomas Mann (rev. ed., New York, 1968) ; Marshall Dill, Jr.'s *Germany* (rev. ed., Ann Arbor, Mich., 1970) ; A. J. P. Taylor's *The Course of German History* (rev. ed., New York, 1961).

Pages 10–11 THE NEW BROOM

One of the latest in the voluminous Bismarck literature is the magnificent two-volume work by Otto Pflanze (Princeton, N.J., 1963 and 1972, paperback). Erich Eyck, *Bismarck: Leben und Werk* (Erlenbach-Zurich, 1943) is the full-length portrait. Wilhelm Mommsen, *Bismarck* (Berlin, 1967, paperback) is a digest of his bigger opus.

Henry Kissinger's essay on Bismarck: "The White Revolutionary: Reflections on Bismarck" in *Daedalus*, Summer 1968, is fascinating.

Pages 12–17 THE THREE WARS

Wilhelm Müller, *Deutschlands Einigungskriege, 1864–1871* (Leipzig, 1889) is an early history of the wars.

Theo Aronson's *The Fall of the Third Napoleon* (Indianapolis, 1970) is the latest study.

Bismarck's speeches and writing are available in their collected edition: his classic *Gedanken und Erinnerungen* (Reflections and Reminiscences) (2 vols., London, 1898). The third volume was published in 1919.

Pages 18–19 FOUNDATION OF THE REICH

The foundation of the Reich is described in Heinrich von Sybel's massive seven-volume history, *Die Begründung des deutschen Reiches durch Wilhelm I* (Munich, 1889–1895) ; it has been translated and published in English.

Egmont Zechlin's *Die Reichsgründung* (Berlin, 1967, paperback) has a detailed German bibliography on the unification and on Bismarck. Ernst Deuerlein, *Die Gründung des deutschen Reiches, 1870–71* (Düsseldorf, 1970) contains eyewitness accounts.

Pages 20–21 THE COMMUNE IN PARIS

La Commune de 1871 (Paris, 1970), a scholarly work by several authors. *The Communards of Paris, 1871*, ed. by Stewart Edwards (Ithaca, N.Y., 1973, paperback), a short study; by the same author: *The Paris Commune, 1871* (New York, 1973), a more comprehensive work.

Pages 22–23 THE VICTORS RETURN

An eyewitness of the event, Baroness Spitz-

enberg, records in her diary, *Das Tagebuch der Baronin Spitzenberg* (Göttingen, 1960), the happenings of that day.

Pages 24–25 BISMARCK'S DOMESTIC POLICIES

Books dealing with the Kulturkampf and Bismarck's labor legislation: Adelheid Constäbel, *Vorgeschichte des Kulturkampfes* (Berlin, 1956) ; F. Toennis, *Der Kampf um das Sozialistengesetz, 1878* (Berlin, 1929) ; Walter Vogel, *Bismarcks Arbeiterversicherung* (Braunschweig, 1951) ; R. Morsey, *Die Oberste Reichsverwaltung unter Bismarck, 1867–1890* (Münster, 1957). See also Otto Pflanze's volumes on Bismarck (previously cited) and A. J. P. Taylor, *Bismarck: The Man and the Statesman* (London, 1955; New York, 1956).

Pages 26–27 THE OLD KAISER DIES

The Prussian historian Wilhelm Oncken pictures the king and his era in his *Das Zeitalter des Kaisers Wilhelm* (Berlin, 1890).

Paul Wiegler, *William the First* (London, 1929). A biography by the art historian.

Pages 28–29 THE NEW KAISER

Biographies of the kaiser: by Emil Ludwig (New York, 1927) ; by Kürenberg (London, 1954) ; by Virginia Cowles (New York, 1963). K. F. Nowak, *Germany's Road to Ruin* (London, 1932) ; Erich Eyck, *Das persönliche Regiment Wilhelm II* (Zurich, 1948).

Pages 30–31 BISMARCK'S REICHSTAG

Erich Eyck, *Bismarck and the German Empire* (New York, 1964, paperback).

Pages 32–33 A BOY BORN TO THE HITLERS

Bradley F. Smith, *Adolf Hitler, His Family, Childhood and Youth* (Palo Alto, Calif., 1967) is the best work on Hitler's early life. Werner Maser's *Adolf Hitler* (Munich, 1971) has detailed information on the family.

Pages 34–35 BISMARCK RESIGNS

Pages 36–37 RECONCILIATION AND DEATH

Works on Bismarck's resignation: Wilhelm Schüssler, *Bismarck's Sturz* (Leipzig, 1921) ; Wilhelm Mommsen, *Bismarck's Sturz und die Parteien* (Stuttgart, 1924) ; Ernst Gagliardi, *Bismarck's Entlassung* (Tübingen, 1927).

Hans Bernard Gisevius, *Der Anfang vom Ende* (Zürich, 1971) is a compelling narrative of William II's early years as emperor.

Moritz Busch, *Bismarck: Secret Pages of His History* (3 vols., London, 1908). Recollections of the chancellor's friend.

Pages 38–41 HOW THEY LIVED

Books about life in Germany before the First World War:

Ray Stannard Baker, *Seen in Germany* (New York, 1901) ; Sidney Whitman, *German Memories* (Leipzig, 1913) ; Price Collier, *Germany and the Germans* (Berlin, 1913) ; Mrs. Alfred Sedgwick, *Home Life in Germany* (New York, 1908).

An outstanding work on the history of the German capital is Gerhard Masur, *Imperial Berlin* (New York, 1970).

Pages 42–43 TWO BOYS GROW UP

Adolf Hitler's *Mein Kampf*, trans. by Ralph Mannheim (Boston, 1943, paperback) recounts the controversy with his father. Of Hitler's early years in Linz: August Kubizek, *Adolf Hitler, Mein Jugendfreund* (Graz and Stuttgart, 1966), which is widely quoted by other biographers and which—although supervised by Nazi authorities—probably gives a correct picture of the young Hitler.

Pages 44–45 KAISER MANEUVERS

Pages 46–47 MARCHING, MARCHING

Pages 48–49 THE LAST YEARS OF PEACE

J. Daniel Chamier, *Fabulous Monster* (London, 1934; rev. German ed., Berlin, 1954), written by an Englishman on the era.

Michael Balfour, *The Kaiser and His Times* (rev. ed., New York, 1972, paperback) is highly commendable.

Pages 50–57 WORLD WAR I

Theodor Wolff, *The Eve of 1914* (London, 1936) ; Barbara Tuchmann, *The Guns of August* (New York, 1962; paperback, 1971) ; *The Defeat of the German Army, 1918*, (Washington, D.C., 1943).

Pages 58–59 A CORPORAL IN THE WAR

This is as good a place as any to mention some of the Hitler biographies. The first lives of the Führer were written by my late friends Konrad Heiden, in 1936 and 1937, and Rudolf Olden, in 1935. I had many discussions with the two while their works were in progress. I let Olden use my interview notes with Reinhold Hanisch, to whom I talked in Vienna about the days when he and Hitler were destitute.

Since then many Hitler biographies have appeared—and the flood hasn't stopped. Alan Bullock, *Hitler: A Study in Tyranny* (London, 1952; rev. ed., New York, 1962) tops the list. William L. Shirer's *The Rise and Fall of the Third Reich* (New York, 1960), the pathbreaking popular volume on the Nazis, gives a superb character portrait of the Führer. Other biographies: by

Helmut Heiber (London, 1961); Hans-Bernd Gisevius (Munich, 1963); Werner Maser (Munich, 1971); Robert Payne (New York, 1973); Joachim C. Fest (Munich, 1973).

Of Hitler in the war, see Hans Mend, *Hitler im Felde* (Munich, 1931).

Pages 60–63 THE END IN SIGHT

Pages 64–65 LABOR SPLITS

Most leading figures of the German labor movement—Scheidemann, Noske, Luxemburg, Müller, Löbe, Braun, Severing, Grzesinsky—wrote their memoirs.

Harry Schumann, *Karl Liebknecht* (Dresden, 1919)—an unpolitical picture.

The party history is recounted and analyzed by two American scholars, A. Joseph Berlau, *The German Social Democratic Party, 1914–1921* (New York, 1949), and Carl E. Schorske, *German Social Democracy, 1905–1907* (Cambridge, Mass., 1955).

Pages 66–67 REVOLUTION IN BERLIN

Illustrierte Geschichte der November Revolution in Deutschland (East Berlin, 1968); Walter Nimitz, *Die November Revolution 1918 in Deutschland* (East Berlin, 1965) are Communist interpretations.

Hermann Müller-Franken, the Social Democrat who later became chancellor, wrote his reminiscences on *Die November Revolution* (Berlin, 1931). Philipp Scheidemann, another Social Democratic leader, wrote about *Der Zusammenbruch* (Berlin, 1951). A solid description of the day is by René Schickele, *Der neunte November* (Berlin, 1919). Count Kuno von Westarp, the Nationalist politician, penned *Das Ende der Monarchie am 9. November 1918* (Rauschenbusch, 1952).

Pages 68–69 THE MONARCHY TOPPLES

Pages 70–71 THE HEROIC DAYS ARE OVER

Pages 72–73 RETURN FROM THE WAR

Pages 74–75 WORKERS' COUNCILS

Pages 76–77 FIGHTING AT THE PALACE

Pages 78–81 BROTHER AGAINST BROTHER

The first weeks of the revolution had many chroniclers:

Hainer Rasmuss, *Die Januarkämpfe 1919 in Berlin* (East Berlin, 1956); Rudolf Rotheit, *Der Berliner Schloss im Zeichen der Novemberrevolution* (Berlin, 1923); Harald von Koenigswald, *Revolution 1918* (Breslau, 1933); Emil Ludwig, *An die Laterne! Bilder aus der Revolution* (Berlin, 1919); *Causes of the German Collapse*, selected by R. H. Lutz (Stanford, 1934), is a translation of extracts from the large twelve-volume German work (Berlin, 1928).

Of the Workers' Councils: Walter Tormin, *Zwischen Rätediktatur und sozial Demokratie* (Düsseldorf, 1954).

Pages 82–85 FIRST VOTING FOR THE REPUBLIC

Philipp Scheidemann, *The Making of New Germany* (2 vols., New York, 1929), the memoirs of the Social Democratic chancellor; Ernst Scheiding, *Das erste Jahr der deutschen Revolution* (Leipzig, 1920).

Pages 86–87 THE WEIMAR PARLIAMENT

Erich Eyck, *A History of the Weimar Republic* (New York, 1967, paperback), two superbly written volumes.

William S. Halperin, *Germany Tried Democracy* (New York, 1946, paperback).

Pages 88–91 SOVIET IN BAVARIA

A good compendium on the Bavarian Soviet rule was issued by the Stadtarchiv of Munich: *Revolution und Räteherrschaft in München* (Munich, 1968).

Müller-Meiningen, *Aus Bayern Schwersten Tagen* (Berlin, 1923). An eyewitness account.

Rosa Meyer Leviné, the wife of the revolutionary, corrects the picture of her husband in her biography *Leviné* (Munich, 1972).

Ernst Toller, *I Was a German* (London, 1934). The sensitive memoirs of the poet-revolutionary.

Pages 92–93 THE PEACE TERMS

Pages 94–95 THE SIGNING OF THE TREATY

Pages 96–97 AGAINST THE TREATY

E. J. Dillon, *The Inside Story of the Peace Conference* (New York, 1920); Robert Lansing, *The Peace Negotiations* (Boston, 1921); Harold Nicolson, *Peacemaking 1919* (London, 1933); Karl Friedrich Nowak, *Versailles* (Berlin, 1927).

Edgar Stern Rubarth, *Graf Brockdorff Rantzau, Wanderer zwischen zwei Welten* (Berlin, 1929); Erich Kern, *Von Versailles zu Adolf Hitler: Der schreckliche Friede* (Göttingen, 1961); Viscount d'Abernon, *An Ambassador of Peace, 1918–1919* (London, 1929).

Pages 98–99 THE WEIMAR CONSTITUTION

On the Republic of Weimar: Erich Eyck, *A History of the Weimar Republic*, and S. William Halperin, *Germany Tried Democracy*, both in paperback, previously cited. In German: Hans Herzfeld, *Die Weimarer Republik* (Berlin, 1969); Helmut Heiber, *The Republic of Weimar* (Munich, 1966); F. A. Krummacher and Albert Wucher, *Die Weimarer Republik* (Munich, Vienna, and Basel, 1965).

Pages 100–101 GERMAN PEOPLE

August Sander, *Menschen ohne Maske* (Lucerne and Frankfurt, 1971) with the best photographs of Sander. A magnificent work. See also: *Deutschenspiegel* (Guetersloh, 1962).

Pages 102–103 THE LEFT FIGHTS ON

Maurice Berger, *Germany After the Armistice* (New York, 1920); Gustav Noske, *Von Kiel bis Kapp* (Berlin, 1920); Rittmeister Schaede, *Berlin schiesst, spielt und tanzt!* (Berlin, 1923).

Pages 104–105 NO MORE WAR!

K. Schwendemann, *Abrüstung und Sicherheit* (2 vols., Berlin, 1933), a document collection; Stewart Roddie, *Peace Patrol* (London, 1932); Von Oertzen, *Das ist die Abrüstung* (Oldenburg, 1931).

Page 106 "STAB IN THE BACK"

Army Service Forces Information Branch, *The Defeat of the German Army, 1918* (Washington, D.C., 1943); "Der Dolchstoss" in the *Süddeutsche Monatshefte*, April 1924; Joachim Petzold, *Die Dolchstosslegende* (East Berlin, 1963).

Page 107 A FATEFUL TRIAL

Karl Helfferich's venomous pamphlet *Fort mit Erzberger* (Berlin, 1919); Karl von Lumm's

biography, *Karl Helfferich als Währungspolitiker und Gerehrter* (Leipzig, 1926).

Der Erzberger Process. A 1056-page transcript of the trial (Berlin, 1920).

Der Erzberger Mord (Bühl, 1921).

Pages 108–109 TO KEEP ALIVE

Graf A. Stenbock-Fermor, *Deutschland von unten* (Stuttgart, 1931). A unique chronicle of the working people and the poor.

Pages 110–113 THE KAPP PUTSCH

Page 114 THE REDS STRIKE BACK

Page 115 A SWING TO THE RIGHT

Erwin Könnemann and Hans-Joachim Krusch, *Aktionseinheit contra Kapp Putsch* (East Berlin, 1972). A Communist interpretation. Gustav Noske, *Von Kiel bis Kapp* (Berlin, 1920). The memoirs of the man who fought the putschists. Oberst Bauer's short report, *Der 13. März 1920* (Munich, 1920). The recollections of someone who was there. Erich Knauf, *Ca Ira!* (Berlin, 1930), a journalistic novel of the putsch.

D. J. Goodspeed, *The Conspirators: A Study of the Coup d'Etat* (New York, 1961); Ludwig Schemann, *Wolfgang Kapp und das Märzunternehmen vom Jahre 1920* (Munich, 1937).

General Seeckt's official biography was written by Friedrich von Rabenau (Leipzig, 1940). Robert G. L. Waite's volume, *The Free Corps Movement in Postwar Germany* (Cambridge, Mass., 1952), is excellent.

The revolutionary Max Hoelz wrote *Vom "Weissen Kreuz" zur Roten Fahne* (Berlin, 1929). In English the title is *From White Cross to Red Flag* (London, 1930). Hoelz's letters from prison had also been published.

Page 116 THE REPARATIONS ISSUE

L. L. B. Angas, *Germany and Her Debts* (London, 1923); Normal Angell, *The Peace Treaty and the Economic Chaos of Europe* (London, 1920); John Maynard Keynes, *The Economic Consequences of the Peace* (London, 1920).

Page 117 PLEBISCITE IN SILESIA

Rudolf Schricker, *Blut—Erz—Kohle* (Berlin, 1930); Karl Hoefer, *Oberschlesien in der Aufstandszeit, 1918–1921, A Collection of Documents and Reminiscences* (Berlin, 1938).

Pages 118–119 IS THIS A REPUBLIC?

Kurt Tucholsky, *Deutschland, Deutschland über Alles* (Reinbek, 1964). The fascinating work of the great satirist which has been translated and published in English as well.

Page 120 A NEW POLITICAL PARTY

Dietrich Orlow, *The History of the Nazi Party* (2 vols., Pittsburgh, 1969–1973), a magnificent work. Werner Maser, *Die Frühgeschichte der NSDAP* (Frankfurt, 1965), a detailed study.

Page 121 RATHENAU MURDERED

David Felix, *Walther Rathenau and the Weimar Republic* (Baltimore, 1971). Excellent, with a comprehensive bibliography (pages 191–205).

Biographies of Walther Rathenau: Count Harry Kessler (Berlin, 1928; New York, 1930); Alfred Kerr (Amsterdam, 1935); Helmuth M. Böttcher (Bonn, 1958).

Rathenau's collected speeches, writings, and letters were published by S. Fischer, Berlin.

Pages 122–123 THE MARCH ON ROME

Richard Collier, *Duce!* (New York, 1971) has a comprehensive bibliography (pages 395–419). Ernst Nolte, *Der Faschismus von Mussolini zum Hitler* (Munich, 1968).

Pages 124–125 THE FRENCH OCCUPY THE RUHR

Hannes Pyszka, *Der Ruhrkrieg* (Munich, 1923); Friedrich Grimm, *Vom Ruhrkrieg zur Rheinland Räumung* (Hamburg, 1930). The memoirs of the German defense counsel.

Pages 126–127 THE FIRST PARTY DAY

Dietrich Orlov, *The History of the Nazi Party, 1919–1933*, previously cited.
Hitler's Weg bis 1924 (Frankfurt and Bonn, 1965), and Ernst Deuerlein, *Der Aufstieg der NSDAP, 1919–1933* (Düsseldorf, 1968) are meticulously researched studies.

Pages 128–129 PHILOSOPHERS OF NAZISM

Dietrich Eckart, *Der Bolschevismus von Moses bis Lenin: Zwiegespräch zwischen Adolf Hitler und mir* (Munich, 1924); Wilhelm Gruen, *Dietrich Eckart als Publicist* (Munich, 1941) has a comprehensive Eckart bibliography. Albert Rosenberg, ed., *Dietrich Eckart: Ein Vermächtnis* (Munich, 1935).
Houston Stewart Chamberlain, *Die Grundlagen des XIX. Jahrhunderts* (Munich, 1906).
Of "Lanz von Liebenfels": Wilfried Daim, *Der Mann der Hitler die Ideen gab* (Munich, 1958). Of Richard Wagner: *In selbstzeugnissen und im Urteil der Zeitgenossen* (Zurich, 1972).
Georg Lukács, *Von Nietzsche bis Hitler, oder der Irrationalismus in der Deutschen Politik* (Frankfurt and Hamburg, 1966).

Pages 130–131 INFLATION

Pages 132–133 THE PEOPLE SUFFER

Hans Ostwald, *Sittengeschichte der Inflation* (Berlin, 1931); Morus, *Histoire de l'Inflation* (Paris, 1926); Harry Graf Kessler, *Tagebücher 1918–1937* (Frankfurt, 1961). Perceptive memoirs of the era, also in English.

Pages 134–135 MILITARISM ON THE STAGE

Thilo Koch, *Die goldenen Zwanziger Jahre* (Berlin, 1970).

Pages 136–137 GERMAN DAY IN NÜRNBERG

A good description of the day is in William Shirer's *The Rise and Fall of the Third Reich*, previously cited.

Page 138 STRESEMANN TURNS THE TIDE

Page 139 TROUBLES EVERYWHERE

Stresemann's writings, speeches, and letters have been issued in many volumes. His life attracted many biographers, among them Heinrich Bauer, Marvin L. Edwards, Walter Görlitz, Hubertus Prinz zu Löwenstein, Rudolf Olden, Edgar Stern-Rubarth, Annelise Thimme, Antonina Valentin.
Hans W. Gatzke, *Stresemann and the Rearmament of Germany* (Baltimore, 1954) is a particularly interesting study.
A bibliography on Stresemann compiled by Gerhard Zwoch appeared in Düsseldorf (1953).

Pages 140–141 THE PUTSCH

Pages 142–143 THE TRIAL IN MUNICH

Harold J. Gordon, Jr., *Hitler and the Beer Hall Putsch* (Princeton, N.J., 1972) is a recent work on the subject. (Bibliography, pages 633–647). Documents of the putsch in Ernst Deuerlein, *The Hitler Putsch* (Stuttgart, 1962). Richard Hauser, *Putsch! How Hitler Made Revolution* (New York, 1971, paperback) is a vividly written account. Hans Hubert Hofmann, *Der Hitlerputsch* (Munich, 1961); General Erich Ludendorff's self-published memoirs, *Auf dem Wege zur Feldhernhalle* (Munich, 1937).
Two highly critical studies were written by my late good friend Leo Lania: *Der Hitler-Ludendorff Prozess* (Berlin, 1925) and *Die Totengräber Deutschlands* (Berlin, 1924).

Pages 144–145 FILM—THE NEW ART FORM

Heinrich Fraenkel, *Unsterblicher Film* (Munich, 1956), by a man who experienced the beginnings of the German film. Paul Rotha, *The Film Till Now* (London, 1967), a vast compendium. Rolf Hempel, *Carl Mayer* (Berlin, 1968), a biography of the pioneer script writer.

Page 146 VOTING FOR THE SECOND REICHSTAG

Page 147 VOTING FOR THE THIRD REICHSTAG

Der Reichstag, ed. by Ernst Deuerlein (Bonn, 1963).
Friedrich Stampfer, *Die vierzehn Jahre der ersten deutschen Republik* (Karlsbad, 1936). By the leading Social Democratic editor.

Pages 148–149 IN PRISON

Otto Lurker, *Hitler hinter Festungsmauern* (Berlin, 1933); *Mit Adolf Hitler auf Festung Landsberg*, memories of Hans Kallenbach, one of the imprisoned with the Führer.

Pages 150–151 NUDES AND JAZZ

Otto Friedrich, *Before the Deluge* (New York, 1972), a brilliant compendium on the life in Berlin in the twenties.
"Pem," *Heimweh nach dem Kurfürstendamm: Aus Berlin Glanzvollsten Tagen und Naechten* (Berlin, 1962). The nostalgic reminiscences of a journalist who lived there.
Hermann Behr, *Die Goldenen Zwanziger Jahre* (Hamburg, 1964).

Pages 152–153 THE PRESIDENT DIES

Friedrich Ebert, *Kämpfe und Ziele* (Dresden, no date); also Ebert's *Schriften, Aufzeichnungen, Reden* (2 vols., Dresden, 1926).
There are biographies of Ebert by Georg Haschke and Norbert Tönnies (Preetz, Holstein, 1961); by Georg Kotowski (Wiesbaden, 1963); by Max Peters (Berlin, 1950).

Pages 154–155 ELECTING A PRESIDENT

Pages 156–157 THE NEW PRESIDENT

Biographies of Hindenburg:
Walter Bloem, *Hindenburg der Deutsche* (Berlin, 1932); Margaret Goldsmith and Frederick Voigt, *Hindenburg—The Man and the Legend* (London, 1930); Rudolf Olden, *Hindenburg, oder der Geist der Preussischen Armee* (Paris, 1935); A. M. K. Watson, *The Biography of President von Hindenburg* (London, 1930); John W. Wheeler-Bennett, *Hindenburg, The Wooden Titan* (London, 1936).
A Hindenburg bibliography was published by the Bibliographic Institute (Leipzig, 1938).

Pages 158–159 A BOOK IS BORN

The first volume of Adolf Hitler's *Mein Kampf* appeared in Munich in 1925, the second volume in 1929. In America it was published in Boston in 1943 in the translation of Ralph Mannheim.

Pages 160–161 WORKING FOR PEACE

Paul Seabury, *The Wilhelmstrasse: A Study of German Diplomats under the Nazi Regime* (Berkeley, 1954).
Anthony Eden, *Facing the Dictators* (Boston, 1962).

Page 162 ROCKING THE REPUBLIC

Erich Eyck, *A History of the Weimar Republic*, previously cited.

Page 163 GENEVA

Gustav Stresemann, *Vermächtnis* (3 vols., Berlin, 1932); *Diaries, Letters and Papers* (3 vols., London, 1935–1940); *Ursachen und Folgen vom Deutschen Zusammenbruch . . .* (Documents), 8 vols.; F. P. Walters, *A History of the League of Nations* (London, 1952).

Pages 164–165 REORGANIZING THE PARTY

See the works of Maser and Orlov.

Page 166 VOTING FOR THE FOURTH REICHSTAG

Chart of the election in Pinson: *Modern Germany*, previously cited, page 603.

Page 167 THÉ DANSANT

Hedda Adlon, *Hotel Adlon* (Munich, 1955). The reminiscences of the wife of the Berlin hotelier.
Hans Erman, *Bei Kempinski* (Berlin, 1956). The story of the popular restaurant.
Walther Kiaulehn, *Berlin: Schicksal einer Weltstadt* (Munich, 1958). A massive volume on the city's history.

Pages 168–169 THE "BAVARIAN"

Ernst Hanfstaengl, *Zwischen Weissen und Braunen Hans* (Munich, 1970); Otto Strasser, *Hitler and I* (London, 1940), the recollections of a former friend who turned into an enemy.

Pages 170–171 WRITERS, POETS

Werner Mahrholz, *Deutsche Literatur der Gegenwart* (Berlin, 1931); Paul Wiegler, *Geschichte der neuen Deutschen Literatur* (2 vols., Berlin, 1930); Kurt R. Grossman, *Ossietzky: Ein Deutscher Patriot* (Munich, 1963); Carl Zuckmayer, *Als wär's ein Stück von mir* (Frankfurt, 1966; English translation, New York, 1970); Hans Bürgin and Hans-Otto Mayer, *Thomas Mann: Eine Chronik seines Lebens* (Frankfurt, 1965); Max Osborn, *Der bunte Spiegel* (New York, 1945), recollections of a Berlin literary editor.
Peter Gay, *Weimar Culture* (New York, 1968). A superlative work with a long and excellent bibliography (pages 165–197).

Pages 172–173 REPARATIONS REVISED

Carl Bergmann, *Der Weg der Reparation* (Frankfurt, 1926); George P. Auld, *The Dawes Plan and the New Economics* (New York, 1927); Harold G. Moulton, *The Reparation Plan* (New York, 1924).

Pages 174–175 AGAINST THE YOUNG PLAN

Der Young Plan (the official text) (Frankfurt, 1929).

Pages 176–177 THE RISE OF THE DRUMMER

See Bullock, Orlov, Shirer, cited before.

Pages 178–179 A STAR IS BORN

Leslie Frewin, *Dietrich—The Story of a Star* (New York, 1970).

Pages 180–181 HARD TIMES

Bruno Nelissen Haken, *Stempel Chronik* (Hamburg, 1932). Stories of the unemployed.

Pages 182–183 THE CRY FOR LAW AND ORDER

See Hitler's speeches about the issue, ed. by Max Domarus, previously cited. Also see the memoirs of Count Kessler, Arnold Brecht.

Pages 184–185 BRÜNING STRUGGLES

Pages 186–189 VOTING FOR THE FIFTH REICHSTAG

Heinrich Brüning, *Memoiren 1918–1934* (Stuttgart, 1970). By the former chancellor.

Page 190 THE WITNESS

F. W. Oertzen, *In Namen der Geschichte!* (Hamburg, 1934). A book on the German political trials after World War I, with a chapter on the Ulmer trial.

Page 191 HIS MOVIE STARS

Siegfried Kracauer, *From Caligari to Hitler* (Princeton, N.J., 1947); Stefan Lorant, *Wir von Film* (Berlin, 1927).

Pages 192–193 HITLER GAINS

Wilhelm Frick, *Die Nationalsozialisten im Reichstag, 1924–1931* (Munich, 1932).

Pages 194–195 THE NATIONAL OPPOSITION

Alfred Pfaff, *Der Young Plan in 67 Fragen und Antworten* (Munich, 1930); Alfred Hugenberg, *Streichlichter aus Vergangenheit und Gegenwart* (Berlin, 1927); Otto Kriegk, *Hugenberg* (Leipzig, 1932).

Pages 196–197 VOTING FOR PRESIDENT

See the works of Bullock, Eyck, Halperin, Shirer, previously cited.

Pages 198–199 ONCE MORE—REPARATIONS

See Eyck, previously cited.

Pages 200–201 FIGHTING IT OUT

See the speeches of Goebbels and Hitler.

Pages 202–203 THE SQUIRE OF NEUDECK

Gestalten ringsum Hindenburg (Dresden, 1930); Franz von Papen, *Memoirs* (London, 1952; in German, *Der Wahrheit eine Gasse*, Munich, 1952); Bruno Buchta, *Die Junker und die Weimarer Republik* (East Berlin, 1959).

Pages 204–205 THE NAZIS GET THE MOST VOTES

Pages 206–207 THE REICHSTAG IS DISSOLVED

Pages 208–209 VOTING FOR THE SEVENTH REICHSTAG

Oswald Dutch, *The Errant Diplomat* (London, 1940); H. W. Blood-Ryan, *Franz von Papen, His Life and Times* (London, 1940); Von Papen's *Memoirs* (New York, 1953). Wilhelm Frick, *Die Nationalsozialisten im Reichstag, 1924–1931* (Munich, 1932).

Pages 210–213 THE NEW CHANCELLOR

Karl Dietrich Bracher: *The German Dictatorship* (New York, 1970). A superb analysis of National Socialism with a comprehensive bibliography (pages 503–533). Richard Grünberger, *The Twelve-Year Reich: A Social History of Nazi Germany, 1933–1945* (New York, 1971). Joachim C. Fest, *Das Gesicht des Dritten Reiches* (Berlin, 1969). Also in English.

Pages 214–215 THE REICHSTAG BURNS

Fritz Tobias, *The Reichstag Fire* (New York, 1964); Douglas Reed, *The Burning of the Reichstag* (New York, 1934).

Pages 216–217 HITLER HAS THE POWER

Hans Otto Meissner and Harry Wilde, *Die Machtergreifung* (Stuttgart, 1958). A commentary on the Nazi coup d'état.

Pages 218–219 THE DAY OF POTSDAM

The accounts in the Nazi newspapers and magazines, like the *Völkischer Beobachter* or *Illustrierte Beobachter*, described and pictured the event fully. The pictorial reportages in the *Berliner Illustrirte Zeitung* and the *Münchner Illustrierte Presse* show everything that happened on that day.

Pages 220–221 THE NATION ABANDONS ITS FREEDOM

Max Domarus, ed., *Hitler: Reden und Proklamationen, 1932–1940* (4 vols., Munich, 1965). It contains Hitler's speech in full.

Pages 222–223 THE BURNING OF BOOKS

Dr. Goebbels's *Der Angriff* has a detailed reportage of the burning.

Pages 224–225 AGAINST THE JEWS

The Wiener Library in London issued in 1958 a bibliography of over 3,500 books and pamphlets under the title *German Jewry, Its History, Life and Culture*. *The Murderers among Us*. The Simon Wiesenthal memoirs, ed. by Joseph Wechsberg (New York, 1967). The book by and of the man who hunted down Nazi criminals.

Pages 226–229 REICHSTAG FIRE TRIAL

Georgi Dimitroff, *Reichstagsbrandprozess* (East Berlin, 1966). *The Reichstag Fire Trial: The Second Brown Book of the Hitler Terror* (London, 1934). *Reichstagsbrandprozess*, ed. by Michael Mansfield (Frankfurt, no date, paperback).

Pages 230–231 NEW YEAR'S CELEBRATION IN THE PRESIDENTIAL PALACE

Emil Ludwig, *Hindenburg und die Sage von der Deutschen Republik* (Amsterdam 1935); Otto Meissner, *Staatssekretär unter Ebert, Hindenburg, Hitler* (Hamburg, 1950).

Pages 232–233 VISITING MUSSOLINI

Ivone Kirkpatrick, *Mussolini: A Study in Power* (New York, 1964); Galeazzo Ciano, *The Ciano Diaries, 1939–1943* (New York, 1947).

Pages 234–235 THE NIGHT OF THE LONG KNIVES

Nicolay Tolstoy, *The Night of the Long Knives* (New York, 1972, paperback). Max Gallo, *Der schwarze Freitag der S.A.* (Munich, 1972).

Pages 236–237 THE MURDER OF DOLLFUSS

William L. Shirer, *Berlin Diary* (New York, 1941, paperback).

Pages 238–239 HINDENBURG DIES

Emil Ludwig, *Hindenburg* (Hamburg, 1962).

Pages 240–241 THE NEW HEAD OF STATE

Hitler taking the power is described in his biographies cited previously. William Shirer gives a particularly good account.

Pages 242–243 GÖRING THE PLAYBOY

Emmy Göring, *An der Seite meines Mannes* (Göttingen, 1967). A whitewash of the man by his loving wife. Roger Manvell and Heinrich Fraenkel, *Hermann Göring* (London, 1962).

Pages 244–245 GOEBBELS THE PROPAGANDIST

Helmut Heiber, *Joseph Goebbels* (Berlin, 1962); Prinz zu Schaumberg-Lippe, *Dr. G.* (Wiesbaden, 1963); Victor Reimann, *Dr. Joseph Goebbels* (Vienna, 1971); Roger Manvell and Heinrich Fraenkel, *Goebbels* (New York, 1960, paperback). Publications containing Goebbels's words, diary entries, and articles: *His Speeches*, vol. I, 1932–1939 (Düsseldorf, 1971); *The Diary of Joseph Goebbels, 1925–26* (London, 1962); *The Goebbels Diaries, 1942–43* (Garden City, N.Y., 1948); *Kampf um Berlin* (Munich, 1934); *My Part in Germany's Fight* (London, 1935); *Vom Kaiserhof zur Reichskanzlei* (Munich, 1937).

Pages 246–247 HIMMLER THE BLOODHOUND

Bradley F. Smith, *Heinrich Himmler: A Nazi in the Making, 1900–26* (Palo Alto, Calif., 1971) is a scholarly account. See also the interesting article in *The American Historical Review*, June 1971, by Peter Loewenberg, "The Unsuccessful Adolescence of Heinrich Himmler"; *Reichsführer: Briefe an und von Himmler* (Munich, 1970), ed. by Helmut Heiber. Heinz Hoehne, *The Order of the Death's Head: The Story of Hitler's S.S.* (New York, 1970).

Pages 248–249 BORMANN THE BUREAUCRAT

Joseph Wulf's *Martin Bormann: Hitler's Schatten* (Guetersloh, 1962) is a well documented biography. The life of Bormann in English: James McGovern, *Martin Bormann* (New York, 1968). *The Bormann Letters* (London, 1954) contains correspondence with his wife, 1943–1945.

Pages 250–251 PARTY DAY IN NÜRNBERG

The *Berliner Illustrirte Zeitung* and *Münchner Illustrierte Presse* published special issues. *Reichstagung in Nürnberg, 1934* (Berlin, 1934). A profusely illustrated volume printed by order of Julius Streicher.

Pages 252–253 THE SHACKLES OF VERSAILLES ARE BROKEN

Bullock, Shirer, and other biographers of Hitler recount the event in detail.

Pages 254–255 DISCUSSING PEACE

See works by Eyck, Halperin, Shirer, previously cited.

Pages 256–257 "I WANT PEACE"

Pages 258–259 WAR OR PEACE?

Hitler's speech is in Max Domarus, *Reden und Proklamationen, 1932–1940* (Munich, 1965). Elizabeth Wiskemann, *The Rome-Berlin Axis* (London, 1969).

Pages 260–261 GÖRING'S OPERA BALL

Emmy Göring's *Memoirs* (Göttingen, 1967); Ewan Butler and Gordon Young, *Marshal Without Glory* (London, 1951); Martin H. Somerfeldt, *Göring, was fällt Ihnen ein!* (Berlin, 1932).

Pages 262–263 THEY ALL CAME TO SEE HIM

Dorothy Thompson, *I Saw Hitler* (New York, 1932). The famous encounter of the American journalist with the Führer.

Pages 264–267 AUSTRIA IS TAKEN

Kurt Schuschnigg, *Austrian Requiem* (New York, 1946); *Im Kampf gegen Hitler* (Vienna, 1969); Gordon Brook-Shepherd, *Anschluss* (London, 1963); Ernst Rüdiger Stahremberg, *Memoiren* (Vienna and Munich, 1971).

Pages 268–269 THE FÜHRER'S BIRTHDAY

Heinrich Hoffmann, *Hitler Was My Friend* (London).

Pages 270–279 THE CZECH CRISIS

Henry Nogueres, *Munich: "Peace for Our Time"* (New York, 1965); Keith Robbins, *Muenchen 1938* (Guetersloh, 1969); Paul Schmidt, *Statist auf diplomatischer Bühne* (Frankfurt and Bonn, 1964); a partial English translation of Dr. Schmidt's recollections is titled *Hitler's Interpreter* (New York, 1951); André François-Poncet, *The Fateful Years* (New York, 1949), memoirs of the French ambassador; Nevile Henderson, *The Failure of a Mission* (New York, 1940), memoirs of the British ambassador; Keith Feiling, *The Life of Neville Chamberlain* (London, 1946).

Pages 280–281 WOMAN CHARMER

Walter C. Langer, *The Mind of Adolf Hitler* (New York, 1972). Some interesting but highly incorrect psychoanalytic interpretations of Hitler's sex life. Felix Gross, *Hitler's Girls, Guns and Gangsters* (London, 1941). An amusingly superficial, sensation-seeking account.

Pages 282–283 THE NIGHT OF THE BROKEN GLASS

William Shirer, *The Rise and Fall of the Third Reich* (New York, 1960) has a masterly description of the event.

Friedrich Karl Kaul, *Der Fall des Herschel Grynszpan* (Berlin, 1965). All the facts about the assassin of vom Rath, his trial etc.

Pages 284–285 THE RAPE OF CZECHOSLOVAKIA

Eduard Benes, *Memoirs of Dr. Eduard Benes* (London, 1954).

Pages 286–287 FOR BISMARCK— AGAINST FDR

Hitler's tirade against FDR is in full in Max Domarus, ed., *Hitler: Reden und Proklamationen, 1932–1940* (4 vols., Munich, 1965).

See also William Shirer, *Berlin Diary* (New York, 1941, paperback).

Pages 288–289 THE NAZI-SOVIET PACT

Joachim von Ribbentrop, *Zwischen London und Moskau* (Leone near Starnberg, 1953). Memoirs of the ambassador Peter Kleist, *Zwischen Hitler und Stalin* (Bonn, 1950). Gustav Hillger and Alfred G. Meyer, *The Incompatible Allies—A Memoir History of German Soviet Relations, 1918–1941* (New York, 1953).

Pages 290–291 MOVING INTO POLAND

Das war der Krieg in Polen, ed. by Rolf Heller (Berlin, 1939). Also B. H. Liddell Hart, *History of the Second World War* (New York, 1971).

Pages 292–293 A MEAL IN THE TEAHOUSE

Nerin Gun, *Eva Braun: Hitler's Mistress* (New York, 1968). A gossipy biography.

Pages 294–295 HITLER'S BLITZKRIEG AGAINST EUROPE

B. H. Liddell Hart, *History of the Second World War* (New York, 1971); Theodore Draper, *The Six Week's War* (New York, 1944); *Die Deutsche Besetzung von Daenemark und Norwegen, 1940* (Göttingen, 1952); Major General J. F. C. Fuller, *The Second World War* (New York, 1949); A. J. P. Taylor, *The Origins of the Second World War* (London, 1963).

Pages 296–297 HE LOVED THE CHILDREN HE KNEW

The text is based on interviews. I am particularly grateful to Leni Riefenstahl, and to Mrs. Max Kimmich, the sister of Dr. Goebbels, with whom I had repeated talks.

Pages 298–299 MIRACLE AT DUNKIRK

Winston S. Churchill, *Their Finest Hour* (Boston, 1949) gives a magnificent description.

Pages 300–301 THE FRENCH SURRENDER

Jacques Benoist-Mechin, *Sixty Days That Shook the West: The Fall of France, 1940* (New York, 1963).

Pages 302–303 HITLER IN PARIS

Albert Speer, *Inside the Third Reich* (New York, 1970) describes the visit.

Pages 304–305 THE BATTLE OF BRITAIN

The Times and other English newspapers.

Pages 306–307 THE SUPREME WARLORD

Franz Halder, *Hitler als Feldherr* (Munich, 1969); Felix Gilbert, ed., *Hitler Directs His War* (New York, 1950); Walter Goerlitz, *History of the German General Staff* (New York, 1953); Walter Warlimont, *Inside Hitler's Headquarters, 1939–1945* (New York, 1964); H. R. Trevor-Roper, *Blitzkrieg to Defeat: Hitler's War Directives, 1939–1945* (New York, 1971).

Pages 308–309 THE WAR IN RUSSIA

Alan Clark, *The Russian-German Conflict, 1941–1945* (New York, 1965).

Paul Carell, *Scorched Earth: The Russian-German War, 1943–1944* (New York, 1971, paperback).

Page 310 HESS FLIES TO ENGLAND

James Douglas-Hamilton, *Motive for a Mission* (London, 1971). The story by the son of the Duke of Hamilton. (Selected bibliography, pages 281–284.)

Page 311 CAMPAIGN IN AFRICA

Dwight D. Eisenhower, *Crusade in Europe* (New York, 1948); Desmond Young, *Rommel—The Desert Fox* (New York, 1950); *The Rommel Papers*, ed. by B. H. Liddell Hart (New York, 1953); Ronald Lewin, *Rommel as Military Commander* (New York, 1970, paperback).

Pages 312–313 PAULUS' ARMY DEFEATED IN RUSSIA

Wladyslaw Anders, *Hitler's Defeat in Russia* (Chicago, 1953); Geoffrey Jukes, *Stalingrad: The Turning Point* (New York, 1968, paperback); John Keegan, *Barbarossa: Invasion of Russia* (New York, 1971, paperback).

Pages 314–315 THE END OF THE WARSAW GHETTO

Gerald Reitlinger, *The Final Solution* (New York, 1961); Rosa Levin, *The Holocaust: The Destruction of European Jewry, 1933–1945* (New York, 1968).

Pages 316–317 D-DAY

D-Day, The Normandy Invasion in Retrospect (Lawrence, Kans., 1971); Dwight D. Eisenhower, *Crusade in Europe* (New York, 1948); General Hans Speidel, *Invasion 1944* (Chicago, 1950).

Pages 318–319 AMERICANS IN GERMANY

Harry C. Butcher, *My Three Years with Eisenhower* (New York, 1946).

Dwight D. Eisenhower, *Crusade in Europe* (New York, 1948).

Pages 320–321 AN ATTEMPT ON HITLER'S LIFE

Pages 322–323 THE TRIAL OF THE PLOTTERS

Many books and memoirs have appeared on the ill-fated plot. H. G. Gisevius, *To the Bitter End* (Boston, 1947), and *The Van Hassell Diaries, 1938–1944* (Garden City, N.Y., 1947) are written by two of the participants. John Wheeler-Bennet, *The Nemesis of Power* (pages 634–693) (New York, 1953) gives an excellent description. Allen W. Dulles's *Germany's Underground* (New York, 1947), and Fabian Schlabrendorff's and Gero Gaevernitz's *They Almost Killed Hitler* (New York, 1947), Heinrich Fraenkel's and Roger Manvell's *Der 20. Juli* (Berlin, 1964) are useful. Joachim Kramarz, *Stauffenberg* (Frankfurt, 1965). The life story of the chief conspirator.

Pages 324–329 THE CLOCK RUNS OUT ON HITLER'S GERMANY

Pages 330–333 WHAT NAZISM WROUGHT

Rudolf Hoess, *Commandant of Auschwitz* (New York, 1960); Hannah Arendt, *The Origins of Totalitarianism* (New York, 1959).

Milton Schulman, *Defeat in the West* (London, 1949).

Pages 334–335 THE END OF A DICTATOR

Ivone Kirkpatrick, *Mussolini: A Study in Power* (New York, 1944).

F. W. Deakin, *The Six Hundred Days of Mussolini* (New York, 1966, paperback).

Pages 336–337 GÖTTERDÄMMERUNG

Pages 338–345 THIS WAS THE END

Gerhard Boldt, *In the Shelter with Hitler* (London, 1948), American edition titled *The Last Ten Days* (New York, 1973, paperback); Karl Koller, *Der letzte Monat* (Mannheim, 1949); H. R. Trevor-Roper, *The Last Days of Hitler* (2nd ed., London, 1950); Hans Dollinger, *Die letzten hundert Tage* (Munich, 1965); Marshal Wassily Tschuikov, *Das Ende des Dritten Reiches* (Munich, 1966); Marlis G. Steinert, *23 Days: The Final Collapse of Nazi Germany* (New York, 1967); Lev A. Besymensky, *The Death of Adolf Hitler* (New York, 1968).

Register of Names